Praise for *Date Night In*, by Ashley Rodriguez:

"Every recipe in *Date Night In* makes me hungry. Potato chips with fennel coriander salt. Thyme and pancetta roasted sweet potatoes. Honey and sriracha chicken wings. This is the most flavorful date night food I can imagine. Since I have the good fortune to count Ashley and Gabe as friends, I know that their love for each other is real and their food is unbelievably good. My husband and I have been inspired to start making each other date night dinners and so will you."

—SHAUNA JAMES AHERN, author of *Gluten-Free Girl and the Chef*

"Ashley has woven her creative and delicious recipes between sweet, honest stories about marriage and family. I will move this cookbook between my bedside and kitchen counter. A cookbook and a love story: this book is truly a treasure."

—SARA FORTE, author of *The Sprouted Kitchen*

"I have long followed Ashley's blog Not Without Salt. There is a nourishing quality to her being, words, and most certainly, food. *Date Night In* is full of universal tales of love and Ashley's recipes are sure to ignite, and better even, refuel passion. Food of love."

—ARAN GOYOAGA, author of *Small Plates and Sweet Treats*

"Rare is the book that not only moves us to cook, but to change our very lives. *Date Night In* is that book! With honesty, humility, and killer recipes for everything from Roasted Strawberry Jam to Dulce de Leche and Nectarine Creamsicles and the best roasted chicken you'll ever eat (really!), Ashley Rodriguez will inspire you to find the romance in your every day."

—MOLLY WIZENBERG, author of *Delancey* and *A Homemade Life*

"Ashley (and Gabe) are as delicious as her recipes. In *Date Night In* she reminds us that our relationships should be savored, and stirred with love."

—SHERRY YARD, pastry chef and author

Date Night In

More Than 120 Recipes to Nourish Your Relationship

Ashley Rodriguez
creator of NotWithoutSalt.com

RUNNING PRESS
PHILADELPHIA · LONDON

Books published by Running Press are available at special discounts for bulk purchases in the United States by corporations, institutions, and other organizations. For more information, please contact the Special Markets Department at the Perseus Books Group, 2300 Chestnut Street, Suite 200, Philadelphia, PA 19103, or call (800) 810-4145, ext. 5000, or e-mail special.markets@perseusbooks.com.

ISBN 978-0-7624-5246-0

Library of Congress Control Number: 2013951218

E-book ISBN 978-0-7624-5531-7

9   8   7   6   5   4   3
Digit on the right indicates the number of this printing

Photographs by Ashley Rodriguez and Boone Rodriguez

Cover and interior design by Joshua McDonnell
Edited by Kristen Green Wiewora
Typography: Avenir, Bembo, Lato, and Maxwell Slab

Running Press Book Publishers
2300 Chestnut Street
Philadelphia, PA 19103-4371

Visit us on the web!
www.offthemenublog.com

To my husband, Gabe.
You always have been and will
continue to be my favorite date.

Introduction
7

Basics
14

SPRING

Feasting on Spring
23

My Birthday
35

A Touch of Thai
46

His Birthday
54

Somewhere in Italy
64

Take It Outside
73

FALL

Eat with Your Hands
159

Wooed by Fried Chicken
168

Breakfast for Dinner
179

An Elegant Classic
188

Fall Comfort
198

A Roman Engagement
207

SUMMER

A Soup for Summer
87

By the Fire
96

Too Hot to Cook
105

It Gets Him
118

A Taste of Home
129

A Sort-Of Fairy Tale
139

Our Burger
149

WINTER

A Winter BBQ
217

All Over the Mediterranean
228

Dinner and a Movie
238

A Flemish Feast
246

A Little French
259

Renewal
268

Introduction

Gabe and I met when we were young. I noticed him early in my freshman year of college. He was hard not to notice, as he was often surrounded by other girls who were also drawn to his sleek black hair, deep olive skin, and tender smile. I offered casual glances as we passed in the hall, and in return he gave me a smile. It was then that I first noticed his shallow dimples and artistically crafted facial hair that framed his face (he was known for his beard and sideburns, which he changed weekly). I walked away with quickened breath and weak knees, wondering if he thought about me as much as I thought about him.

Undeterred by my competition, I managed to get his instant messaging name by spying over the shoulder of a friend. That same evening, with the flutters of butterfly wings in my stomach making me feel nearly ill, I started a casual conversation with him on instant messenger. It was this conversation that led to his asking me out on our first date.

Each in our separate dorm rooms, we shut off our computers, buttoned up our winter coats, and met for a brisk walk on a cold December evening, making our way to a rundown 7-Eleven just off campus. There we shared a cherry Slurpee, without noticing its icy freeze, and many laughs trying on $5 sunglasses. He wore a navy blue peacoat with the stiff collar pulled up and resting gently against his neck. Rather shyly, I caught a glimpse of him parading around in the convenience store aviators. He looked at me and in an instant I took him all in: his quiet confidence, his ability to laugh at himself, and the way he looked at me with kindness and interest. I was hooked. I went home that night wanting to date Gabe for as long as he'd let me.

As our relationship evolved, so did our dates, all of which centered on food. In addition to Gabe, food had become the love of my life. Food and I began courting at my mom's apron strings, but our relationship really ignited when I was in college, living and studying in Italy. Gabe and I were engaged in Italy; he gave me a ring and I introduced him to carbonara. Eventually, I went on to train as a professional pastry chef at Spago Beverly Hills and worked in kitchens such as the Essential Baking Company, Ciao Thyme Kitchen and Catering, and Delancey, as well as running my own wedding cake and dessert catering business.

Just out of college and newly married, we had a standing date night every Friday, and I looked forward to it every week. We were new to each other, and new to the appreciation of great food. On one particularly memorable Friday night, we cozied up to the bar at a little French café downtown, making fast friends with the bartender, who recommended a lovely Champagne and delighted us with Raclette. He served us a bowl of bubbling melted cheese with roasted potatoes, crisp and golden around the edges, and tangy cornichons for dipping (see page 268). Steam rose as the bubbles broke on the surface, releasing an alpine scent before we descended on it eagerly with forks and fingers.

Later that night, we lingered at the bar over a deep cup of rich, dark chocolate and methodically dipped our spoons into the cool whipped cream before plunging them into the warm, melted chocolate. It was the best thing I had ever tasted. After one last sip of crisp Champagne, we paid the bill and slid off our stools. I tucked my arm into his as we left the restaurant, full, and more in love than when we

had first come in.

Those leisurely romantic meals in fabulous restaurants quickly became memories of what felt like a past life as our current life grew full of children, diapers, Legos, laughter, and chaos. We once sipped cocktails at 5 o'clock; now that's our family dinnertime. This is our new reality. It's joyful, yes, but life often leaves Gabe and me with little energy and time for each other. We both look forward to the rare quiet hours of the evening when the kids are settled into bed and the house is still.

It was in those quiet hours that I started to notice a very *un*-romantic routine forming. Gabe would retreat to his computer and I to mine. After a long day spent caring for three small children, I had nothing more to give; I felt like this time was mine. But the neglect to our marriage started to become clear, as we began to feel more like roommates than husband and wife.

As I nursed a newborn, exhausted, I longingly recalled those date nights of the past. I was transported to the memories of pepper-flecked pasta we'd shared in Rome over a red-and-white-checked tablecloth (page 212) and how, after dinner, we had roamed the cobbled streets with our fingers woven tightly together, just happy to be with each other. I remembered playful conversation and laughter as we lingered

over a crisp wedge of iceberg lettuce with blue cheese dressing (page 54) pooling in between the citron-hued leaves at a diner in L.A. Even recalling the simple dates in our dorm rooms with store-bought pizza eaten off paper plates, nacho-flavored chips, and a pint of Ben & Jerry's shared straight from the container reminded me of the fun we had just being together. It wasn't the expense of these meals or the locations that made them memorable, or even the food in some cases; it was the time and experiences we were having together. So, as I sat there caring for our third baby, I felt the desire to re-create those days when we had more time together. Those early dates had nurtured our relationship, and I wanted to make time for us again.

It was then that I decided things had to change. We needed more than the quarterly date we were trying to squeeze into our budget and our schedule. Our finances were tight, and babysitters were not lining up at the door eager to hang out with our three young children. We had to get creative. So we turned to our modest kitchen as a new, romantic setting where we could begin to date again.

With a mutual commitment to making it happen, we have made this a reality. Instead of retreating to our computers and iPhones, once a week (usually on Thursday) you can find us casually pouring each other a drink and lingering over the stove, relishing the quiet, our time together, and the excitement of a delicious meal. Most important, we are talking, laughing, eating, drinking, and enjoying each other, giving our marriage the time it deserves and needs to be sustained and to continue to grow.

These days, I find myself eager to plan our dates at home. I choose a hoppy beer to start, knowing that it is my husband's favorite. When I see a perfectly ripe avocado with dimpled skin and a vibrant jewel-toned citrus at the store, I dream up a simple salad to start our evening. Once home, I roll up my sleeves and rub fragrant spices onto a pork shoulder weaved with white fat (page 221).

I am practically giddy preparing for our dates, in the same way I was as a young college student, when Gabe and I first met. I think about him more often, eager to spend time with him and happy to love him through my passion for food. With three children and ten years of marriage behind us, I can appreciate the necessity of putting in the time and intention our marriage needs in order to thrive as we grow older together.

Date Night In tells our story of cultivating romance while sautéing and roasting in our kitchen. It's a journey in figuring out how to continue to grow in love with each other while mixing and dicing. It's about connecting around the table in the midst of simple, thoughtful meals. *Date Night In* invites the reader into our home as we fall deeper in love through great food. The recipes are easy to make and are combined with honest, fresh observations about life, marriage, and finding joy in the simple pleasures of cooking, dining, and being together.

Each chapter in *Date Night In* centers on a date we've enjoyed. It opens with an intimate and honest portrait of the joyful and not-so-joyful reality of life together, telling stories through the recipes. The menus are simple yet different than your typical weekday fare. They are easy to make and include helpful tips; the "Timeline" lays out a clear plan for each menu.

Keeping a love-filled marriage takes work. Gabe and I continually struggle not to let the reality of our lives overwhelm the most important relationship we have: that of being husband and wife, parents to three children under the age of eight, and the same two nineteen-year-olds who fell in love in college and promised to stay with each other forever. While I will never claim to be a marriage expert (sometimes I feel just as confused and overwhelmed as I did on day 1), I can say that, as a result of creating intentional time for each other through these date nights, we've already felt our relationship strengthen and our love deepen.

The idea for this book was born out of a series I created on my award-winning blog, NotWithoutSalt.com. When I started this monthly series just over four years ago, I had no idea that our dates would resonate with people so deeply. These posts are often my most visited and most commented on, and the subject of the most emails. Because we shared the reality of the work involved in maintaining a marriage, I've had people tell me how they have renewed their relationships after reading these posts and starting the weekly tradition themselves.

Like many of my readers' marriages, our marriage was starved for time and connection. For Gabe and me, these evenings help us stay connected, feed our marriage, and give us the space to fall deeper in love. Based on the movement we see forming through those who follow this series, it's clear that it is not just us, but many couples, who have the need and desire to date. *Date Night In* is the story of nourishing a relationship and the food that brings us together.

You'll hear me talk a lot about my 12-inch cast-iron pan. I love it, and frankly it never leaves my stove. It and my 6-quart Le Creuset are staples.

When it comes to hard cheeses like Parmesan and pecorino, a microplane is best for getting those frilly, fine, and wispy curls that softly melt into the bubbly cheese on top of a pizza or that blend beautifully into a crust, as is the case with the Bacon and Leek Tart with Ricotta Custard (page 164).

Masaharu Morimoto says, "A kitchen is not a kitchen without a knife." A good, sharp chef's knife makes the dinner prep tasks so much easier.

Keep a well-supplied stash of baking sheets and parchment paper. Besides helping cookies slide off the tray, parchment makes cleanup much simpler. I'm a big advocate. I buy my parchment in bulk at restaurant-supply shops. It's cheap, it comes in big sheets (which I then cut to size), and it doubles as tracing paper for the kids. Bonus: It also works as a light diffuser on the rare occasion that I need to block out the Seattle sun when I shoot food photos.

A scale is really the best tool for accurate baking. For cooking, I don't bother too much with it.

Toasted nuts and spices: To get the most flavor out of nuts and spices, they should be toasted first. I toast spices in my cast-iron skillet over medium heat. I move them around frequently to avoid scorching; the moment I smell them, I remove them from the pan and let them cool a few moments before I grind them. I toast nuts in a 350°F oven on a parchment-lined sheet tray for 10 to 15 minutes, or until I can smell them and their flesh has been tinted golden brown.

Brown butter: There's quite a bit of brown butter in this book, and I have been asked, "Why?" To which I reply, "Why not?" When butter is browned it takes on a completely new taste: one that I happen to love. It's nutty and caramelized, and tastes almost of toffee. I was taught early on that "color equals flavor," so I try to add color as much as I can. By that I mean changing something that was once pale, like butter and nuts, into a deeper shade to caramelize the natural sugars.

It's best to brown the butter in a light-colored pan. That way you can see the color of the milk solids as they start to turn golden. Cut the butter into smaller chunks to speed up the process and then melt over medium to medium-high heat. The milk solids in the butter will foam up and then subside. As they do this, they will fall to the bottom of the pan and caramelize. Again, trust your nose. When you smell a soft nuttiness, turn off the heat. The residual heat will continue to caramelize the butter. The milk solids should be lightly browned when you turn off the heat.

They will continue to cook to a deeper amber. If they become blackened, you've gone too far and may have to start over; the milk solids will taste burnt, but taste the butter first to see if the flavor is off.

Roasted red peppers: You can easily buy roasted red peppers and that's fine, but, when the markets are filled with peppers in various heat levels and colors, it's fun to roast a bunch and then save them for later. They freeze well and can also be canned. Of course, this only happens if I'm really planning ahead; most of the time I simply roast what I need right then and there.

To do so, I use one of two methods that I've grown to love. The more showy and dramatic way is to roast them right on the gas stove over a high flame, turning the peppers to blacken them on all sides. They char and wilt and scent the house with a sweet spice and smokiness. Once completely blackened, place them in a paper bag, close it up tight, and wait for 15 minutes. After that time, the skins should easily peel off. Don't rinse them in water, however, otherwise you'll wash away some of that robust smokiness that you've just worked so hard to create.

The other method is to bake them on a parchment-lined sheet tray (for ease of cleaning up) in a 375°F oven for about an hour. Their skins will char slightly and wrinkle, and their interiors will slump and become sweet and soft.

Once cool, slip off the skins and discard them and store or use the peppers straight away.

PANTRY

For ease of planning, I've created a grocery list and a list of pantry items needed for each date. These are the items that I assume are already in your pantry:

PRODUCE

Lemons
Garlic
Yellow onions

DAIRY

Whole milk
Unsalted butter
Eggs (large)

BAKING

All-purpose flour
Granulated sugar (white refined sugar)
Dark brown sugar
Confectioners' sugar
Cocoa powder
Instant espresso powder
Gelatin
Cornstarch
Baking powder
Baking soda
Vanilla extract
Active dry yeast

SPICES / GRAINS

Kosher salt
Flake salt
Freshly ground black pepper
Cinnamon, ground and sticks
Dried oregano
Cumin, ground and seeds
Whole nutmeg
Ground ginger
Dried bay leaves
Allspice, ground and berries
Smoked paprika (hot and regular)
Sweet paprika
Cayenne
Garlic powder
Star anise
Whole cloves
Caraway seeds
Red pepper flakes
Coriander, ground and seeds
Fennel seeds
Mustard seeds
Vanilla beans
Coffee beans
Chicken stock
Vegetable stock
Arborio rice
Panko breadcrumbs

OILS/VINEGARS, ETC.

Extra-virgin olive oil

Olive oil

Neutral oil (such as canola or vegetable)

Toasted sesame oil

Sherry vinegar

Apple cider vinegar

Champagne vinegar

Red wine vinegar

Rice vinegar

Soy sauce

Maple syrup

Honey

Molasses

Corn syrup

Yellow mustard

Dijon mustard

Grainy mustard

Ketchup

Mayonnaise

Smooth peanut butter

Liquid smoke

Capers

BAR/BEVERAGE

Triple sec

Brandy

Grand Marnier/Cointreau

Whiskey

Gin

Tequila

Vodka

Bourbon

Rum

Soda water

Basics

The recipes below are ones that I use in several places throughout the book. They've become standards in our home, and when I'm on top of things I'll make a batch or two and then freeze what I don't need for another use.

Most doughs can easily be frozen, if well wrapped, for at least a month. If it's a yeasted dough, I recommend freezing it after the first rise.

One final note before you get to it. When I measure flour, I scoop the flour into the cup measure and then sweep off the excess. Using this method, 1 cup generally weighs around 140 g.

Using a scale in baking is definitely the most accurate, but if you follow the recipes using the scoop-and-sweep method you shouldn't have any problems.

Olive Oil Pizza Dough

I've tried many variations of pizza dough at home, and this one has been the longest-running favorite. It's soft, it's easy to stretch to a wafer-thin crust, and it has a complex flavor (especially once it's been sitting in the fridge for a couple days). It's also the base of my Pretzel Rolls (page 51).

MAKES TWO 12-INCH PIZZAS

1 teaspoon active dry yeast

½ teaspoon granulated sugar

2 tablespoons olive oil

¾ cup / 180 ml lukewarm water

2¼ cups / 310 g all-purpose flour

1½ teaspoons kosher salt

Start this dough the day before or up to 2 days before you plan to use it.

In the bowl of a stand mixer fitted with the dough hook, combine the yeast, sugar, olive oil, and water. Dump in the flour and salt. Start by mixing the dough on low until everything is well combined. Increase the speed of the mixer to medium low and knead for 5 minutes. Alternatively, you can knead for 7 to 10 minutes by hand, on a lightly floured surface.

The dough should pull away from the sides of the bowl and be smooth and elastic.

Transfer to a container with a lid and refrigerate 24 to 48 hours. Make sure the container allows room for the dough to double in size. After this first slow rise, dough balls can be frozen until ready to use. Defrost in the refrigerator for 6 to 8 hours.

Burger Buns

I like a bun that isn't too tender but also one that doesn't make you fight for a bite. It needed to be bread-like without being too chewy. These buns are just that. The extra protein in the bread flour gives them a nice chew, while the presence of butter, milk, and honey tenderizes and sweetens, offering a nice, easy, and gently sweet bite.

MAKES 8 TO 12 BUNS,
DEPENDING ON FINISHED SIZE

DOUGH

1 cup / 240 ml warm water

3 tablespoons whole milk

2 teaspoons active dry yeast

2 tablespoons honey

1 large egg

3¼ cups / 460 g bread flour

2 teaspoons kosher salt

2 tablespoons unsalted butter, at room temperature

Neutral oil, for brushing (optional)

EGG WASH

1 whole egg

1 egg yolk

1 teaspoon water

2 tablespoons sesame seeds (optional; recommended if using them for the burgers on page 000)

Start this dough the day before you plan to use it.

In the bowl of an electric mixer, whisk together the water, milk, yeast, honey, and egg. Now, with the dough hook attached, add the flour and salt all at once and mix for 5 minutes on medium low. Add the butter and mix for another 2 minutes. The dough should be soft, smooth, and not too sticky.

Dump the dough into a sealable container and place straight into the refrigerator.

When you are ready to bake the buns, remove the dough from the refrigerator and divide into eight to twelve equal portions (2½-inch balls yield about twelve buns; 3½-inch balls yield eight buns). Roll each portion of dough into a ball by covering the dough with one hand and gently rotating that hand in a circular motion. As your hand is moving, use your fingertips to tuck the edges of the dough under itself. Do this on an unfloured countertop with lightly floured hands.

Place the rolled buns on a parchment-lined sheet tray. Spray the buns lightly with nonstick cooking spray or brush them lightly with a neutral oil and cover the tray loosely with plastic wrap, to prevent the dough from drying out.

Allow to rise in a warm spot until doubled, about 1½ to 2 hours.

Preheat the oven to 400°F.

Whisk together the egg, egg yolk, and water.

Once the buns have doubled in size, carefully remove the plastic wrap and brush the buns with the egg wash and sprinkle with sesame seeds, if using. Bake for 15 to 20 minutes, or until the buns are golden on the top and bottom, rotating the pan once during baking. The buns should feel hollow when gently tapped. Cool on a wire rack.

These buns will keep in an airtight container for up to 2 days at room temperature or up to 1 month in the freezer.

Roasted Strawberry Jam

I've been making jams in the oven for the past two seasons now, and I can't get enough of it. I've always loved how roasting adds a caramelized flavor to foods and how it adds more depth and sweetness to the food that basks in its warmth, and so one day I thought, "Why not jam?"

I like my jams tart and quite loose. Feel free to adjust this recipe to suit your tastes. This method also works beautifully with apricots.

MAKES 3½ CUPS / 910 G

2 pounds / 910 g frozen strawberries

¾ cup / 150 g granulated sugar

1 vanilla bean, split (optional)

1 tablespoon freshly squeezed lemon juice

Pinch of kosher salt

Preheat the oven to 325°F. Line a baking sheet with parchment paper so that it comes up the sides or use a shallow roasting pan in order to catch all the juices.

In a large bowl combine the strawberries, sugar, vanilla bean, lemon juice, and salt. Stir to combine. Turn out onto the parchment-lined baking sheet.

Roast for 1 to 1½ hours, or until the berries are slumped and the juices nearly flood the pan. Stir the berries a few times throughout the roasting to ensure even cooking. It will look very wet, but, as it cools and you mash the berries slightly, it will thicken. If you prefer a tighter jam, you may drain off some of the juice, but save it for making strawberry sodas or for pouring over vanilla ice cream.

While still warm, squish the berries into the juice so that they break up a bit and thicken the jam. You can use a potato masher or the back of a wooden spoon. You can also process the jam in a food processor or blender once it has cooled if you prefer a smooth jam.

Let the jam cool in the pan before storing in a sealable container. The jam will keep in the fridge for up to 2 weeks.

Ricotta

This recipe can easily be halved, as it makes quite a bit of ricotta. I see no problem with having enough ricotta to last for the week. Ever since living in Italy, my favorite breakfast is stale bread with fresh ricotta and jam. Or, if we're out of jam, terrible as it may be, a drizzle of olive oil and a sprinkle of salt is a fine substitute. So, go ahead and just make the full batch.

MAKES 2¼ CUPS / 550 G

4 cups / 950 ml whole milk

2 cups / 470 ml heavy whipping cream

3 tablespoons freshly squeezed lemon juice

½ teaspoon kosher salt

Line a sieve (or colander) with two layers of cheesecloth and set it over a large bowl.

In a large, heavy saucepan, combine the milk and cream and set over medium heat. Warm the milk and cream just to a gentle boil and then turn off the heat. Add the lemon juice and give the whole pot a soft stir. Curds will begin to form immediately, so you don't want to disturb them too much with stirring.

Let the pot sit undisturbed for 1 to 2 minutes. At this point, you should see the curds and whey separating. Gently pour the mixture onto the sieve and allow the whey to drain until the ricotta has reached the consistency you like. This usually takes about 20 minutes.

Place the ricotta in a bowl and stir in the salt.

If you aren't using the ricotta right away, just cover it and place it in the fridge. It will keep for up to 1 week in the fridge.

Crème Fraîche

You will find that I use a lot of crème fraîche in the book, mostly as a nice creamy component for serving alongside dessert. You can buy crème fraîche, but I find that it is quite pricey and I mostly stopped buying it when I realized how easy it can be made at home. The classic crème fraîche uses a cultured starter in the form of buttermilk or yogurt, but, in a pinch, lemon juice thickens the cream quite nicely while adding a soft tang. If you can find it, use pasteurized cream rather than ultra-pasteurized.

MAKES 1 CUP

1 cup / 240 ml heavy whipping cream

2 tablespoons plain cultured yogurt or buttermilk

Combine the cream and yogurt in a small bowl, cover loosely with a towel or plastic wrap, and allow to sit at room temperature for several hours or overnight, until the cream is thick and tastes tangy. Taste it as it sits so you can best determine when you think it's done.

If you are strapped for time, you can make a quick crème fraîche using 1 cup / 240 ml heavy whipping cream and 1 tablespoon freshly squeezed lemon juice. It won't have the same cultured tang, but it will be a lovely substitute and it thickens much quicker.

Crème fraîche will keep for 1 week, covered, in the refrigerator.

Chicken Stock

There are two methods that I use for making chicken stock. One involves using a fresh, uncooked bird. The second involves using a spent carcass from, say, last night's roasted chicken dinner. I've made both with great success. Either way you choose, the next steps are the same.

Add aromatics to a large pot. This is the time to use those unsightly onion bits that you've collected, the bruised and slightly bitter outer celery stalks that preserve the sweet interior ones, herb stems, carrot stubs, fennel fronds, et cetera. Of course, if you don't save all those scraps and bits (which can be stored in the freezer for your next stock-making escapade), using roughly chopped fresh vegetables and herbs is great too, and what I often use, being the poor saver of scraps that I am. For one chicken, I use 1 roughly chopped large onion, 4 garlic cloves (no need to peel), 3 to 4 stalks celery, and 3 to 4 carrots. If I have fennel lying around, I use that too.

After that I add some peppercorns, a bay leaf, and a few other dried herbs that are in reach. If I have herb stems lying around, I toss those in as well. Beyond that, you can add red pepper flakes, coriander, and cumin. I add a pinch of salt here too, as I like to lightly season everything along the way so that the final dish doesn't taste salty but rather is properly seasoned.

Add the chicken, fresh or roasted. Cover with water. Bring to a rolling boil and then reduce the heat and simmer for at least 4 hours. The longer it cooks, the more strongly flavored the stock will be.

Let it cool a bit before you strain out the spent vegetables.

Refrigerate the stock until completely chilled, about 3 hours, and then skim off the layer of fat that rests at the top.

Chicken stock will keep in the fridge for up to 1 week or in the freezer for up to 3 months.

Note: For a more robust and roasted-tasting stock, sauté the vegetables first before adding the water.

Vegetable Stock

The method for a vegetable stock is the same as for a chicken stock, except that you'd omit the bird, of course. I often sauté or roast the vegetables first in a bit of olive oil so that the stock has a bit more heft to it. I almost always add mushrooms to a vegetable stock for that same reason.

Quick Puff Pastry

If you don't have a stand mixer, you can do this by hand, which is the method I used for a long time until I realized how much quicker it is when using the mixer. My favorite tool when I make this by hand is a bench scraper. It's how I keep the dough together and how I cut up the cubes of cold butter. This recipe can easily be halved. Whatever is not used can be wrapped well and frozen for up to 2 months.

MAKES 2½ POUNDS, ENOUGH FOR FOUR (10-OUNCE / 280 G) 10 X 15 SHEETS

4 cups / 565 g all-purpose flour

2 teaspoons kosher salt

3 cups / 680 g unsalted butter, diced into ½-inch cubes, chilled

1 cup / 240 ml cold water

Combine the flour and salt in the bowl of a stand mixer fitted with the paddle attachment. Add all the butter to the bowl at once and mix for 30 seconds on low speed. You want the butter to just start to break up and incorporate into the flour. Add the cold water and mix for 15 seconds.

This mix will be crumbly and dry. You may be cursing me for getting you into this mess, but I assure you, when you pull the airy, puffed dough out of the oven, I will be your best friend.

Turn the dough out onto an unfloured counter or large cutting board. Roughly shape the crumbly dough into a rectangle. Fold over the right third of the dough to the center, like folding a business letter. A bench scraper helps with the folding at this point. Fold the left third over the dough and turn 90 degrees. This was your first turn. It will likely fall apart through the first three turns, and when it does, simply use your hands to press the dough back together.

Using the palm of your hands, push the dough back to a flattened rectangle and repeat the process two more times for a total of three turns. If at any point you feel the butter getting soft or the dough becomes too tough to work with, just place it in the fridge to rest for at least 30 minutes.

After three turns, place the dough in the fridge to rest for at least 30 minutes or up to 1 hour. You can leave the dough at this state overnight if time is an issue; just let it rest on the counter for 10 minutes to remove the chill from the butter slightly before starting the turning process again.

Once rested, continue with three more turns. After that first rest, the water will have hydrated much of the flour and it should resemble a dough. This is when I start to use the rolling pin rather than my hands to work with the dough. After the final three turns (for a total of six turns), let it rest again for 30 minutes in the fridge.

At this point your dough is ready to use.

Most often recipes call for a sheet of puff pastry. Roll out your dough to ¼-inch thickness and cut to any size that the recipe calls for.

19

Shortcakes

This recipe has been made no fewer than a hundred times in our house. These shortcakes are our scones, the cobbler on top of our baked fruit, and sometimes, with the addition of herbs or cheese, savory biscuits to accompany dinner.

The trick here is not to overwork the dough. It's a very crumbly mass once it comes out of the bowl, but that's why the finished texture is so light and tender. Don't knead the dough together, but rather press it until it just holds.

This dough can be made by hand, in a food processor, as it is written, or in a stand mixer.

MAKES 8 SHORTCAKES

2 cups / 270 g all-purpose flour

1 teaspoon kosher salt

1 tablespoon aluminum-free baking powder

3 tablespoons granulated sugar

½ cup / 115 g unsalted butter, diced into ½-inch cubes, chilled

1 cup / 240 ml plus 2 tablespoons heavy whipping cream, divided

3 tablespoons turbinado or granulated sugar (optional, if using the dough for a dessert or breakfast pastries)

> **Note:** Often I make these by hand and simply grate the chilled butter into the dry ingredients with a cheese grater. From there I toss the butter and dry ingredients together, breaking up any large clumps with my hands, and then stir in the cream.
>
> For extra flaky layers, give this dough 1 or 2 turns as you do in the Quick Puff Pastry recipe (page 19).

In the bowl of a food processor, combine the flour, salt, baking powder, and granulated sugar. Pulse a few times to combine and break up any clumps.

Add the butter, scattering it over the flour. Pulse 15 times to break up the butter. The mixture will look sandy, with some larger pieces of butter throughout.

Pour 1 cup / 240 ml cream over the dough and pulse an additional 20 times. The dough will look crumbly and dry.

Dump the dough onto an unfloured work surface and use the palm of your hand to work the dough just until it holds together. You don't want to overwork the dough, as this can make it tough. Gather the dough together into a 6- to 8-inch round (for making wedge-shaped scones) or a rectangle (for cutting out round biscuits).

Use a brush or your fingers to spread the remaining 2 tablespoons cream in an even layer on top. Sprinkle the extra sugar, if using, on top of the cream. Chill the dough for 30 minutes.

Preheat the oven to 400°F. Line a baking sheet with parchment paper.

Cut the dough into the desired shapes and then place them on the baking sheet. Bake for 20 to 25 minutes, or until deep golden along the edges.

Cool to room temperature on a wire rack.

These are best served the day they are baked. Unbaked dough can be wrapped and frozen for up to 1 month.

Pickled Sweet Peppers

These are modeled after my favorite pickled peppers by Mama Lil's. I love having a jar around and use them often; one year I even served some alongside my turkey at Thanksgiving. In the book, you'll see them used in my German Pretzel Sandwich (page 100) and on the White Pizza with Sausage (page 243).

MAKES 1 CUP / 440 G

1 cup / 240 ml apple cider vinegar

1 teaspoon kosher salt

2 tablespoons dark brown sugar

½ teaspoon dried oregano

3 garlic cloves

1 red jalapeño pepper, sliced into thin rounds

¼ cup / 60 ml extra-virgin olive oil

8 ounces / 230 g Italian roasting peppers or colorful mini peppers, sliced into ¼-inch rounds

In a medium saucepan over medium heat, combine the vinegar, salt, sugar, oregano, garlic, jalapeño, and olive oil and bring to a simmer. Add the sliced peppers and simmer for 15 minutes, or until the peppers are tender and have swelled in the pickling liquid.

Cool to room temperature in the saucepan. Transfer the cooled peppers into a jar with a slotted spoon, pour the liquid on top, and cover. Will keep in the refrigerator for up to 1 month.

SPRING

Feasting on Spring

Rhubarb Sour

27

Spring Green Salad with Creamy Shallot Vinaigrette

28

Herb-Butter Roasted Chicken with Tarragon Aioli

30

Maple Coriander Roasted Carrots

33

Strawberry Shortcake Trifle

34

With three kids all old enough to sit around the table and eat, but not yet old enough to get in the kitchen and fend for themselves, I feel like I spend most of my time at the stove, floating from one meal to the next. As I clear away dishes from breakfast, the kids start to ask, "When is it lunch time? I'm hungry." Five minutes later, or so it seems, they are asking for dinner.

In a moment of exhaustion, I once asked Gabe if he would do some of the cooking. I knew then that I was agreeing to repeated dinners of quesadillas and grilled cheese. He said yes even though he generally loathes the idea of cooking. I thought a few cooking classes might make him excited about the idea, and I signed him up for some lessons with the chef I was working with at the time. I'm happy to report that Gabe now makes a mean vinaigrette. But he still stresses in the face of determining what's for dinner. I'll see him trudge into the kitchen, open up the fridge door, look inside already feeling defeated, and then five minutes later he is still standing there when I come to the rescue.

Although preparing three meals a day, seven days a week, can be a daunting and sometimes undesirable task, I've come to realize that it doesn't make me nearly as frantic as it does Gabe—in fact, most of the time I enjoy it. So why should I make him do it? (The other truth to this arrangement is that I tend to be controlling

and downright mean in the kitchen: I'll blame my stint working in commercial kitchens for that.) It's best for our marriage if I do the cooking and he stays out of the way, unless he's doing the dishes.

Date nights are often the same; I cook while Gabe puts the kids to bed or mixes us a drink. This meal was no different. Until it came time to make the aioli.

As the chicken roasted in a buttery and herb-scented bath and the carrots blistered and caramelized in the oven, I coated the greens in a tangy dressing and found myself in the midst of doing too many things at one time. So I asked Gabe to help with the aioli.

Being a romantic in and out of the kitchen, I love the idea of making mayonnaise and aioli by hand with nothing but a bowl and a whisk. However, if you've set out to do this task alone, you quickly realize that it doesn't take much whisking before you feel like your arm is either on fire or about to disconnect from your shoulder. So Gabe and I took turns. He held the bowl while I whisked until my arm was nearly numb, and then he took over.

The whole process takes a while; if more than one drop of oil falls into the bowl at a time, the aioli will not emulsify. As I whisked and he steadily dribbled in the oil, I wondered if Gabe thought I was crazy. I wondered if he understood why I'd chosen to make aioli by hand rather than mixing a bit of tarragon with store-bought mayonnaise—which is a perfectly legitimate alternative. I wondered if he felt the giddiness I felt when the oil, garlic, and lemon juice became pale yellow and perfectly creamy. Or did he think this was just a giant waste of time and he'd rather be sitting at the table with his cocktail?

Gabe didn't complain about helping me or ask why I was being so ridiculous by insisting the aioli needed to be made by hand. He was there and willing to join in the process, no matter how daunting the task. Even though it was such a silly thing—aioli—he loved me as he took part in my passion.

The chicken came out of the oven with a crisped caramel-colored skin. Carefully, and with a bit of flair, I flipped the bird to reveal an even deeper color on the breast side. The fragrant butter sputtered in the bottom of the pan while I marveled at the skin: pleasantly charred in parts, protecting the tender meat inside. I slid the carrots to the top of the oven to give their tender flesh a bit more heat under the broiler. As the chicken rested and lapped up some of the butter that had escaped while roasting, I put the last bit of fresh herbs on our salad while Gabe poured us each a vibrant, pink cocktail.

When we sat down, it took a moment to take in the seasonal feast before us. The brief moments between one season and the next are my favorite. In early spring, days retain just the right amount of winter to warrant both a hot oven and a salad of soft-stemmed herbs that have pushed their way through the nearly frozen earth to remind us that things are growing. Their flavor is delicate, subtle as if to slowly and tenderly awaken our senses while we emerge from a season of simmered roasts and root vegetables.

Sitting down to dinner I thought about which flavor most represents this season. If it were to have a mascot, rhubarb and fresh herbs would have to vie for the title. A sip of our tangy, pink Sour pulls rhubarb in the lead before I bite into the greens dressed in vinaigrette and flecked heavily with herbs. In this meal I think herbs take the lead, as they've made their way into the salad, the chicken, and the carrots. And yet, perhaps it's strawberries that should speak for spring. They border the start of summer so it's hard to say where they belong except in a bowl along with buttery biscuits and sweetened cream.

I couldn't help feeling a little proud as Gabe plunged the sweet, spiced carrots into our aioli. His love for the tangy, rich sauce might never match mine, but I appreciated his willingness to experience something that means so much to me.

TIMELINE

1 TO 3 DAYS IN ADVANCE
Season chicken
Make shortcake dough
Make tarragon aioli
Make rhubarb syrup
Make vinaigrette

DATE DAY
Prep strawberries
Prep salad
Bake shortcakes

DINNER TIME
Roast chicken
Make rhubarb sours
Roast carrots
Assemble trifles
Assemble salad

GROCERY

1 pound / 450 g rhubarb
1 head butter lettuce
1 pint / 225 g strawberries
1 shallot
1 small bunch carrots (7 to 8)
1 package or small bunch dill
1 bunch fresh flat-leaf parsley
1 package or small bunch chives
1 package or small bunch mint (optional)
1 package or small bunch tarragon
1 package or small bunch cilantro
1 package or small bunch basil
1 small bunch radishes
1 avocado
1 (3 to 4 pound / 1.4 to 1.8 kg) whole
    chicken
Heavy whipping cream
Crème fraîche (optional)
3 ounces / 90 g goat cheese

PANTRY

2 lemons
Garlic
Eggs
Unsalted butter
Granulated sugar
Dark brown sugar
All-purpose flour
Baking powder
Whole nutmeg (optional)
Cinnamon sticks
Ground coriander
Kosher salt
Flake salt
Black pepper
Red pepper flakes
Vanilla bean
Extra-virgin olive oil
Neutral oil (such as canola or vegetable)
Champagne vinegar
Maple syrup
Honey
Dijon mustard
Grainy mustard
Gin

Rhubarb Sour

In the spring I make countless batches of this syrup, and many cocktails are born out of it. Mixed with a bit of rum and mint it becomes a pink, vanilla-flecked mojito. But here I love the added lemon in the sour because it plays off rhubarb's natural tartness.

I often add a few things to this syrup to enhance the rhubarb's flavor: cinnamon sticks, vanilla bean, lemon or orange peel, cardamom, juniper berries, nutmeg, or star anise. For a refreshing, nonalcoholic drink, make rhubarb soda with the syrup and some soda water. Add a splash of cream to the soda for an Italian rhubarb soda or, my favorite, add a scoop of vanilla ice cream to craft a flushed rhubarb float.

SERVES 2

3 ounces / 90 ml gin

3 ounces / 90 ml Rhubarb Syrup (recipe follows)

1½ ounces / 40 ml freshly squeezed lemon juice

Lemon peel (optional)

¼ teaspoon freshly ground nutmeg (optional)

Combine the gin, rhubarb syrup, and lemon juice in a cocktail shaker filled with ice and shake vigorously. Strain into two small coupe glasses. Garnish with lemon peel and a little freshly grated nutmeg, if desired.

Rhubarb Syrup

MAKES 2½ CUPS / 650 G

1 pound / 450 g chopped rhubarb

1 cup / 200 g granulated sugar

2 cups / 470 ml water

Additional flavorings: cinnamon stick, freshly grated nutmeg, vanilla bean, or citrus peel

Note: Don't throw out that rhubarb. It might look stringy and spent, but that rhubarb will burst with sweet, tart flavor that goes beautifully atop yogurt, oatmeal, toasted bread, or ice cream.

Place the rhubarb, sugar, water, and your choice of flavorings into a medium saucepan and bring to a boil. Reduce the heat slightly so the mixture continues to boil gently for 15 minutes, or until it is reduced by nearly half. The rhubarb will break down and the liquid will get syrupy. Remove the pan from the heat and let the syrup cool to room temperature.

When cool, strain the syrup through a fine-mesh sieve. Transfer the syrup to a storage container with a lid. It will keep covered in the fridge for up to 2 weeks.

Spring Green Salad WITH Creamy Shallot Vinaigrette

This is a simple salad with a deceptive amount of flavor, tasting of mint, licorice, sweet grass, and spring. Use whatever soft, fresh herbs you have, but I especially recommend mint, tarragon, and dill.

SERVES 2

VINAIGRETTE

1 tablespoon minced shallot

2 teaspoons honey

2 teaspoons Dijon mustard

2 tablespoons crème fraîche or heavy whipping cream

2 tablespoons Champagne vinegar

¼ cup / 60 ml extra-virgin olive oil

¼ teaspoon kosher salt

⅛ teaspoon freshly ground black pepper

SALAD

½ head butter lettuce, washed and dried

3 radishes, thinly sliced

½ avocado, thinly sliced

½ cup / 10 g roughly chopped assorted fresh herbs (such as tarragon, dill, mint, chives, parsley, and cilantro)

3 ounces / 90 g soft goat cheese, crumbled (optional)

Flake salt and freshly ground black pepper

For the vinaigrette:

Whisk together the shallot, honey, mustard, crème fraîche, and vinegar. Continue to whisk while pouring in the oil. Alternatively, combine all the ingredients in a jar and then shake until combined. Add the salt and pepper. Taste and adjust seasonings to your desire.

For the salad:

Place the lettuce leaves in a medium bowl and toss with ¼ cup / 60 g of the vinaigrette. Arrange the leaves on two plates and then top with the radishes, avocado, and herbs. Finish with crumbled goat cheese, if desired. Sprinkle with flake salt and freshly ground black pepper to taste.

Note: The vinaigrette recipe makes enough dressing for four salads. It also makes a great marinade or sauce for grilled chicken or shrimp. Leftover dressing can be stored in the refrigerator for up to 1 week.

Herb-Butter Roasted Chicken with Tarragon Aioli

This is my go-to method for roasting a chicken. In a 12-inch cast-iron skillet, I sear the chicken breast-side down to ensure a deeply caramelized skin and to allow juices from the dark meat to drip into the white meat, which tends to get dry and lack flavor. Salting the chicken anytime from 1 to 3 days before you roast it gives the salt time to soak into all of the meat; if you salt the chicken right before roasting, only the skin is seasoned.

Roast the carrots on the lower rack of your oven at the same time as you roast the chicken.

SERVES 4

1 (3 to 4 pound / 1.4 to 1.8 kg) whole chicken

2 teaspoons kosher salt

1 teaspoon freshly ground black pepper

¼ cup / 5 g finely chopped herbs, plus more for garnish (such as chives, parsley, tarragon, and basil)

3 garlic cloves, minced

1 tablespoon grainy mustard

3 tablespoons unsalted butter, at room temperature

2 tablespoons extra-virgin olive oil

Prepare your chicken 1 to 3 days ahead: remove the giblets and sprinkle the chicken with salt and pepper inside and out. Place in a small roasting pan and refrigerate, uncovered.

Remove the chicken from the fridge 30 minutes prior to roasting. Pat dry with paper towels.

Preheat the oven to 400°F.

In a small bowl, stir together the herbs, garlic, mustard, and butter. Carefully separate the chicken skin from the breast and tuck some of the herbed butter under it, massaging to move it all around the breast. Spread the remaining butter over the chicken skin and in the cavity.

Heat the olive oil in a large, oven-safe skillet over high heat until the oil is just starting to smoke. Carefully add the chicken to the pan, breast-side down. Allow the breast to sear for 4 minutes without moving. Remove from the heat and place the pan in the preheated oven.

Every 20 minutes, spoon the butter-and-herb-laced drippings from the pan over the chicken, coating the skin. Roast for a total of 60 minutes, or until a thermometer reads 165°F deep in the thigh, away from the bone.

Remove the chicken from the pan and let rest on a cutting board for 15 minutes before carving.

Serve the chicken with the golden, crisped breast-side up and garnish with chopped fresh herbs.

Note: Refrigerating the chicken without a covering such as plastic wrap dries out the skin and gives you an extra-crispy chicken.

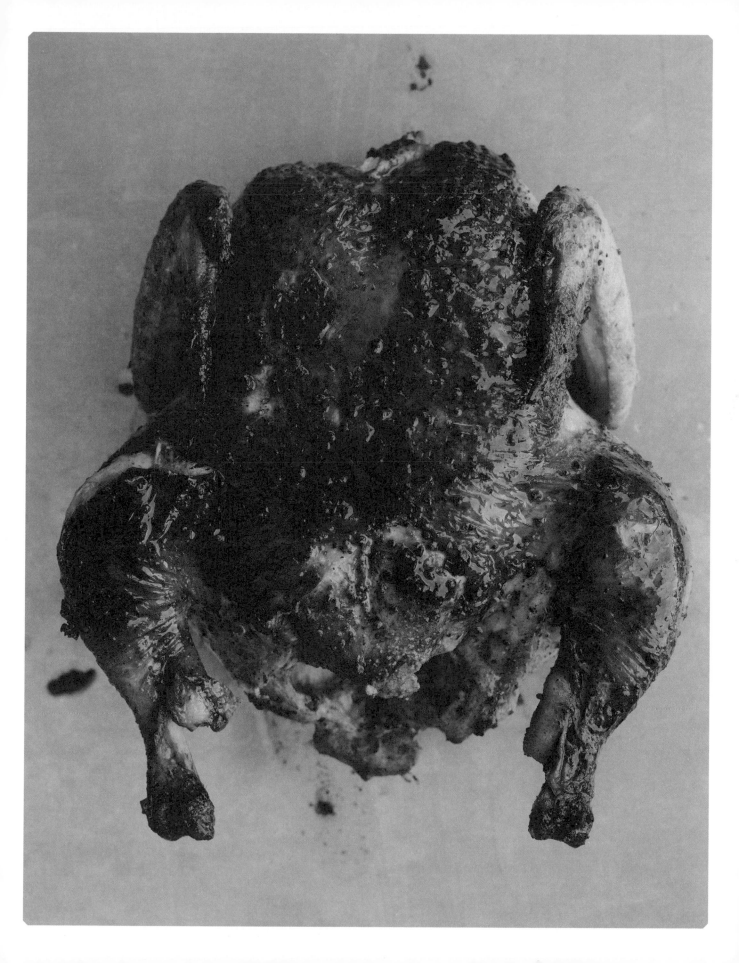

Tarragon Aioli

This aioli, although time-consuming and tiring to whisk together, makes the chicken sing and the carrots shine. I went back to the bowl for many more dips before my plate was clean. If you'd rather not tire out your arm, you could combine the garlic, salt, Dijon, lemon juice, and tarragon with a scant ½ cup good-quality store-bought mayonnaise. If you don't have someone available to help with the whisk, form a damp kitchen towel into a ring and rest the base of the bowl in the center. This will keep it from slipping and sliding.

MAKES ABOUT ½ CUP / 120 G

1 garlic clove

¼ teaspoon kosher salt

1 teaspoon Dijon mustard

2 teaspoons freshly squeezed lemon juice

1 egg yolk

¼ cup / 60 ml extra-virgin olive oil

3 tablespoons neutral oil (such as canola or vegetable)

2 tablespoons chopped tarragon

Mince the garlic very fine. Add the salt directly to the garlic. Use the flat part of the knife to press it against the board seven to ten times until a fine paste forms. Add this to a medium bowl along with the mustard, lemon juice, and egg yolk. Whisk to combine.

Begin adding the oils, one drop at a time, whisking continuously. Once an emulsion begins to form, start to pour in a steady stream of oil. After you add all the oil, it should look like very loose mayonnaise. Stir in the tarragon. Taste and add more salt if needed.

Serve alongside the roasted chicken and roasted carrots.

Note: Combine leftover tarragon aioli, cubed leftover chicken, and halved grapes for a simple chicken salad. Serve on butter-toasted bread with fresh herbs.

Maple Coriander Roasted Carrots

By the time these carrots come out of the oven, they look a bit frazzled, gnarled, and charred in parts, which is exactly what makes them so sweet, crisp, and addictive. Here I dip them, with abandon, into the tarragon aioli, but I've also been known to serve them on a bed of ricotta (page 17).

SERVES 2

1½ tablespoons extra-virgin olive oil

2 tablespoons maple syrup

2 teaspoons ground coriander

1 teaspoon kosher salt

Pinch of red pepper flakes

7 to 8 small carrots, halved

Preheat the oven to 400°F. Line a baking sheet with parchment paper.

In a small bowl, combine the oil, syrup, coriander, salt, and red pepper flakes. Pour the mixture over the carrots and toss until evenly coated.

Roast for 35 to 40 minutes, or until the carrots are tender and caramelized in parts, turning them once. If they are tender but not yet caramelized, turn the broiler on high and broil for 3 to 5 minutes, or until charred in parts. Watch closely so they don't burn.

Strawberry Shortcake Trifle

Certain dishes mark the passing of time. It isn't late spring or early summer in the Northwest until the first strawberry shortcake has been served. My version turns the shortcake into a trifle with juicy berries bathed in brown sugar and lemon juice. I've also made this trifle using raspberries and cherries. This is a wonderful picnic dessert that packs beautifully in jars.

SERVES 2

STRAWBERRIES

1 pint / 225 g strawberries, quartered

2 to 3 tablespoons dark brown sugar (depending on sweetness of berries)

1 teaspoon freshly grated lemon zest

1 tablespoon freshly squeezed lemon juice

WHIPPED CREAM

½ vanilla bean (or 1 teaspoon vanilla extract)

⅔ cup / 160 ml heavy whipping cream

1 tablespoon granulated sugar

TO ASSEMBLE THE TRIFLE

2 shortcakes (page 20), scones, or biscuits, broken into small and medium pieces (see recipe below)

For the strawberries:

In a medium bowl, toss the strawberries with the sugar, lemon zest, and lemon juice. Let sit for at least 30 minutes. This will allow the juices to release.

For the whipped cream:

For the whipped cream: Scrape the seeds of the vanilla bean into a large bowl, add the cream and sugar, and whip on medium-low speed with an electric mixer until soft peaks form.

To assemble:

Add one quarter of the berries to each of two glasses or bowls. Add a spoonful of whipped cream on top of that and put one quarter of the shortcake pieces into each cup. Divide between the bowls the remaining strawberries, including the juices from the bowl they were sitting in, whipped cream, and shortcake pieces.

Refrigerate until ready to eat. Can be made 2 to 3 hours in advance; much more than that and the strawberries start to wilt.

My Birthday

Hot Dates with Olive Oil and Sea Salt
39

Fresh Herb Risotto
41

Fennel-Crusted Lamb Chops
42

Crème Fraîche Panna Cotta with
Ginger-Roasted Rhubarb
44

We celebrated my birthday on an actual go-out-to-a-restaurant date. I like those too. And while the food was incredible—a table scattered with creamy hummus, crispy fried falafel, pistachio-studded lamb kefta, and fragrant tabbouleh—we ate most of it in between harsh words, awkward silences, and unfulfilled expectations.

I had known I wasn't in the best shape for going out. I had been on the East Coast for a couple days. I was tired and overly hungry, and my ability to control my emotions was like that of my two-year-old. Yes, I almost had an adult tantrum and, if it had been socially acceptable, I would have thrown my body onto the floor while flailing my arms and legs. Adding to the list of complications, it was also my birthday, which for me brings along a host of expectations. "It only happens once a year," I told myself, "so it better be good."

I felt bad for the waitress who had to cut through the stale, tense air just to pour water into our glasses. "How's everything doing here?" she asked. I returned her staged question with an equally staged smile, "We're great." We all knew otherwise.

After some sleep and distance from the argument, we continued our conversation with much more adult-like behavior. But I still wanted a redo.

A few nights later we sat down to dinner at home. We welcomed the evening with pan-roasted dates as the kids made their way to bed. The dates offered a warm bite, with an overwhelming sweetness set off with flakes of sea salt. Already I could feel that this night was different.

Gabe herded the kids upstairs with their usual moans over the injustice of it all, while batting away their last-ditch efforts at postponing the inevitable: "Mom, can you scratch my back?" "I'm thirsty." "But I'm still huuuuuungry."

It wasn't long before the only sound I could hear was the soft swish and swirl of a wooden spoon turning rice into rich and creamy risotto. I stirred the rice into sautéed onions and butter, pleading with each grain to soak up the scent coming from the pan. To entice the grains of rice, I added white wine, and everyone in the pot was happy. Heady herbal scents from the food processor lured me over for yet another sniff of its mashed up contents, a deep green blend of parsley, mint, chives, and cilantro. I smelled

35

spring in my kitchen. My mind wandered to picnics, plucking summertime strawberries from their tender vines, and vibrant rhubarb. The rhubarb! I opened the oven door and set the pan to cool on the stove. Sweet, honeyed rhubarb and ginger overwhelmed the kitchen. While I continued to stir the risotto, I stared at the sheet tray covered in pink and quietly said a farewell and good riddance to winter, knowing full well that, in Seattle, even though the calendar showed that spring was nearing, the gray and cold would be around for a while. But for the moment, chives thrived in the garden, the cold wasn't as biting as it once was, and we were having rhubarb for dessert.

Gabe trudged down the stairs, exiting the world of chaos and whines and entering into a kitchen flooded with sweet and herby smells. A tall glass of Cava reminded us that tonight was date night. In between return trips upstairs to further settle the kids into bed, Gabe set the table and put music on softly in the background. I covered the lamb chops with more fresh herbs, sharp pecorino, and toasted fennel seeds. The fennel seeds danced and sputtered in the pan and gave off an unmistakable floral, licorice scent. I stirred herbs into the risotto as the lamb rested, and Gabe sat eagerly at the table, tired from the day but excited for dinner and another chance to celebrate my birthday.

"There's one more little gift I have for you," he said as I set a plate in front of him.

"Ohhhh!!" I said with the excitement of a child. I really do love presents.

"I bought you an Enneagram test."

For some, this might be the equivalent of getting a vacuum cleaner for Christmas. But for me, it was the perfect gift. I love personality tests: answering endless seemingly unrelated questions to have them reveal truths about myself that I couldn't have put into words. There's something comforting about reading the words and insights of a complete stranger (albeit a highly trained and knowledgeable stranger) and finding that they fit you perfectly.

The other part of this gift was that Gabe was going to take the test too. He doesn't get the same thrill from the moment the results come in like I do. After dinner, we snuggled up next to each other on the couch, with dirty plates still on the table and piled up in the kitchen. We worked through the 145 questions quickly, while I laughed to myself thinking about how drastically different our answers to the same questions must be.

When the results were tallied, we eagerly poured over them. We marveled at their accuracy and stopped to share some of the more powerful points, knowing that the other would completely understand how accurate it was.

"My greatest desire is to find myself and my significance," I tell Gabe, thrilled to find that someone else had the words that I so often tried to say myself or was too afraid to admit. But, because these words were not mine and just part of the test results, it felt safe to reveal them.

"Sixes are engaging, friendly, and playful—truly likable, dependable people," Gabe says proudly. I roll my eyes at his giddiness in revealing his personality, while inwardly agreeing heartily before continuing to read deeper into my test results.

"The individualist Four wants to express herself and her individuality, to create and surround herself with beauty, to maintain certain moods and feelings, to withdraw to protect her self-image, to take care of emotional needs before attending to anything else, to attract a 'rescuer.'"

When Gabe and I first met, I loved that he had fun no matter what we were doing. In a stale dorm room surrounded by pizza that tasted little better than cardboard, he could laugh so infectiously that the entire room would fill with people. He turned our less-than-ideal "first date," a trip to 7-Eleven, into one of the most fun evenings I've ever had.

I was drawn toward his ability to be carefree. What other people thought of him didn't matter; he didn't care if someone thought he was weird for wearing two button-up shirts with every other button undone or if someone didn't understand his "leave the last bite rule" because "it's always that last bite that puts you over the edge." He played bass, very well actually, but he played because he loved it. To Gabe, it was just playing music for pleasure: he didn't do it for approval.

Gabe was so vastly different from me. When we first met, the differences drew me to him. They made our relationship exciting and mysterious. But then we got married. Suddenly, the differences drove me crazy and quickly became the source of our conflict.

"Why can't he take anything seriously?" I'd ask myself, quickly forgetting that it was his fun-loving attitude that attracted me to him in the first place. His ability to be content drove me crazy. My emotions take dips and dives faster than a roller coaster, and I was trying to drag him onto the ride.

While I moaned about my job and our future plans, he desperately tried to make a joke in order to lighten the tone. Instead of appreciating how well his personality suited mine, I felt as if he didn't care to listen to me and understand how I was really feeling. I withdrew and felt resentment for what he wasn't giving me rather than loving who he was.

Ten years later, we're still different. But over time I've been able to see how our differences make us perfectly suited for marriage. If Gabe was as emotional and introspective as I am, we'd both be living with little gray rain clouds over our heads.

Gabe makes me laugh when I need to laugh. He reminds me that "this too shall pass" and helps to put things into perspective. Alternatively, I can remind Gabe to think more deeply, which grows our relationship and makes us better parents and better people. We, and I'm talking all of us now, have created this romantic notion of "soul mates." We date people and search for "the one." If we are lucky to find that one, we marry and expect things to be perfect because we think we were made for each other. Yet when our "soul mate" unintentionally hurts us and dissatisfies us in some way—which will happen because we are all imperfect people—we are crushed and confused, and we question whether "the one" was really the soul mate.

I've found that it's through the course of marriage that you become soul mates. It's through deep sadness that we learn to grieve together, through great joy we learn to celebrate together, and simply through the day-to-day that we learn how to use who we are to create a stronger unit that works for both.

Somehow, in the midst of being married to Gabe, he's managed to make me more "me." He has encouraged me to embrace who I am while gently inspiring me to see things differently: he refines who it is that makes me *me*. Together we are electric, introspective, creative, and funny—basically one hell of a person. A decade into this crazy thing called marriage, I no longer wish for Gabe to be different, or more like me. Instead, I'm able to see the very reason why we are a team. Our differences attracted me to Gabe, drove me absolutely crazy, and made us strong. Gabe and I are soul mates, but we worked damn hard to get here.

TIMELINE

1 TO 3 DAYS IN ADVANCE
Season lamb chops
Roast rhubarb
Make panna cotta

DATE DAY
Make fennel rub for lamb

DINNER TIME
Open sparkling wine
Sauté dates
Make risotto
Cook chops

GROCERY

4 to 6 Medjool dates
1 package or small bunch fresh thyme
1 package or small bunch fresh mint
1 bunch fresh cilantro
1 bunch fresh flat-leaf parsley
1 package or small bunch fresh chives
8 ounces / 230 g rhubarb
½-inch / 1-cm piece fresh ginger
2 double-cut lamb chops (about 5 ounces / 140 g each)
2 ounces / 60 g pecorino
Heavy whipping cream
8 ounces / 230 g crème fraîche, homemade (page 17) or store-bought
Dry white wine
1 bottle Cava or favorite sparkling wine

PANTRY

1 yellow onion
Garlic
Unsalted butter
Granulated sugar
Vanilla bean
Vanilla extract
1 package powdered gelatin
Honey
Extra-virgin olive oil
Kosher salt
Flake salt
Freshly ground black pepper
1 tablespoon fennel seeds
4½ cups / 1.1 L chicken or vegetable stock, homemade (page 18) or store-bought
10 ounces / 280 g short-grain rice (such as arborio)

Hot Dates with Olive Oil and Sea Salt

I had my first taste of a warm date served with nothing but crunchy salt on top at the Walrus and the Carpenter, one of my favorite restaurants in Seattle. I wouldn't have ordered the dates had it not been for a friend who demanded we add them to our long list of "must gets." They are so simple, so magical that they've become my go-to meal opener. People might give you a weird look when you declare "hot dates!" but after one taste, they'll get it: soft, salty, sweet, and fragrant from a bit of grassy olive oil. Hot dates are the perfect start to a hot date.

SERVES 2

1 tablespoon extra-virgin olive oil, plus more for finishing (use the good stuff here)

4 to 6 Medjool dates

Flake sea salt (such as Maldon)

Add the olive oil to a sauté pan over medium heat. Add the dates and stir to coat. Keep the dates moving so that they don't scorch but rather get warm and soft and blister slightly. After 3 to 4 minutes in the pan, place the hot dates on a plate and drizzle with the olive oil from the pan. Add a bit more olive oil if you'd like. Sprinkle with a pinch of flake salt. Serve immediately.

MY BIRTHDAY

Fresh Herb Risotto

In spring, herbs feel like a luxury. They are among the first fresh produce to arrive at the market that isn't a root vegetable or a winter green, and to me that is cause for celebration. Highlighted with a bright pop of salty pecorino, herbs take center stage in this risotto. When I make risotto, I like to make enough for leftovers; a warm bowl of leftover risotto with a fried egg on top makes waking up a bit easier. You can easily halve the recipe if you'd rather not have leftovers.

SERVES 4

½ cup / 10 g loosely packed fresh mint leaves

½ cup / 10 g loosely packed fresh flat-leaf parsley leaves

½ cup / 5 g loosely packed fresh cilantro leaves

½ cup / 25 g roughly chopped, loosely packed fresh chives

2 tablespoons unsalted butter

1 medium-size yellow onion, diced

½ teaspoon kosher salt, divided

3 garlic cloves, minced

4½ cups / 1,070 ml low-sodium chicken or vegetable stock (page 18)

1½ cups / 300 g short-grain rice (such as arborio)

½ cup / 120 ml dry white wine

1 cup / 20 g finely grated pecorino, plus more for finishing

1 tablespoon extra-virgin olive oil

½ teaspoon freshly ground black pepper

Add the herbs, reserving 2 tablespoons for garnish, to the bowl of a food processor and process for about 30 seconds. Scrape down the sides of the bowl once or twice to ensure the processor has finely chopped all the herbs.

Melt the butter in a large saucepan or Dutch oven over medium heat. Add the onion and ¼ teaspoon kosher salt and sauté until just golden around the edges and translucent throughout, about 10 minutes. Add the garlic to the pan and cook an additional 2 minutes.

While the onions and garlic cook, bring the chicken stock to a simmer in a small saucepan over medium-high heat. Reduce the heat to low.

Add the rice to the onions and garlic. Stir until well incorporated and coated with butter, about 1 minute. Add the wine and cook until fully absorbed, stirring slowly. One cup at a time, pour the stock into the mixture and continue to stir; pour in the next cup once the liquid has been absorbed, 5 to 10 minutes. Continue in this way until the rice is nearly tender, stirring continuously, 16 to 18 minutes total. The risotto will continue to soften as it sits. You may not need to add all of the liquid.

Remove the saucepan from the heat and stir in the pecorino and fresh herb purée. Finish with a drizzle of olive oil. Add the remaining ¼ teaspoon salt and freshly ground black pepper. Taste and adjust the seasonings as needed.

Serve the risotto immediately and garnish with additional herbs and finely grated pecorino.

Fennel-Crusted Lamb Chops

Every year (maybe I'm exaggerating), my mother would sing, "It's my party and I'll cry if I want to" at my birthday party. When I was eight this was terribly embarrassing, but, when I was planning what I wanted to eat for my birthday dinner, I couldn't help singing to myself, "It's my party and I'll eat what I want to." I'm the lamb fan in the family, and Gabe doesn't really care much for large doses of rhubarb and herbs. Needless to say, this menu, and in particular these lamb chops, is all about Ashley.

SERVES 2

2 double-cut lamb chops (about 5 ounces / 140 g each)

½ teaspoon kosher salt

¼ teaspoon freshly ground black pepper

1 tablespoon fennel seeds, toasted (see technique on page 11)

1 teaspoon chopped fresh thyme leaves

1 tablespoon chopped fresh flat-leaf parsley

2½ tablespoons extra-virgin olive oil, divided

1 tablespoon finely grated pecorino

Up to three days before dinner, sprinkle the lamb chops with salt and pepper. Cover and refrigerate.

When you are ready to cook, preheat the oven to 400°F.

For the fennel rub, combine the fennel seeds, thyme, parsley, ½ tablespoon oil, and pecorino in a small bowl. The rub can be made earlier in the day and refrigerated until ready to use. Coat the lamb chops with this mixture and let sit for 15 minutes.

Add the remaining 2 tablespoons oil to a medium, oven-safe sauté pan or skillet over medium-high heat. Once hot, add the lamb chops and let sear, undisturbed, on each side for 4 minutes. Finish in the oven for 5 minutes for perfect medium-rare doneness.

Remove the chops from the pan and let rest for 10 minutes before serving.

Crème Fraîche Panna Cotta WITH Ginger-Roasted Rhubarb

I'm a big fan of custard desserts: frozen, baked, or torched, I'll take them all. But there are times, quite often, when I don't want to deal with tempering egg yolks. For those times, I turn to panna cotta. With panna cotta there is the satisfaction of a creamy custard without dealing with fragile egg yolks. This version yields a softly sweet and tangy creaminess that suits roasted rhubarb perfectly. When rhubarb isn't available, try roasted strawberries, peaches, or plums. A lovely jam on top makes for an even simpler dessert. Warm the jam before serving to contrast the cool panna cotta.

SERVES 2

3 tablespoons cold water

1 teaspoon powdered gelatin

½ cup / 120 ml heavy whipping cream

½ cup/ 120 g crème fraîche, homemade (page 17) or store-bought

2 tablespoons granulated sugar

½ vanilla bean, split and scraped, bean reserved for rhubarb (substitute ½ teaspoon vanilla extract)

Pinch of kosher salt

In a small bowl, combine the cold water with the gelatin. Allow to bloom for 10 minutes.

In a small saucepan over medium heat, stir together the cream, crème fraîche, sugar, and vanilla bean seeds (if using). Bring to a simmer and stir until the sugar is dissolved.

Add the gelatin to the warm cream mixture, throw in a pinch of salt, and stir to combine. Add the vanilla extract if you didn't use a vanilla bean (or go crazy and use both).

Pour the custard mixture into two 6-ounce ramekins or bowls. If you want to unmold the panna cotta once set, spray the ramekins with a bit of cooking spray before pouring in the custard mixture. Loosely cover the bowls with plastic wrap.

Refrigerate until set, about 2 hours. The panna cotta can be made up to 3 days in advance.

Remove the panna cotta from the refrigerator 30 minutes before serving to let it warm up just slightly. If unmolding, run a knife around each ramekin and invert onto a plate. Top with warm ginger-roasted rhubarb.

Ginger-Roasted Rhubarb

A little sweet but mostly tart: that's how I like my rhubarb. Leftovers are fantastic on morning toast, in yogurt, or atop vanilla or strawberry ice cream.

MAKES 2 CUPS / 190 G

2 cups / 225 g rhubarb, cut into 2-inch pieces

3 tablespoons honey

3 tablespoons granulated sugar

1 teaspoon minced fresh ginger (from a ½-inch / 1-cm piece of ginger)

Preheat the oven to 400°F. Line a sheet tray with parchment paper.

Place the rhubarb on the parchment–lined sheet tray. Add the honey, sugar, ginger, and reserved vanilla bean pod (if using) and toss to combine.

Roast for 20 minutes, or until the rhubarb is tender and deeply blushed and the juices just start to bubble. Serve warm, over the panna cotta.

The compote can be made up to 3 days in advance. Cover and refrigerate, then gently warm before serving. Leftover rhubarb can be covered and refrigerated for up to 1 week.

A Touch of Thai

Fresh Spring Rolls with Ginger and Sesame

49

Spring Vegetable Green Curry

51

Thai Iced Coffee Affogato with
Spiced Coconut Ice Cream

53

"What have we done in our marriage that you all have taken into your own marriages?" My dad asks as my brothers, their wives, my husband, and I share dinner together to celebrate my parents' fortieth wedding anniversary.

We sit under towering walnut trees in their front yard. In the distance, a couple of cows and a horse wander the fields while we finish melon salad with basil vinaigrette and roasted pork tenderloin over creamy Parmesan polenta.

The weight of my dad's question makes me tense. I busy myself with the last bit of polenta left on my plate. Forty years of marriage is a lot to process in a short moment and, honestly, I had spent more time analyzing how I wanted my marriage to be different. Then it hits me.

"You always strive for intimacy," I start. "It's not always perfect and doesn't often look like what you want, but the desire to have shared interests and to spend time together is there; neither of you settle for anything but the other to be your best friend." As the words stumble from my mouth into a clumsy puddle on the table, I become even more aware of their truth.

My parents' marriage was never complacent. In disconnected seasons, they fought their way back to intimacy. As their child and an observer of their marriage, I see how their need for connection inspires the same in my marriage.

As I thought about our own marriage, I remembered a conversation with my son Baron when Gabe and I had just started dating at home. Baron watched intently as I cleaned up stray noodles that dotted the floor from their dinner and set the table for Gabe's and my dinner.

"What are you doing?" He asked while I placed a couple of unfamiliar cloth napkins next to the plates.

"I'm setting the table for a special date with your dad," I told him.

The kids were all watching now as I set out a bowl of frilly lettuce leaves lightly dressed. I couldn't help but feel a little guilty as their eyes followed my every move. I was taking great care to taste the food at each step, making sure everything was just right even though they had eaten a simple pasta with butter and Parmesan for dinner.

Since then, they've seen us setting up for dozens of dates. Sometimes there are cloth napkins, candles, and a set table. Other times they just see me in the kitchen chopping onions while they bring empty plates to the sink after their dinner. One night while I was in between date night preparations, I tucked Baron into bed and he asked, "What are you making for Daddy tonight?" I recited the menu in great detail and assured him that there would be leftovers that he could try in the morning.

I was cleaning out Baron's school folder recently and found a piece of paper divided into four squares. The top left square said "morning," next to that "afternoon," below that "evening," and then "night." In each square Baron had drawn a picture.

"Baron, what is this?" I asked, eager for him to decipher the stick-figure drawings.

"This is me brushing my teeth in the morning," he said while pointing to the first box. "This is me eating lunch in the afternoon. This is me and Roman wrestling in the evening, and this is you and Daddy having a date when we're in bed," he told me proudly while pointing to the last box.

I hadn't realized it before that moment: these date nights at home not only benefit us as a couple but also are a tangible image for our kids to see that a relationship takes work. So often I feel bad that we rush the kids off to bed early with a dinner far simpler than the one we are about to enjoy. But as I looked at Baron's drawing of Gabe and me sitting down to dinner—just the two of us—I realized that they needed to see this. As important as our daily family dinners are, they needed to see Gabe and me making time for each other and not just for them.

When I think of Baron's picture, I hope that each one of them will do the same in their relationships; I put each of their faces on top of those stick-figured bodies and imagine them

sitting down to a great meal with someone they love and working for intimacy in the same way we do and in the same way I watched my parents do throughout their marriage.

On some date nights, the little voices upstairs that interrupt our conversation annoy and irritate me. But tonight, as we sit down to a bowl of green curry and its warm ginger, lemongrass, and lime fragrance, they are a reminder that the kids can hear their mom and dad downstairs laughing, enjoying a great meal, and fighting for a close, loving marriage. By the time the spiced coconut ice cream sits in front of us, melting in little pools of hot coffee, the house is perfectly quiet. We are silent too as we savor the ice cream's mix of coolness and warmth. I feel whole, happy to have had time with my husband, proud to be an example for our kids, and, admittedly, a bit daunted by the sink filled with dishes. If only the kids could see the great example their dad sets by doing the dishes . . . I'm sure I'll tell them about it in the morning.

A TOUCH OF THAI

TIMELINE

1 TO 3 DAYS IN ADVANCE
Make green curry paste
Make curry
Make dipping sauce
Make ice cream base

DATE DAY
Churn ice cream

DINNER TIME
Make rice
Assemble fresh rolls
Heat curry
Make coffee
Assemble affogatos

PANTRY

Garlic
Eggs
Dark brown sugar
Granulated sugar
Ground cumin
Ground coriander
1 vanilla bean
1 cinnamon stick
Whole nutmeg
Kosher salt
Rice vinegar
Neutral oil (such as vegetable or canola)

GROCERY

2 medium-size carrots
1 English cucumber
1 bunch scallions
5- to 6-inch piece fresh ginger
1 package or small bunch fresh basil
1 package or small bunch fresh mint
2 bunches fresh cilantro
1 avocado
4 Thai or serrano chiles (or more if you like more spice)
1 red jalapeño pepper
2 stalks lemongrass
1 package lime leaves
1 red bell pepper
1 zucchini
1 small bunch asparagus
½ cup / 65 g shelled green peas, fresh or frozen
1 shallot
3 to 4 limes
2 tablespoons toasted sesame seeds
5 cardamom pods
Ground cardamom
Heavy whipping cream
Rice noodles (optional)
Rice paper wrappers
2 (13.5-ounce / 380 g) cans full-fat coconut milk
Fish sauce
Sesame oil
Jasmine rice
Coffee or espresso

Fresh Spring Rolls with Ginger and Sesame

Gabe and I used to make variations of this recipe all the time when we were dating. To us it felt sort of fancy and grown-up because we were using an ingredient—rice paper wrappers—that many of our friends never knew existed. But it was also cheap and gave us the chance to clean out the fridge with all the bits of vegetables and leftovers that accumulate. Like us, this recipe has grown up a bit, and this is the version we're sticking with.

These can easily be made into a meal itself with the addition of tofu, shrimp, or chicken. Gabe likes his with rice noodles; I prefer just vegetables.

SERVES 2

DIPPING SAUCE

½ cup / 120 g rice vinegar

2 tablespoons dark brown sugar

1 garlic clove, minced

1 scallion, thinly sliced (white and green parts)

½ teaspoon sesame oil

½ teaspoon fresh ginger, minced

½ red jalapeño pepper, finely diced (more or less depending on desired amount of heat)

Zest and juice of 1 lime

ROLLS

1 carrot, julienned

½ large English cucumber, julienned

1-inch piece fresh ginger, finely julienned

½ avocado, thinly sliced

1 cup / 30 g total of fresh basil, mint, and cilantro leaves

2 tablespoons toasted sesame seeds

2 ounces / 60 g rice noodles (optional), cooked according to package directions and cooled

6 large rice paper wrappers

For the dipping sauce:

Whisk together the rice vinegar, brown sugar, garlic, scallion, sesame oil, ginger, jalapeño, lime zest, and lime juice. Can be made up to 2 days in advance.

For the rolls:

In a medium bowl, combine the carrot, cucumber, and ginger. Toss with 1 tablespoon of the dipping sauce. Set aside to marinate for at least 15 minutes.

Prep the remaining roll ingredients and place on a tray or large platter. You'll want everything together for the assembly.

To assemble the rolls, have a pan larger than the size of the rice paper wrappers (like a large pie plate) filled with hot water. Dip one of the wrappers in the hot water and keep submerged until translucent and pliable, about 20 to 30 seconds. Carefully lay the wrapper on a cutting board or other flat surface. Grab a small amount of the marinated vegetable mixture, some fresh herbs, two slices of avocado, and some rice noodles, if using, and place in the middle of the wrapper. Finish with a sprinkling of toasted sesame seeds. Roll the top of the wrapper over the filling, using your fingers to pull the filling together tightly. Fold in the sides to seal the edges and continue to roll as you would a burrito. The finished product should be a neat, tight roll about 1 inch thick. But if yours are like my husband's—oversized, covered with holes, and packed way too full—no problem; they are still delicious.

Serve the fresh rolls immediately with the dipping sauce.

Green Curry Paste

This recipe makes quite a bit of paste because, if I'm going to make my own curry paste, I'm going to make a lot and freeze the rest. Then some random Monday night, when I'm still reeling from the weekend and the looming to-do list for the week threatens to make me run into a corner and weep, well then, at least I won't have to worry much about dinner.

MAKES 1 GENEROUS CUP / 240 G

1 bunch cilantro, leaves and stems roughly chopped

1 cup basil leaves

1 medium-size shallot, roughly chopped

5 large garlic cloves

2 stalks lemongrass, all hard dry outer leaves and root end removed, roughly chopped

4- to 5-inch piece fresh ginger, peeled and roughly chopped

4 Thai or serrano chiles, seeded (more or less depending on desired level of heat)

¼ cup / 60 g freshly squeezed lime juice

1 teaspoon freshly grated lime zest

¼ cup / 60 g fish sauce (if vegetarian, use soy sauce)

2 teaspoons ground cumin

1 teaspoon ground cardamom

2 teaspoons ground coriander

1 teaspoon dark brown sugar

Combine the cilantro, basil, shallot, garlic, lemongrass, ginger, chiles, lime juice, lime zest, fish sauce, cumin, cardamom, coriander, and brown sugar in a food processor or blender and blend until a fine paste is formed, for 1 to 2 minutes. If you need to, you can add a couple tablespoons of coconut milk to get a smooth purée. Blend everything really well, as lemongrass and ginger can be stringy if the paste isn't blended enough. The flavor of the curry paste improves if made ahead. You can make the paste up to 1 week in advance. Leftover paste can be frozen for up to 1 month.

Spring Vegetable Green Curry

For the sake of this recipe, you'll need to seek out a few ingredients that you may not normally have on hand. Fish sauce should be easily found in the ethnic aisle of your grocery store or at an Asian market. Most stores sell lemongrass and lime leaves alongside other packaged herbs; check the freezer case too. They can be a bit pricey, but you won't use up everything in this recipe. Store what you don't use in the freezer alongside the leftover green curry paste for a healthful and flavorful dinner in a hurry.

SERVES 4

1 tablespoon neutral oil (such as vegetable or canola)

½ cup green curry paste / 120 g (page 50)

1 carrot, diced small

1 teaspoon kosher salt, divided

1 (13.5-ounce / 380 g) can full-fat coconut milk

4 lime leaves (substitute 2 teaspoons freshly grated lime zest)

1 red bell pepper, cut into thin strips

1 small zucchini, diced

½ cup / 65 g shelled green peas, fresh or frozen

1 cup / 120 g diced tender asparagus (about 7 to 8 stalks)

1 cup / 30 g assorted herb leaves, plus more for garnish (mint, basil, and cilantro work well)

1 teaspoon fish sauce, plus more for serving

2 teaspoons freshly squeezed lime juice

1 cup / 200 g jasmine rice, cooked according to package directions, for serving

Lime wedges, for serving

In a large sauté pan or wok, heat the oil over medium-high heat and stir in the curry paste. Cook until fragrant, about 1 minute. Add the carrot and ½ teaspoon salt and sauté 2 minutes more before adding the coconut milk and lime leaves. Bring the curry to a simmer and then add the bell pepper and zucchini and the remaining ½ teaspoon salt. Cook for 2 minutes. Add the peas and asparagus and cook until the asparagus is just tender, about 10 minutes more. Finish by stirring in the fresh herbs, fish sauce, and lime juice.

Taste and adjust the seasonings to your liking.

Serve over cooked jasmine rice and garnish with more fresh herbs. Serve with lime wedges and keep the fish sauce on hand. The curry can be made up to 3 days in advance.

Thai Iced Coffee Affogato WITH Spiced Coconut Ice Cream

There's rarely an order of Thai takeout that doesn't include either a Thai iced coffee or tea for me. I love the sweet and bitter drink and the way it soothes the spiciness still lingering from the meal. My version marries that drink I love so much with one of my favorite desserts: affogato. Affogato, an Italian dessert, is a shot of espresso served over ice cream. For a Thai take on affogato, pour strong, hot coffee over coconut ice cream laced with cardamom, vanilla, and other warming spices.

MAKES 1 GENEROUS PINT

1 cup / 240 ml heavy whipping cream

1 (13.5-ounce / 380 g) can full-fat coconut milk

1 vanilla bean, split and seeds scraped

1 cinnamon stick

5 cardamom pods, lightly crushed so the seeds can release into the custard

¼ teaspoon freshly grated nutmeg

3 egg yolks

½ cup / 100 g granulated sugar

¼ teaspoon kosher salt

⅔ cup / 160 ml freshly brewed strong coffee or 2 shots espresso (you could also use a strong black tea to make a Thai tea affogato), for serving

Combine the cream, coconut milk, vanilla seeds and the pod, cinnamon, cardamom, and nutmeg in a medium saucepan and bring to a simmer over medium heat. Turn off the heat and let stand for 15 minutes to allow the spices to infuse the cream.

In a large bowl, whisk together the egg yolks, sugar, and salt for 2 minutes, or until the sugar is dissolved and the color is pale yellow.

Return the cream mixture to a simmer and gently pour about one quarter of it into the egg mixture. Then slowly whisk the egg mixture into the saucepan of simmering cream mixture. Cook over medium heat until it has thickened enough to coat the back of a spoon, about 3 minutes, stirring constantly.

Cool the custard to room temperature. To do this quickly, pour the custard into a bowl and then place the bowl in a bigger bowl of ice water. Stir until cool. The ice cream base can be made up to 3 days in advance, but I recommend churning it the day you plan to serve it, as that's when the texture is best.

Place the custard in a sealable container, cover, and then refrigerate until completely cold.

To churn the ice cream, strain the ice cream base through a fine-mesh sieve and then process in your ice cream machine according to the manufacturer's instructions.

Freeze the coconut ice cream until firm, at least 1 hour. To serve, add a scoop or two to a small bowl or cup. Pour ⅓ cup / 80 ml strong hot coffee or a shot of espresso over each bowl of ice cream. Serve right away.

His Birthday

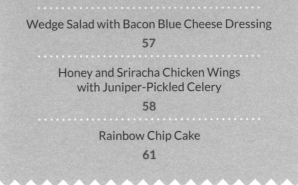

Wedge Salad with Bacon Blue Cheese Dressing
57

Honey and Sriracha Chicken Wings
with Juniper-Pickled Celery
58

Rainbow Chip Cake
61

Every year, I'd start asking him about a month before his actual birthday, "What kind of cake do you want this year?"

"Well, umm," Gabe would stall, knowing that what he really wanted was often different from what I wanted to make for him.

"No really, whatever you want," I'd say, trying to ease his fear of disappointing me.

"Rainbow chip."

"Seriously?! I bake cakes for a living. I'm willing to make you whatever you could possibly want, towering layers of dark chocolate devil's food layered with sweet vanilla cream and bittersweet ganache, and you want a boxed cake?!"

"Whatever you want to make is fine." He'd quickly change his answer.

A month later I'd humble myself to the boxed cake mix, a rainbow chip cake with rainbow chip frosting that is NOT to be confused with Funfetti. Gabe would dig into the fluffy, artificial white cake with the same sort of abandon I imagine he did when he indulged in the sweet cake as a young boy. I'm not above boxed cakes; the truth is, they infuriate me with their perfect texture. They might taste like cloyingly sweet cardboard and chemicals, but I marvel at their structure and crumb, the texture I had tried tirelessly to match when I was baking wedding cakes.

The other truth is that I felt I wasn't loving my husband well enough by just adding eggs and oil. I wanted to spend hours constructing a perfectly balanced cake with many components that each, in their own way, say, "You are loved." Because, whether he realizes it or not, it's through my food that I love him most honestly. I am terrible at kissing him in public, and I get all weird and red in the face when trying to use my words to tell him how I feel. But creaming butter and sugar together until they're the color of marshmallows and folding in flour so that the cake has enough structure and tenderness? Now that's how I say, "I love you."

For years I made him that boxed cake because that's what he wanted. Sometimes he'd let me make him homemade carrot cake, which he liked too, especially when the amount of tangy cream cheese frosting piled on top rivaled the quantity of cake it hid below, but mostly it was boxed rainbow chip. Until, one year, I decided I was going to face my greatest cake-making challenge and come up with a homemade recipe that matched the nostalgic rainbow chip he longed to taste year after year.

The process began nearly two months before Gabe's birthday and it started with the chips, which make up the bulk of rainbow chip's cake and frosting layers. Unlike Funfetti, rainbow chips are soft and waxy and gradually melt as you roll them around your tongue. They are tinted in rainbow hues and stand strikingly against the fluffy white cake and pillowy peaks of white frosting.

To start, I melted a bag of white chocolate chips in a large bowl and divided the contents into five small bowls. Next, drops of bright food coloring went into each bowl. With five separate spoons, I stirred the chocolate until striations of chocolate and food coloring blended into one mass of brightly colored chocolate. I poured each color out onto parchment and spread it thinly with an offset spatula. After they had set up in the freezer, I chopped the brightly colored chocolate into small flecks. They ranged in size and looked very homemade, and, when I saw the pile of brightly colored boxed cake-like chips, I knew I was onto something good.

Then there was the cake itself. It needed to be white, so no egg yolks, but the butter had to stay; while I love the texture of oil-based cakes, I love the taste of butter-based cakes more. The cake would be pristinely white and wonderfully buttery, yet still I fretted about its texture. I wanted a spongy, light, and tender cake just like the boxed version but without the chemicals that made it that way. Usually cake bakers then turn to cake flour but I don't like the flavor and never have it on hand, I always have all-purpose in my pantry. Like so many of my cooking and baking decisions, this one was partly made based on laziness. After a bit of research, I found a way to mimic the texture of a cake-flour cake by using a mix of cornstarch and flour.

Finally, I needed to address the frosting. This, I knew, was the part that Gabe would be most critical about; I would often buy an extra container of his beloved rainbow chip frosting just so there would be enough left over for him to drag graham crackers through its chip-laced contents. And it needed to be sweet, much sweeter than I prefer to make frosting. In the bowl of a stand mixer, I blended three packages of soft cream cheese along with soft, pliable butter. I finished the frosting with confectioners' sugar, a hefty pinch of salt in my attempt to balance the sweetness, and a vanilla bean's speckled seeds because I couldn't help myself.

I started the mixer on low speed and watched confectioners' sugar float up and over the bowl while the other ingredients mingled with the cream cheese and butter. Little black specks scattered throughout the soft frosting before I turned up the mixer and watched it lighten. It spurted and smacked against the bowl while I marveled at its familiar texture. I poured in the brightly colored, randomly sized chips and, in that moment, I knew I had done it. A quick taste affirmed my rainbow chip success, and I laughed, delighted to cast off my boxed-cake chains.

Gabe sat on the couch nearby. "Try this!" I demanded, practically shoving a spoonful into his mouth.

"Mmm. Dat's good," he said with his mouth full.

By the time his birthday arrived, I had perfected the cake. When we sat down that night with our cake, Gabe confirmed that I had indeed done it. He was so happy with this version that he declared we would never need a boxed cake again. Perhaps he was just loving me well by letting me make him this cake; maybe the truth is he'd rather have cake from a box with a tub of frosting on the side. If that is the case, I love that he's letting me love him. From the melted chocolate rainbow chips to the roasted strawberry jam I tuck between the cake's layers to the generous amount of slightly tangy but mostly sweet, chip-speckled frosting, I am loving him in the way I do. We all give and feel love differently. Recognizing how the other loves you and allowing them to love you well in their own way is just as loving as their own actions.

TIMELINE

1 TO 3 DAYS IN ADVANCE

Make rainbow chips

Bake cake

Make frosting

Make dressing

Make pickled celery

Make wing sauce

Make marinade

DATE DAY

Assemble cake

DINNER TIME

Roast chicken wings

Toss salad

GROCERY

1 head iceberg lettuce

Cherry tomatoes

1 package or small bunch chives

1 lime

8 ounces / 230 g celery (about 6 to 7 stalks)

½ cup / 130 g roasted strawberry jam (page 16) or store-bought strawberry jam

3 strips bacon

Sour cream

3 ounces / 90 g crumbled blue cheese (Rogue River Blue works well)

3 (8-ounce) packages / 680 g cream cheese

2 pounds / 900 g chicken wings

1 (11-ounce / 310 g) bag white chocolate chips

Food coloring (red, yellow, blue, and green)

Cornstarch

1½ tablespoons juniper berries

Sriracha (or other hot sauce)

Fish sauce

PANTRY

Garlic

Unsalted butter

Whole milk

Eggs

Granulated sugar

Confectioners' sugar

All-purpose flour

Baking powder

Vanilla extract

Vanilla bean

Ground cumin

Ground coriander

Red pepper flakes

Cumin seeds

Kosher salt

Freshly ground black pepper

Extra-virgin olive oil

Neutral oil (such as canola or vegetable)

Apple cider vinegar

Mayonnaise

Honey

Wedge Salad WITH Bacon Blue Cheese Dressing

If tomatoes are in season, I love throwing in a few halved cherry tomatoes or diced heirloom tomatoes. If they aren't, sun-dried or roasted tomatoes work well and taste tangy. Feel free to crisp up a bit of extra bacon to throw on top; I won't tell.

SERVES 2

DRESSING

½ cup / 120 g mayonnaise

½ cup / 120 g sour cream

½ cup / 120 ml whole milk

½ teaspoon kosher salt

½ teaspoon freshly ground black pepper

3 ounces / 90 g crumbled blue cheese (Rogue River Blue works well)

3 strips bacon, cooked until crisp and finely chopped

SALAD

½ head of iceberg lettuce, halved

½ cup / 80 g halved cherry tomatoes

2 tablespoons chopped fresh chives (optional)

For the dressing:

Whisk together the mayonnaise, sour cream, whole milk, salt, and pepper. Fold in the blue cheese and crumbled bacon (reserve a tablespoon of crumbled bacon to top the salads), making sure the blue cheese stays in big crumbles. Taste and adjust the seasonings to your liking.

Cover and refrigerate until ready to serve. Dressing will keep for 1 week in the fridge.

For the salad:

Set a wedge of lettuce on two salad plates. Spoon a generous amount of the dressing over each wedge and garnish with halved cherry tomatoes, reserved bacon, and fresh chives. Serve with extra dressing on the side.

Honey AND Sriracha Chicken Wings WITH Juniper-Pickled Celery

This recipe will make more than enough for two so that you'll have leftovers the next day. I LOVE cold chicken wings.

SERVES 4

MARINADE

1 tablespoon Sriracha (or other hot sauce)

1 teaspoon freshly grated lime zest

1 teaspoon ground cumin

1 teaspoon ground coriander

2 garlic cloves, minced

1½ teaspoons kosher salt

2 tablespoons extra-virgin olive oil

2 pounds / 900 g chicken wings

WING SAUCE

¼ cup / 65 g Sriracha (or other hot sauce)

¼ cup / 80 g honey

1 to 2 tablespoons freshly squeezed lime juice (from 1 lime)

1 tablespoon fish sauce

3 tablespoons unsalted butter, melted

For the marinade:

Stir together the Sriracha, lime zest, cumin, coriander, garlic, salt, and olive oil in a large bowl. Toss in the wings. Cover and refrigerate for at least 2 hours or overnight. The marinade can be made 1 to 3 days in advance.

Preheat the oven to 400°F. Place an oven rack in the top third of the oven.

Lay the marinated chicken wings on a baking sheet and roast for 30 minutes.

For the wing sauce:

Meanwhile, make the wing sauce: Whisk together the Sriracha, honey, lime juice, fish sauce, and melted butter. The wing sauce can be made 1 to 3 days in advance.

Remove the wings from the oven and transfer them to a medium bowl. Toss well with two thirds of the wing sauce. Return the wings to the baking sheet. Set the baking sheet 4 to 6 inches from the broiler and broil for 3 to 5 minutes, or until crispy and charred in parts.

Serve the wings with the remaining sauce and Juniper-Pickled Celery (**recipe follows**).

Juniper-Pickled Celery

Traditionally, wings are served with fresh celery, but I rarely miss an opportunity to pickle something. The celery remains crisp, serving its vital role of toning down the heat from the wings, but it brings a delightful complexity with a sweet and sour taste and an herbal flavor from the juniper. It would also do well as a garnish for chili, on top of a salad, or on a cheese plate alongside a sharp Cheddar.

MAKES 2 CUPS / 260 G

1 cup / 240 ml water

1 cup / 240 ml apple cider vinegar

¼ cup / 50 g granulated sugar

2 teaspoons kosher salt

2 garlic cloves, smashed

1½ tablespoons juniper berries

¼ teaspoon red pepper flakes

1 teaspoon cumin seeds

8 ounces / 230 g celery, sliced ⅛ inch thick
    (about 6 to 7 large stalks)

Combine the water, apple cider vinegar, sugar, salt, garlic, juniper berries, red pepper flakes, and cumin seeds in a medium saucepan. Bring to a boil. Turn off the heat and add the celery.

Let cool slightly, pour into a container, cover, and refrigerate until cold. Pickles will keep in the refrigerator for up to 1 month.

Note: The brine can be reheated to make another batch of pickles once all the celery has been enjoyed.

Rainbow Chip Cake

I had a wedding cake business when Baron, my oldest, was a baby. Even after all those years of experience, I still find cakes maddening. I want a cake the texture of a cake made from a box—springy, tender, and light—without using a boxed cake mix. This cake in particular needed to resemble the rainbow chip cake mix that my husband craves every time his birthday rolls around. For years I would make him the boxed cake. ME?! The one with the cake business! Then one year I decided, that's it! I'm making boxed cake myself.

MAKES ONE 2-LAYER 8-INCH CAKE

RAINBOW CHIPS

1 (11-ounce / 310 g) bag white chocolate chips

1 tablespoon neutral oil (such as canola or vegetable)

Food coloring (red, yellow, blue, and green)

CAKE

1 cup / 240 ml whole milk, at room temperature, divided

5 egg whites

2 teaspoons vanilla extract

¼ cup / 30 g cornstarch

2¾ cups / 370 g all-purpose flour

1 tablespoon plus 1 teaspoon baking powder

1 teaspoon kosher salt

1¾ cups / 350 g granulated sugar

¾ cup / 170 g unsalted butter, at room temperature, plus more for the pans

½ cup / 70 g homemade rainbow chips

FROSTING

3 (8-ounce) packages / 680 g cream cheese, at room temperature

½ cup / 115 g unsalted butter, at room temperature

3 cups / 340 g confectioners' sugar

¼ teaspoon kosher salt

1 teaspoon vanilla extract or the seeds from 1 vanilla bean

1 cup / 135 g homemade rainbow chips

ASSEMBLY

½ cup / 130 g roasted strawberry jam (page 16) or store-bought strawberry jam

For the rainbow chips:

In a microwave-safe bowl, melt the white chocolate with the oil in 20-second intervals, three or four at the most, and stir well. Be careful: the chocolate burns easily. Continue to heat and stir until all the chips are melted. The white chocolate will be thick and stiff but smooth.

Divide the melted white chocolate into four small bowls. Add five to seven drops of color into each bowl, one color per bowl. Stir to combine. The white chocolate may seize up a bit but should still be pliable. If not, pop it back into the microwave for about 10 seconds.

Empty each bowl of colored chocolate onto a parchment-lined baking sheet. Using your hands or an offset spatula, form it into a rough rectangle about ¼ inch thick. Do this with all the colors. They should all be able to fit on one large baking sheet.

Place in the freezer for about 10 minutes, or until set. Once set, chop up each color into little pieces. Rainbow chips can be made 1 week ahead and stored, covered, in the refrigerator.

For the cake:

Preheat the oven to 350°F. Butter two 8-inch cake pans and line the bottom with parchment paper. Butter the parchment.

In a medium bowl, whisk to combine ¼ cup / 60 ml of the milk with the egg whites and vanilla extract.

In the bowl of an electric mixer fitted with the paddle attachment, add the cornstarch, flour, baking powder, salt, and sugar and mix on low speed for 30 seconds. Add the butter and the remaining ¾ cup / 180 ml milk. Mix on low until combined and then increase the speed to medium and beat for 1 minute.

With a rubber spatula, scrape down the sides of the bowl and mix again just to combine. With the mixer on low, add one third of the egg white mixture and mix until incorporated. Add half of the remaining egg white mixture, beat well, and then add the remaining egg white mixture, beating until everything is combined.

Scrape down the sides of the bowl again and finish mixing on low.

Fold in the rainbow chips.

Divide the batter equally between the pans (1 pound 6 ounces / 620 g of batter per pan).

Bake for 35 to 40 minutes, or until the edges are golden and the cake springs back when gently pressed in the middle.

Let the cakes cool on a wire rack for 10 minutes before you remove them from the pans. They should pop out easily when you invert the pans. Cool completely before frosting.

The cakes can be made a day in advance. Wrap the cooled cakes completely in plastic wrap. I actually think the texture of the cake dramatically improves the day after it's baked. However, I recommend frosting the cake the day you plan on serving it.

For the frosting:

Beat the cream cheese and butter in a large bowl with an electric mixer until smooth. Stop the machine and add the confectioners' sugar, salt, and vanilla. Turn on low and mix until combined.

Turn up the speed to medium and beat 4 minutes more.

Turn off the machine and add the rainbow chips. Mix on low until just combined.

The frosting can be made up to 1 week in advance and stored, covered, in the fridge.

To assemble the cake:

Place one of the cake layers on a cake stand or platter. Use a serrated knife to even out the domed top of the layer and cut off the crisp edges; this also exposes the softer inside of the cake, allowing it to soak up more of the jam. Spoon ¼ cup / 65 g strawberry jam on the cake and spread in a thin, even layer. On top of the jam, spread about ½ cup/ 130 g frosting evenly across the cake. Leave the outer ½-inch edge of the cake unfrosted.

Trim the top of the second cake layer in the same way and add ¼ cup jam to the exposed cake top. Place the cake, jam-side down, on top of the first layer.

On top of the cake, add about 2 cups / 520 g frosting, pushing the frosting to the edges with an offset spatula. Continue to frost the cake until evenly covered. Add more frosting as needed. If the frosting gets too soft, pop it into the fridge for 10 to 20 minutes before continuing to frost.

Somewhere in Italy

Aperol Spritz

67

Crostini with Ricotta, Prosciutto, and Peas

69

Pasta e Fagioli with Crispy Prosciutto

70

Grapefruit and Olive Oil Cake
with Bittersweet Chocolate

72

"It's just one dinner," I think as the temptation to retreat to the couch once the kids have been tucked in threatens to derail our plans. Sometimes it's the deceptive simplicity of these date nights that is my greatest excuse for not having them. "How can one evening really make a difference?" I ask myself.

As I stir swooped orecchiette into an oregano-laced broth, I think about what I can do tonight to make the evening feel different, more special. "I could write him a sweet note." I say to myself as I set the last few peas onto the creamy, ricotta-topped crostini.

The pan on the stove begins to smoke, reminding me it's ready. I slide two pieces of prosciutto into the pan. Instantly the fat hisses and bubbles and then melts, turning the once wriggly prosciutto into a crisp, ruffled sheet. I forget that just moments ago I was fretting about making the night feel special, and now I focus on the food and the person I am making it for.

With a certain amount of flair and a great amount of pride, I nestle the crisped prosciutto in between tender white beans and tangy tomatoes. The prosciutto stands tall and proud, looking as if it were a flag marking its conquest over the soup. Over it all, I shower salty Parmesan and then set it on the table in front of Gabe, who waits with an orange-tinted Spritz.

Hungry and exhausted, we eat. In silence first as we lap up the soup and bite into the crisped bread that releases a biting garlic scent. Then we start to talk. The sort of conversation that happens when you make the space for it. The conversation that I crave during the one or two minutes that we find ourselves alone throughout the day, only to be quickly interrupted by a little voice that needs our attention.

Tonight there's the time for both of us to talk and for both of us to listen. We talk until the sun dips behind our neighbor's house. He reaches for the light switch when the shade dims the room. "Nuh uh, I've got a better idea," I say, reaching for a few candles instead. The wax rolls down the candle and pools on the table as we continue to connect with growing honesty and intimacy.

We talk like best friends and I never want it to end. It feels like the times when we were dating and we'd stay up for hours discussing complete nonsense just so we could continue to be in the same room with each other; except this is better because the awkwardness, the questioning about feelings and where the relationship is

Great things are done by a series of small things brought together.

Vincent van Gogh

going is gone. When the flame finally succumbs to the puddle of melted wax, we move to the couch and continue to talk. Then finally, when our words are few, we head up to bed.

I'm not naive to think every date night from here on out will be this intimate and wonderful, and there are definitely times when a little more effort for romance is needed, but tonight I walk away feeling downright giddy and grateful for our time together. It was just us sitting over a great meal, connecting, and that was enough. There were no bells or whistles. Just us, some crispy pork, a bit of gin, and great conversation.

In Anne Lamott's book on writing, *Bird by Bird*, she bases the premise of the book off some advice her brother received from their dad. He was fretting over a school report about birds the night before it was due. He had barely begun and sat numb in the vastness of the project. His dad put his arm around his desperate son and said, "Just take it bird by bird."

I've been known to say that in many circumstances: when tackling the laundry pile, in parenting, with work, and in my relationship with Gabe.

Sometimes the distance between us felt too big to be bridged by a seemingly simple date night at home, but then I stopped looking at the big picture and took it one date at a time. One night a week? That I can give. What I found is that that is enough. It's small, but over time those small things, these simple evenings at home, equate to something big. Bird by bird, one night at a time.

Tonight we said yes to dinner, yes to us, and that was enough. All we really need for our relationship is this time together, and quite possibly, more crispy pork.

TIMELINE

1 TO 3 DAYS IN ADVANCE

Make ricotta

Make olive oil cake

Make pasta e fagioli (if you wish), but don't add the pasta

DINNER TIME

Make pea salad

Make Aperol spritzes

Make crostini

Crisp prosciutto

Make pasta e fagioli, or if you've made the soup ahead, simply bring to a boil then cook the pasta

PANTRY

Garlic

3 lemons

1 yellow onion

Unsalted butter

Whole milk (for ricotta, page 17, or purchase 3 ounces / 90 g store-bought ricotta)

Eggs

Granulated sugar

Confectioners' sugar

All-purpose flour

Baking soda

Baking powder

Dried oregano

Kosher salt

Extra-virgin olive oil

Gin

Soda water

GROCERY

1 orange

1 grapefruit

1 package or small bunch fresh mint

1 package or small bunch fresh thyme

1 bunch fresh flat-leaf parsley

1 stalk celery

1 cup / 130 g peas, fresh or frozen

4 ounces / 110 g whole-milk plain yogurt

Crème fraîche (optional, to serve with dessert)

Heavy whipping cream (for ricotta, page 17, or purchase 3 ounces / 85 g store-bought ricotta)

4 ounces / 110 g Parmesan

4 slices prosciutto

4 ounces / 110 g bittersweet chocolate

¼ cup / 40 g chopped walnuts

¾ cup / 70 g dried orecchiette pasta

1 (15-ounce / 430 g) can cannellini beans

1 (14.5-ounce / 410 g) can diced tomatoes

2 cups / 470 ml low-sodium chicken stock, homemade (page 18) or store-bought

1 rustic country loaf of bread

Aperol

Prosecco

Aperol Spritz

Imagine yourself sitting outside at a table at a little café in Italy. You're on the edge of the piazza watching life pass by as you sip on an orange-colored spritz: lightly bitter, bubbly, and bright. This is what I do when I drink a spritz, while all around me, kids are melting down at the thought of going to bed and dishes are piling up in the sink: then I add gin. I suggest you do the same.

SERVES 2

½ cup / 120 ml Aperol

¾ cup / 180 ml Prosecco

¼ cup / 60 ml gin

Splash of soda water

2 orange slices

Fill two large white wine glasses with ice. Add to each glass half of the Aperol, the Prosecco, and the gin. Give a gentle stir and then finish each drink with a splash of soda water and an orange slice.

Crostini with Ricotta, Prosciutto, and Peas

When peas are at their best, this simple dish is quite often my lunch. I love the salt and fat the prosciutto adds, but it's fine if it's just ricotta and the pea salad with a healthy dose of vibrant green olive oil over the top.

MAKES 2

PEA SALAD WITH MINT AND WALNUTS

1 cup / 130 g peas, fresh or frozen, blanched

2 tablespoons extra-virgin olive oil

¼ cup / 60 g chopped walnuts, toasted (see technique on page 11)

½ tablespoon freshly squeezed lemon juice

¼ cup / 5 g chopped fresh mint

¼ teaspoon kosher salt

CROSTINI

1 tablespoon extra-virgin olive oil

2 thick slices of a rustic country loaf of bread

1 garlic clove

⅓ cup / 80 g ricotta, homemade (page 17) or store-bought

2 slices prosciutto

1 recipe pea salad

For the pea salad:

If you are using frozen peas, allow them to thaw by setting them out at room temperature for about 30 minutes or by running them under warm water. Drain well.

In a medium bowl, combine the peas, olive oil, walnuts, lemon juice, mint, and salt. With the back of a wooden spoon, smash some of the peas against the bowl. This will bruise the mint, combine the flavors, and make those peas less likely to roll off your crostini. Do not make this in advance, as the lemon juice will turn the peas brown if left to sit.

For the crostini:

Add the olive oil to a heavy skillet set over medium-high heat. Lay the bread in the pan and cook until golden and crisp, about 2 to 3 minutes per side. While the bread is still warm, rub the garlic clove over the crisp exterior.

Slather half of the ricotta on each crostini, top with a slice of prosciutto, and a few spoonfuls of the pea salad.

Serve immediately.

Pasta e Fagioli WITH Crispy Prosciutto

If you happen to have a piece of Parmesan rind lying at the bottom of your cheese drawer, throw that into the pot as the soup simmers. This soup, like so many, improves the day after it's made. I just reserve the cooking of the pasta until right before I plan to serve the soup so that it doesn't overcook.

SERVES 4

2 tablespoons extra-virgin olive oil

1 small yellow onion, chopped

1 celery stalk, chopped

2 garlic cloves, minced

½ teaspoon kosher salt

1 teaspoon dried oregano

1 teaspoon fresh thyme leaves

2 cups / 470 ml low-sodium chicken stock, homemade (page 18) or store-bought

1 (15-ounce / 430 g) can cannellini beans, drained

1 (14.5-ounce / 410 g) can diced tomatoes

¾ cup / 70 g dried orecchiette pasta

2 slices prosciutto

2 tablespoons chopped fresh flat-leaf parsley

½ cup / 15 g finely grated Parmesan

Add the olive oil to a large pan or Dutch oven over medium heat and sauté the onion, celery, garlic, salt, oregano, and thyme until fragrant and translucent, 8 to 10 minutes. Add the chicken stock, beans, and tomatoes. Bring everything to a gentle simmer and cook for 10 minutes. At this point the soup can cool and then sit in the refrigerator for a couple of days. When you are ready to serve dinner, bring the soup back to a boil and then add the pasta and continue to simmer till it is al dente, about 10 to 12 minutes.

Meanwhile, crisp the prosciutto. Place the prosciutto in a hot skillet and cook until it shrivels and its fat has rendered, about 1 to 2 minutes on each side. The prosciutto will crisp as it cools.

When the pasta is al dente, remove the pot from the heat and stir in the parsley. Taste and adjust the seasonings, keeping in mind that salty Parmesan and prosciutto are coming.

Serve the soup with grated Parmesan and a crispy piece of prosciutto on top.

Grapefruit AND Olive Oil Cake WITH Bittersweet Chocolate

When baking with olive oil, I recommend one that is more grassy and floral than peppery.

SERVES 8 TO 10

Unsalted butter, for the pan

¾ cup / 180 ml freshly squeezed grapefruit juice, divided

1½ tablespoons freshly grated grapefruit zest, divided

½ cup / 125 g whole-milk plain yogurt

3 large eggs

⅔ cup / 160 ml best-quality extra-virgin olive oil

¾ cup / 150 g granulated sugar

1¾ cups / 235 g all-purpose flour

1½ teaspoons baking powder

¼ teaspoon baking soda

1¼ teaspoons kosher salt

4 ounces / 110 g bittersweet chocolate, finely chopped

1½ cups / 170 g confectioners' sugar

Crème fraîche, for serving (optional)

Preheat the oven to 350°F. Butter a 9 x 5-inch loaf pan.

Add ½ cup / 120 ml grapefruit juice to a small saucepan set over medium heat. Bring to a simmer and reduce the juice by half. Cool slightly.

In a medium bowl, combine 1 tablespoon grapefruit zest, yogurt, eggs, olive oil, and reduced grapefruit juice and whisk to mix well.

In a large bowl, add the granulated sugar, flour, baking powder, baking soda, and salt. Whisk to combine.

Add the wet ingredients to the dry ingredients. Mix until everything is well blended. Stir in the chocolate.

Pour the batter into the prepared pan and place in the hot oven. Bake until the cake is deeply brown and set and springs back gently when pressed, 50 to 55 minutes.

While the cake bakes, prepare the glaze. In a bowl, combine the remaining ½ tablespoon grapefruit zest with the remaining ¼ cup / 60 ml grapefruit juice. Gently, in order to prevent a confectioners' sugar snowstorm, stir in the confectioners' sugar and continue to stir until well mixed.

Let the cake cool in the pan for 5 minutes before cooling on a wire rack.

When cooled to room temperature, place the cake on a serving platter and drizzle with half the glaze. Reserve the rest of the glaze for serving along with the sliced cake. Serve with crème fraîche, if desired. The cake can be made 1 day in advance.

Take It Outside

Kickin' Kentucky Mule

76

Potato Chips with Fennel Coriander Salt

79

Roast Beef Tenderloin Sandwiches with
Caramelized Onions, Horseradish Mayonnaise,
and Arugula

81

Salted Chocolate Chip Cookies

84

He held the door for me while the bell rang on the paint-chipped door frame above. A man, arms covered in tattoos, came to the desk.

"We want to get a tattoo," Gabe said with an equal mix of eagerness and terror.

It was the last day of our honeymoon and, although we had said "I do" a week before, getting a tattoo together seemed just as eventful. It would be a visible realization of the permanence in the commitment we had just made.

A week earlier, branches of fresh greens had wrapped the banister and made the entire room smell like the woods after a good rain: fresh, herbal. My dad and I walked down the stairs and aisle slowly, taking in every detail. All eyes were on us, but I focused on Gabe first. He wiped away tears, which relieved us both; I had joked with him the night before: "You better cry."

I tried to make eye contact with everyone in that room, hoping they would know I appreciated their presence. I'm terrible with thank-you cards, but I also wanted them to know how influential they had been and would be in Gabe's and my relationship. They were our people, and we knew we would need them to remind us of the vows we were about to promise to each other.

We said I do, bounded back down the aisle, and sat next to the roaring fireplace holding each other for the first time as husband and wife.

Together, in that tattoo shop, we decided to each get an Old English "R" for Rodriguez on our left wrists. He went first, while I shuffled around the black-and-white-checked floor, acting as if I were an old pro at the whole getting-a-tattoo thing. I had acted on a moment of temporary daring when I was eighteen, getting myself my first tiny tattoo on my back. I often forget it's there.

Just over an hour later, we walked out of the shop with lotion, sore wrists, and a connection through ink forever embedded just below the surface of our skin. I see the "R" as I grip the handle of a pot with my left hand as the right stirs.

As our tenth anniversary approached, Gabe brought up the idea of getting another tattoo. Our anniversary was a few days away, and, as I searched the Internet for ideas, I read that the tenth anniversary is the diamond anniversary. An actual diamond was out of the question, but when it came to tattoo designs a diamond seemed appropriate. Within the hour of the first mention of a tattoo, we had our design picked out and knew we wanted to get another tattoo together.

This time I didn't even blink at the permanence of it. The thought of sharing another forever with Gabe held no fear but instead gratitude. We both got large geometric diamonds on the arms opposite our "R." The shape of the round diamond matches the one I wear on my ring finger, the one Gabe gave me eleven years ago with the money he got from the insurance company after his car was smashed. He was fine; his car was drivable but with a large dent that was never fixed, hugging the driver's side.

There was a great naiveté with that first tattoo—and with our marriage. We were young and had no idea what we had just gotten into. It's like having a baby. People will try to prepare you for what is coming, but, until you live it, you really have no idea. It's okay not to have any idea. In fact, in marriage and in parenting, I think it's best.

It's hard to understand permanence when you are twenty-one and twenty-two. There's no way of knowing what forever is going to look like or what we'll look like in ten years, twenty, thirty, or sixty.

There was a bit more understanding with our diamond tattoos. I have an easier time imagining that round diamond eventually growing a bit oblong and wrinkled around its edges as our skin loosens and sags. I've walked with this man for ten years already. In that time, we've both changed. He drinks coffee now, and beer, has a beard, and takes pictures of people for a living. I am softer around the edges, cut my own bangs (then immediately regret it, every time), and, while I once thought I'd teach art to teenagers, I now want to feed people, take photos of that food, and then write about it all.

When we permanently marked an "R" on our wrists, we thought we knew each other, but now we know there was so much more to learn. I know that Gabe doesn't like sad movies, that he always weighs his coffee beans, and that it's easy to get him to laugh hysterically. Gabe knows that my version of fresh ginger ale makes the back of your throat tingle and your mouth pucker from lime. He knows that when it comes to chocolate it's always dark, and, for my cookies, a sprinkle of salt to finish. I know that Gabe likes everything with bread, and, while he tolerates my meals made up of mostly vegetables, there's not much better to him than a sandwich piled high with meat. And if there are chips on the side, well then he's really happy.

Through all the changes, big and small, we know that for as long as we can help it, there will be an *us*. We've got the tattoos to prove it.

TIMELINE

1 TO 3 DAYS IN ADVANCE

Make ginger syrup

Make seasoned salt

Make potato chips

Roast tenderloin

Make burger bun dough

Make cookie dough

Mix horseradish mayo

Caramelize onions

DATE DAY

Make burger buns

Bake cookies

DINNER TIME

Mix drinks

Assemble sandwiches

GROCERY

10 ounces / 280 g fresh ginger

12 limes

1 large russet potato

1 cup / 30 g arugula (or other peppery
    green such as watercress or mustard
    greens)

1 pound / 450 g beef tenderloin

Bread flour

Turbinado sugar

6 ounces / 170 g bittersweet chocolate

Fennel pollen (optional)

Prepared horseradish

1 pint / 450 g vanilla ice cream (optional;
    for making ice cream sandwiches)

Angostura bitters

PANTRY

1 lemon

1 large yellow onion

Unsalted butter

Whole milk

Eggs

Granulated sugar

Dark brown sugar

All-purpose flour

Baking soda

Active dry yeast

Vanilla extract

Coriander seeds

Fennel seeds

Kosher salt

Black peppercorns

Fresh coarsely ground black pepper

Flake salt

Mayonnaise

Honey

Canola or vegetable oil, for deep-frying

Bourbon

Soda water

Extra-virgin olive oil

Kickin' Kentucky Mule

Originally, we wanted to have a lovely homemade ginger ale for our date, but then we started researching the Moscow Mule (made with vodka), which led us to the Mississippi Mule (gin), which led us to the Kentucky Mule (bourbon). After trying all these, we finally settled on the Kickin' Kentucky Mule (bourbon with bitters), as we liked the bright and bitter citrus pop from the bitters. Whatever booze you decide on, this cocktail is delightfully spicy and fresh, and a great way to get the date kickin'.

SERVES 2

GINGER LIME SYRUP

10 ounces / 280 g fresh ginger, cut into 1-inch pieces (no need to peel!)

1 cup / 200 g granulated sugar

1 cup / 240 ml warm water, divided

1 cup / 240 ml freshly squeezed lime juice (from 8 to 10 limes)

MULE

½ cup / 120 ml bourbon

¼ cup / 60 ml freshly squeezed lime juice

Soda water

Few drops Angostura bitters

For the ginger lime syrup:

Purée the ginger in a food processor until finely chopped. Add the sugar and ½ cup / 120 ml warm water. Process further, until the ginger is very finely minced, about 2 minutes.

Add the puréed ginger mixture to a bowl. Stir in the remaining ½ cup / 120 ml water and the lime juice. Mix to combine.

Strain the ginger syrup through a fine-mesh sieve, pressing out any liquid in the ginger. Store in a sealable container in the fridge for up to 2 weeks. You should have 2½ cups / 590 ml.

For the mule:

Add the bourbon, lime juice, and ¾ cup / 180 ml of the ginger syrup to a cocktail shaker filled with ice. After a few hearty shakes, pour into 2 glasses or copper mugs filled with ice. Finish with a splash of soda water and a few drops of bitters.

Note: To make a simple ginger ale with this syrup, combine ½ cup / 120 ml of the ginger lime syrup with 2 cups / 470 ml soda water. I like mine with extra lime. We keep a jar of the syrup in our fridge all throughout the spring and summer for a quick, refreshing soda or cocktail.

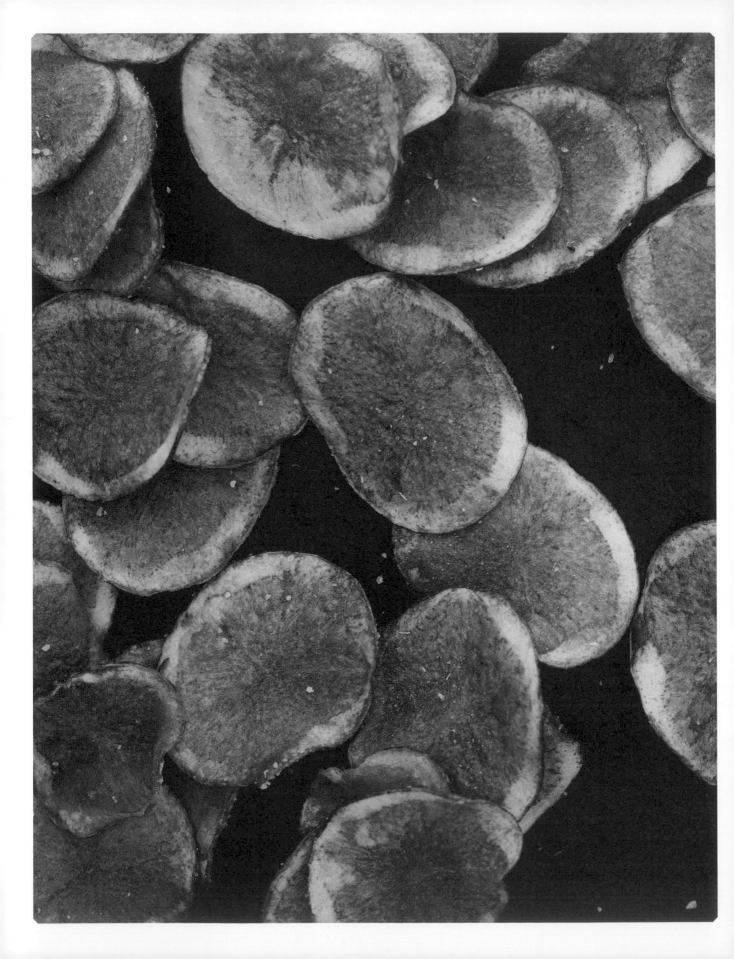

Potato Chips WITH Fennel Coriander Salt

Frying at home seems like a daunting task, but really it's not. Sometimes I wish I still thought it was daunting, so I wouldn't fry so many things at home; it is just so darn satisfying to create a bowl full of homemade potato chips. When you toss the chips with a fragrant sprinkling of toasted fennel seeds and coriander seeds, there is nothing like it.

For frying I use a 7-quart cast-iron Dutch oven. Cast iron retains heat very well, and the wide shape of the Dutch oven provides easy access to the chips. I'm able to fry larger batches without overcrowding the pan and causing the heat to drop drastically.

SERVES 2

1 large russet potato

4 cups / 950 ml canola or vegetable oil, for deep-frying

1 to 2 teaspoons Fennel Coriander Salt
(recipe follows)

Using a mandoline, cut the potato into paper-thin slices (about ⅟₁₆ inch thick) and let the potato slices soak in a bowl of cold water for 5 minutes.

Drain the potato slices. Spread the slices without overlapping on a triple layer of paper towels or a clean dish towel. Blot slices completely dry with another triple layer of paper towels or a clean dish towel.

Add the oil to a large saucepan. It should be about 2 to 3 inches deep in the pan, and you should have at least 3 inches to the top rim of the pan; oil tends to sputter up when hit with the potatoes.

Heat the oil over medium-high heat until a deep-fry thermometer registers 350°F.

Fry the potatoes in batches of 10 to 15 slices. Carefully move the chips around with a slotted spoon or spider so that they cook and color evenly. Continue to fry until they are golden all over and the bubbles have nearly calmed from their initial frenzy (this shows that the water in the potatoes has been cooked out), 2 to 3 minutes total.

Transfer the fried chips to paper towels to dry. Season with Fennel Coriander Salt while the chips are warm so that the salt sticks to the chips. Bring the oil back to 350°F before adding the next batch.

Potato chips can be made and seasoned up to 2 days ahead and kept in an airtight container.

Fennel Coriander Salt

This salt makes the potatoes say, "Hey, we're something special." I love fennel's and coriander's earthiness, but feel free to use any number of spices: cumin and red pepper flakes or rosemary and dried lemon zest, perhaps. I mix up a large batch of the salt so that I have it on hand to season fish, chicken, or roasted vegetables.

MAKES ⅛ CUP

1 teaspoon fennel seeds

¼ teaspoon black peppercorns

¼ teaspoon coriander seeds

2 tablespoons kosher salt

¼ teaspoon fennel pollen (optional)

Grind the fennel, peppercorns, and coriander seeds in a spice grinder or with a mortar and pestle to a fine powder. Transfer to a small bowl or storage container with a lid. Add the salt and fennel pollen, if using, and stir to combine.

Leftover salt will keep, well sealed, for several months.

Tip: For optimal flavor, toast all the spices before you grind them (for technique on how to toast spices, see page 11).

Roast Beef Tenderloin Sandwiches WITH Caramelized Onions, Horseradish Mayonnaise, AND Arugula

Think classic roast beef sandwich with just enough sophistication for date night: tenderloin, arugula, and hot horseradish. Beef tenderloin can be pricey, but for this recipe you don't need much to make a great meal. If you can't find a 1-pound piece of tenderloin, simply buy a 1-pound filet mignon, which is cut from the slender end of the tenderloin.

SERVES 2

TENDERLOIN

1 teaspoon kosher salt

¾ teaspoon fresh coarsely ground black pepper

1 pound / 450 g beef tenderloin

2 tablespoons extra-virgin olive oil

CARAMELIZED ONIONS

2 tablespoons unsalted butter

1 large yellow onion, halved and thinly sliced

Pinch of kosher salt

SANDWICHES

2 burger buns (page 15, or store-bought), split, buttered, and toasted in a hot pan

1 recipe Horseradish Mayonnaise (recipe follows)

1 recipe caramelized onions

1 cup / 30 g arugula leaves (or other peppery green such as watercress or mustard greens)

For the tenderloin:

One to 2 days ahead of time, salt and pepper the beef. Salting beef in advance gives you an incredibly flavorful roast. Place the meat, covered, in a bowl or lipped platter in the fridge to catch any juices. If you are terrible at planning in advance, salting just before still gives you a delicious sandwich. I know this because I'm terrible at planning in advance.

Remove the tenderloin from the fridge an hour before you plan to cook it.

Meanwhile, start caramelizing your onions. Melt the butter in a large skillet over medium-low heat. Add the onion and a pinch of salt. Reduce the heat to low and cook for at least 45 minutes, stirring and scraping up the browned bits on the bottom every 7 to 10 minutes, until the onions are nearly coffee-colored throughout and smell sweet. Caramelized onions can be made 1 to 3 days in advance. Rewarm, slightly, before you add them to the sandwich.

Preheat the oven to 325°F.

Place the olive oil in a large (12-inch), oven-safe skillet over high heat. When the oil smokes, sear the roast over high heat 2 to 3 minutes on all sides, until the entire surface is deep brown and crisp, a total of 8 to 12 minutes.

Place the skillet in the oven for 10 to 15 minutes, or until the temperature reaches 125°F in the thickest part for medium rare.

Remove the tenderloin to a cutting board. Cover with aluminum foil and let rest for 30 minutes before thinly slicing across the grain of the meat. You can roast the tenderloin 1 to 3 days in advance. Remove the cooked tenderloin from the fridge at least 30 minutes prior to serving just to take the chill off.

For the sandwiches:

Spread your butter-toasted buns with a generous amount of horseradish mayonnaise. Assemble each sandwich with half of the caramelized onions, beef, and arugula.

Note: If you are short on time, you can easily grab 8 ounces / 230 g of thinly sliced roast beef from the deli counter.

A note on caramelized onions:

Most recipes will lie to you and tell you to caramelize onions for 10 minutes. Well, let me speak a word of truth: your onions will NOT be caramelized after 10 minutes. For a true caramelization, the kind that practically melts the onion into something wonderfully sweet and rich, you will need to keep them on a steady, low heat for 45 minutes to an hour. All you need to do to encourage the sweetness is cook the onions in butter (the milk solids in the butter encourage caramelization) with a bit of salt and stir every now and again to make sure they brown evenly. *Whew.* I feel much better having righted that horrific lie.

Horseradish Mayonnaise

If you're sensitive to heat, you may want to start with 1 tablespoon horseradish and taste from there. Use prepared grated horseradish with as few additives as possible: that is, just plain jarred horseradish without the addition of a lot of other ingredients (check near the seafood counter).

SERVES 2

¼ cup / 60 g mayonnaise

1 to 1½ tablespoons prepared horseradish

½ tablespoon freshly squeezed lemon juice

⅛ teaspoon kosher salt

Whisk together the mayonnaise, horseradish, lemon juice, and salt in a small bowl. Taste and adjust to your preference, adding more heat as desired. This can be made 1 to 3 days in advance. Cover and refrigerate until ready to use.

Salted Chocolate Chip Cookies

This is my classic cookie. It's what I crave and the reason that I often have butter coming to room temperature on the counter. The dough exists only to hold the chocolate in place. Without the chocolate, this dough makes a great base for any number of cookies: dried cherry, white chocolate and cardamom, chopped dates and walnut, or oatmeal and rum raisin (just replace some of the flour with oatmeal).

Use all three sugars; if you need cookies *now* and don't have turbinado sugar (also known as raw sugar), add more dark brown sugar. You'll miss out on a nice little sugary crunch, but the cookies will still be amazing. Also, don't skimp on the time you spend creaming the butter and sugar. As the sugar cuts through the butter to create bubbles, you build air and structure. Most people think baking soda and baking powder create bubbles in baking, but they only make existing bubbles bigger. So cream until the butter and sugar mixture is very pale and light, which takes a good 5 minutes with your electric mixer on medium speed.

There is a lot of chocolate, good dark chocolate, in this recipe. Chocolate chips work too, but they won't puddle and melt into chocolate layers. To cut down the cost a bit, I often use a combination of a great chocolate bar and chocolate chips.

Finally, don't overbake. The oven temperature is an obnoxious 360°F so that an extra burst of heat sets the outside while the inside remains gooey. The end result is a crispy, gooey, and chewy cookie. Let the cookies cool on the tray for at least 5 minutes before transferring to a wire rack. Any less than that and the cookie will most likely fall apart from all that chocolate and gooeyness. Oh goodness, time to start softening more butter.

The dough is best made a day or two before you plan to bake the cookies; their flavor and texture improves with time. Leftover dough can be rolled into a 2-inch-thick log, wrapped in parchment paper, and then refrigerated for 1 week or frozen for up to 1 month. You can also freeze the baked cookies, but I prefer to freeze the dough.

One final note: I always double this recipe. Just thought you should know.

MAKES 18 TO 24 COOKIES

½ cup / 115 g unsalted butter, at room temperature

2 tablespoons granulated sugar

2 tablespoons turbinado sugar

¾ cup plus 2 tablespoons / 170 g packed dark brown sugar

1 egg, at room temperature

1 teaspoon vanilla extract

1¾ cups / 250 g all-purpose flour

¾ teaspoon baking soda

½ teaspoon kosher salt

6 ounces / 170 g bittersweet chocolate (use the best-quality chocolate you can), cut into roughly ½-inch chunks with a serrated knife

Flake salt (such as Maldon), for finishing

1 pint / 450 g vanilla ice cream (optional; for making ice cream sandwiches)

In a medium bowl, cream the butter and sugars together with an electric mixer on medium speed, until light in color and texture, 5 minutes. Scrape down the sides of the bowl with a rubber spatula as needed. Add the egg and vanilla and mix well to combine. Again, stop the machine and scrape down the bowl with a spatula.

In a medium bowl, whisk the flour, baking soda, and salt to combine.

With the mixer on low, slowly add the flour mixture. Mix until streaks of flour still run throughout. Add the chocolate and mix until everything just comes together. Finish the dough by hand, taking care to scrape the sides and the bottom of the bowl to make sure everything is evenly distributed.

At this point, it is best to refrigerate the dough for 24 hours. Resting the dough intensifies the deep toffee flavors, and the texture of the baked cookie improves.

When ready to bake, preheat the oven to 360°F. Line two baking sheets with parchment paper. Scoop the dough onto the baking sheets. Top the cookies with a pinch of flake salt just before baking.

Bake for 10 to 12 minutes. Rotate the sheets halfway through if they appear to be baking unevenly. The cookies should be lightly golden on the outside but still look quite gooey on the inside. Let the cookies cool on the baking sheets for at least 5 minutes.

Transfer the cookies to a wire rack to finish cooling.

These are best eaten the day of baking but will keep, if well sealed, for up to 2 days. Gabe and I also recommend turning pairs of these little beauties into ice cream sandwiches with the help of some great vanilla ice cream.

SUMMER

A Soup for Summer

Cherry Lime Soda

90

Grilled Mexican Corn with Cotija and Lime

90

Roasted Green Pozole with Chicken

93

Dulce de Leche and Nectarine Creamsicles

94

I peel an onion the same way every time. I grip it in my hand while examining its layers and look for any soft or bruised spots. Then, without much thought, I lay it on the cutting board with the roots to my left and the stem end to my right. I lop off the ruffled stem end, turn it on the flattened end, and slice it in half, directly through the mangled and crisped roots.

With the tips of my fingers, I peel back the papery layers of one of the halves and some of the flesh if it feels a bit tough. If the recipe calls for a dice, I'll follow the curve of the onion with my knife and stop just short of the root end. I change the angle of my knife and cut across the cut lines while the cold blade barely glides past my knuckles and guides me across the onion's pungent flesh.

In professional kitchens I was taught how to cut an onion precisely and quickly, but every so often I slow down this now-instinctive process. I'll grab my camera and take a photo of the way the onions fall on themselves as they slide off the blade. Or I'll stop just before I rip off the rust-colored papery layers and notice how they crinkle like linen and fall over the roots like an elegant gown. On the outside they are rough, cracked, and crisp, but as you peel them back they are smooth and shiny like the satin ribbons I tie in Ivy's hair.

When I lift the freshly cut flesh to my nose, I notice subtleties in its fragrance, not just its ability to make me sob over my cutting board; you can smell the sweetness that you taste after cooking them slowly for a long time. I love noticing these details, and it's a reminder of the beauty in the journey that we tend to miss when we focus only on the end result. We all have our routine, the things we do habitually without taking notice. The alarm clock rages against a restful sleep and suddenly we're flung into the routine; shower, brush teeth, get dressed, eat breakfast, put on shoes, then walk out the door. Driving the same path, it's easy not to take notice of the details unless they radically change. Was that tree there yesterday or did it just begin to sprout its blossoms? Before long we're at the destination without noticing how we got there.

Gabe shakes me out of my thoughts and asks what he can do. "Make me a cocktail, please." He sets up his cocktail station on the dining table; he has learned that I like to use up all of the space in our small kitchen. He hands me my cocktail, puts on some music, and then sets the table.

87

At the table, Gabe sits closest to the window while I sit facing the window. We know our place, we know the process, we know this time.

Our dates have become a habit. We know that once a week we will sit down together whether it's with a cocktail, takeout, a nice full meal, or just something sweet. We know that time is built into our schedule. Sometimes it gets squeezed off the calendar, but more often than not it's on there.

I've never been a big proponent of habits, ritual, and consistency. In fact, when I worked in restaurants, I almost lost my job over my inconsistency. One plate went out with three berries while the next had five. I always feel as if I can be improving; therefore, I rarely see the point in repeating the same action. So you can imagine my frustration in finding these evenings to be routine. Something needs to change, I immediately think. But does it?

The beauty with habit is that it happens without thinking. I slice onions habitually, and I'm pretty sure I could do it blindfolded, although I don't see why I would want to. Our date nights happen now without much planning. Gabe and I sit down with our computers open to our Google calendars and look over the week. After going over the schedule and making sure the kids will be where they need to be, we ask ourselves, "When is date night?" I like Thursday nights; it makes me feel like we are starting the weekend a touch early. But sometimes there are parent/teacher conferences, or a photo shoot, or friends in town. So we adjust the date accordingly.

Fitting in the date is not the challenge it once was because we've made it happen enough that we know it will be there. I love that and have felt this habit's good effects on our marriage more than I could have imagined. But I also realize that it's important to step outside of the habit and see it for what it really is.

When I was eighteen and first swooned over his dark hair and caramel-colored skin, I would never have imagined that thirteen years later he and I would have three children together. Dreamed maybe, but an actual possibility? Never. But each date night, I sit down to dinner with Gabe at the same table where our three kids sat a few hours before. I sit with the same man who held my hand through every birth. Who sat and cried with me in the midst of a very dark season of depression. Who makes me laugh like no one else can, who says, "Yes, let's do that!" to my crazy dreams and who stretches me to do things I don't like to do, like dancing in public or measuring my coffee beans.

Our dates may be a habit, but they're a habit worth slowing down to notice.

TIMELINE

1 TO 3 DAYS IN ADVANCE

Make pozole

Make creamsicles

Make crema sauce for corn

Make cherry soda concentrate

DINNER TIME

Finish sodas

Warm pozole and prep accompaniments

Grill corn and finish with sauce and Cotija

PANTRY

Garlic

2 large yellow onions

Granulated sugar

Mayonnaise

Vegetable oil

Dried oregano

1 teaspoon cumin seeds

1 quart / 950 ml chicken stock, homemade (page 18) or store-bought

Kosher salt

Baking soda

1 vanilla bean

Ground cinnamon or 1 stick cinnamon

Soda water

Olive oil

GROCERY

8 ounces / 230 g bing cherries, fresh or frozen

6 limes

2 ears fresh corn

Cotija cheese

10 ounces / 280 g tomatillos

1 jalapeño pepper

1 bunch fresh cilantro

¾ cup / 90 g roasted, salted pepitas

4 boneless, skinless chicken thighs

1 (15-ounce / 430 g) can hominy

2 radishes

1 avocado

1 nectarine

1 quart / 950 ml whole milk

Sour cream or Mexican crema

A SOUP FOR SUMMER

Cherry Lime Soda

Usually, we like to start the date with cocktails; the drink sets the night apart and helps us ease into the evening while the kids are still clamoring to get out of bed and insisting on another drink of water. But sometimes the uncharacteristic presence of a homemade soda is enough to make the night feel special.

SERVES 2

CHERRY CONCENTRATE

8 ounces / 230 g cherries, fresh or frozen, pitted and halved

¼ cup / 50 g granulated sugar

½ teaspoon freshly grated lime zest

¼ cup / 60 ml water

SODA

¼ cup / 60 ml freshly squeezed lime juice (from 2 to 3 limes)

1 cup / 240 ml soda water

For the cherry concentrate:

Bring the cherries, sugar, lime zest, and water to a boil in a small saucepan over medium heat. Stir until the sugar is dissolved, about 2 minutes. Remove the pan from the stove and chill. The concentrate will keep in the fridge in an airtight container for up to 3 days.

For the soda:

When ready to serve, put ½ cup / 135 g of the cherries and their juice in two pint glasses, add 2 tablespoons lime juice to each glass, fill with ice, and top with soda water.

Variation: Add a splash of cream for a cherry lime creamsicle, or a shot of vodka, gin, or tequila.

Grilled Mexican Corn with Cotija and Lime

Grilled corn with little more than butter and salt is one of my favorite summer tastes. Somehow, grilled corn becomes even tastier with this sweet and tangy mix of mayonnaise and sour cream, lime and salty crumbles of Cotija cheese. Suddenly, just butter and salt don't quite cut it anymore.

SERVES 2

2 ears fresh corn, husks removed

1 tablespoon olive oil

¼ teaspoon kosher salt, plus pinch

2 tablespoons mayonnaise

2 tablespoons Mexican crema or sour cream

Freshly grated zest of 1 lime

1 garlic clove, minced

⅓ cup / 30 g crumbled Cotija cheese

Lime wedges, for serving

Drizzle each ear of corn with olive oil and sprinkle with a pinch of kosher salt.

Whisk together the mayonnaise, crema, lime zest, garlic, and salt in a small bowl. Crema sauce can be made 1 to 3 days in advance and then covered and refrigerated until ready to serve.

Place the Cotija on a large plate.

Grill the corn over high heat until charred in parts and tender throughout, about 10 minutes, rotating halfway through, or once charred on one side.

While the corn is warm, brush each ear generously with the lime crema mixture and then roll it in the Cotija. Serve the corn while still warm with plenty of lime wedges.

Roasted Green Pozole with Chicken

By the time our date rolls around, the sun is nearly set and there's a slight chill in the air that makes this roasted, fragrant stew a perfect late-summer evening meal. It's vibrant and fresh yet pleasantly hearty from roasted and ground pepitas. The original recipe comes from *Gourmet* magazine, but I've since made many changes throughout its life in our home. The biggest change being the pan-roasting of the tomatillos and garlic, which gives the soup a soft smokiness and a bit more complexity.

SERVES 4

½ cup / 60 g roasted, salted pepitas, plus more for garnish

1 teaspoon cumin seeds, toasted (see technique on page 11)

2 tablespoons vegetable oil, divided

10 ounces / 280 g tomatillos (about 4 to 5 medium size), peeled and quartered

3 garlic cloves

1 large yellow onion, roughly chopped, plus more for serving

1 jalapeño pepper, halved and seeded

½ cup / 10 g chopped fresh cilantro, divided

1 to 1½ teaspoons kosher salt

1 teaspoon dried oregano

2½ to 3 cups / 590 to 710 ml chicken stock, homemade (page 18) or store-bought

4 boneless, skinless chicken thighs, thinly sliced

1 (15-ounce / 430 g) can hominy, drained and rinsed

To serve: any combination of thinly sliced radishes, sliced avocado, chopped cilantro, pepitas, lime wedges, diced onion, crumbled Cotija, and sour cream or crema.

Grind the pepitas and cumin seeds in a spice grinder or blender until finely ground.

Add 1 tablespoon oil to a large pot or Dutch oven over medium-high heat.

When the oil is hot, add the tomatillos, garlic, onion, and jalapeño to the pot, along with a pinch of salt. Roast in the pan for 10 to 15 minutes, stirring occasionally, until the vegetables are charred, caramelized in parts, and tender.

Carefully transfer the roasted vegetables to a food processor or blender and process along with ¼ cup / 5 g chopped cilantro and 1 teaspoon salt.

Add the remaining 1 tablespoon oil to the pot over medium heat. Return the purée to the pot and cook, stirring frequently until thickened, for 5 to 7 minutes. Scrape up the deeply flavored browned bits on the bottom of the pot. Stir in the ground pepitas and cumin seeds, along with the oregano and 1 cup / 240 ml stock. Bring to a simmer and then add the remaining 1½ cups / 360 ml stock, chicken, and hominy.

Let this simmer, mostly covered, for 20 minutes. Stir in the remaining ¼ cup / 5 g chopped cilantro. Taste and adjust seasonings, adding more salt if you feel it needs it. I prefer the pozole to be thick, like a stew, but if you want it thinner, add more stock. Pozole can be made 1 to 3 days in advance, and in fact the flavor improves after a rest in the fridge. Leftovers can be refrigerated for up to 1 week.

Serve with the accompaniments.

Dulce de Leche and Nectarine Creamsicles

At Spago we simmered cans of sweetened condensed milk in hot water until their contents turned thick and intensely caramelized. The task always made me fearful that a can might explode in the process. That fear, and a desire to start from scratch using ingredients I always have on hand, prompted me to make my own dulce de leche. It takes a while for the sweetened white milk to turn into a thick, dark caramel, but I don't have to be bothered with it much except for an occasional glance into the pan to marvel at the process.

Slices of ripe nectarine nicely mellow dulce de leche's sweetness.

MAKES 6 TO 8 CREAMSICLES, DEPENDING ON THE SIZE OF YOUR MOLDS

4 cups / 950 ml whole milk, divided

¾ cup / 250 g granulated sugar

¼ teaspoon kosher salt

Scant ½ teaspoon baking soda

1 vanilla bean, split and seeds scraped

Pinch of ground cinnamon or 1 stick cinnamon

1 nectarine, thinly sliced

Combine 3 cups / 710 ml milk with the sugar, salt, baking soda, vanilla bean, and cinnamon in a large saucepan. Bring the mix to a boil and watch it carefully; the baking soda will make the mixture bubble up. Lower the heat to medium low and simmer, stirring occasionally, until reduced to 1½ cups / 360 ml of copper-colored caramel, about 1 hour and 15 minutes. If any scorching happens on the bottom of the pan, be careful not to scrape it up as you are stirring. Add the remaining 1 cup / 240 ml milk to the dulce de leche and then strain into a container with a pour spout.

Add three to five slices of nectarine to each popsicle mold and then pour in the strained dulce de leche mixture, leaving a ½-inch space to allow the popsicles to expand as they freeze. Cover the mold and add popsicle sticks. Freeze until completely firm, at least 4 hours.

Keeps in the freezer for 1 week.

Note: If you'd prefer dulce de leche ice cream instead of a popsicle, replace the final 1 cup / 240 ml addition of milk with cream. Let chill completely. Churn the ice cream according to your manufacturer's instructions and fold in pieces of diced nectarine once it's done.

By the Fire

Fire-Pit Fontina with Tomatoes, Rosemary, and Lemon

99

German Pretzel Sandwiches

100

Smoky Potato Salad with Sour Cream and Dill

102

S'mores Terrine with Smoked Salt

104

"We need to do something about our yard," I said, in one of my not-so-rare moments of desperation. "I can't even look at it."

I *was* actually looking at it and saw creeping vines of choke weed threatening to overtake everything, including us. In between towering kale plants were weeds of many shapes and sizes. Our "grass" was mostly daisies and dandelions, which the kids loved to pluck and give to me. In my good moments I saw the gesture as a gift and put the tender, invasive weeds in water and set them on the counter. But in the moments when our yard felt like a jungle, taunting me with its creeping vines and incessant needs, I felt like the kids had teamed up with our yard. The yard made them parade those dandelions right in front of my face so that the weeds invaded both inside and outside my home.

"Okay, well maybe we can do something with it this summer," Gabe said, trying to talk me off the ledge.

"Let's just swing by the hardware store on the way home from church and see what they have," I said, with my eyes glued to Pinterest, already formulating a plan.

A few hours later we had a car full of cinder blocks and a rough plan for a fire pit and a bench.

Gabe spent the next couple of weeks digging and leveling while I cheered him on with lemonade. We didn't have a lot of free time, and often the work was done in random twenty-minute free moments.

During one of those intervals, Gabe asked, "How did this happen?" He paused and wiped sweat from his brow.

After I stacked a few more blocks, I replied, "What do you mean?"

"One minute you said you wanted to do something with the yard, and then suddenly we have a fire pit."

I smiled while continuing to dig.

Gabe is a planner; maybe a better word is *premeditator*, except that sounds sort of sinister. He wants to make sure everything is in order and all the proper tools are acquired before we even begin to think about proceeding. I get an idea and start working immediately. I would have dug that fire pit out with a spoon if I had to because something needed to be done and it needed to be done right then.

Because Gabe is precise and uses the right tools, our benches are level. Because I am determined and stubborn, we actually have benches.

We celebrated our newly renovated yard with a date centered around the fire. On one of those summer evenings when it seems as if the sun never plans to set, we started a fire in our pit and marveled at ourselves when it actually held the flame.

"We built that!" I said. He and I can take beautiful photos, dress well, make a mean cocktail, and tell you where to go for a great meal, but, when it comes to being handy around the house, we're not your go-to couple.

Gabe poured us a beer while I tucked baby potatoes into a pouch made of several layers of aluminum. I threw in a few cloves of garlic and a few glugs of olive oil for good measure. I nestled the pouch in the coals, and before long the oil was hissing and bubbling within.

He prodded at the fire. "I'm making the perfect sausage-roasting coals," he assured me just before I ran upstairs to check on the kids and gather the rest of our dinner.

In the kitchen, I placed pretzel buns on a tray, still warm from the oven and the color of copper pennies, and anticipated their tender, slightly sweet interior and salty, tangy exterior. Next to the buns I tucked a dish piled high with spicy pickled peppers. I tamed the peppers' kick with olive oil, garlic, and oregano and finished the platter with a small dish filled with mustard-laced cream cheese.

On my way outside, I grabbed our roasting sticks and saw Gabe sitting on the (level) bench we made and still poking at the fire. We crisped the beer-bathed sausages over the fire we had built.

We ate quickly and without many words while the fire warmed the front of our legs and made our faces glow. He shook his head signaling to me that I'd done good, and I nodded in agreement while taking another large bite. With my sandwich in one hand, I reached for a potato: smoky and tender. The potatoes clung together with sour cream and looked almost healthful with the abundance of fresh dill mixed throughout.

Our evening ended with another round of beer and thick slices of chocolate terrine dotted with marshmallows and graham crackers and topped with smoky flake salt. We both nodded in delight.

By the time we ended our meal, the sun had set but the fire was warm and kept us outside.

"This is nice," I said. Our dinner, our date, and our new yard: it was all so nice.

It really was a simple project, a fire pit made from squarely stacked cinder blocks and a cinder block bench, and yet we both felt proud of what we had built together. We had contributed to make something that we were using to spend time together. I've spent nearly half of my life building things with this man. It's enough time to know for sure that in building a life—or a fire pit—we're good together.

TIMELINE

1 TO 3 DAYS IN ADVANCE

Make pickled peppers

Make pretzel roll dough

Make mustard whipped cream cheese

Make s'mores terrine

DATE DAY

Bake pretzel rolls

Prep fontina ingredients

DINNER TIME

Make fire-pit fontina

Make potato salad

Roast sausages and assemble pretzel
sandwiches

PANTRY

Garlic

1 lemon

Unsalted butter

Dark brown sugar

Granulated sugar

All-purpose flour

Kosher salt

Freshly ground black pepper

Active dry yeast

Baking soda

Extra-virgin olive oil

Apple cider vinegar

Dried oregano

Dijon mustard

Grainy mustard

GROCERY

8 ounces / 230 g Italian roasting peppers
or colorful mini peppers

1 red jalapeño pepper

1 red onion

1 pound / 450 g baby red potatoes

2 of your favorite high-quality sausages or
hot dogs, fresh or smoked

1 (8-ounce / 230 g) package cream cheese

Heavy whipping cream

1 pint / 450 g sour cream

1 small shallot

½ cup / 80 g cherry tomatoes

5 ounces / 140 g fontina

Fresh rosemary

1 bunch fresh dill

12 ounces / 340 g dark chocolate

Mini marshmallows

Graham crackers

Instant espresso powder

Smoked flake salt

Liquid smoke (optional)

Fire-Pit Fontina WITH Tomatoes, Rosemary, AND Lemon

For perfect fire-pit fontina, you'll need a flat spot on a bed of hot, glowing coals. When you find the right spot, the shallots will soften in the pan and release their fragrance almost instantly, and the tomatoes will swell just before they burst. Roasted tomato juice helps the cheese melt so it's gooey enough to slide a piece of bread or cracker through. You can easily double or triple this recipe to feed a crowd and make it on the stove top if you don't have access to a fire pit or would like to avoid smelling like smoke. I happen to love smelling a bit smoky.

SERVES 2

1 tablespoon olive oil

1 tablespoon minced shallot

½ cup / 80 g cherry tomatoes, halved

5 ounces / 140 g fontina, cut into ½-inch cubes

½ teaspoon freshly grated lemon zest

½ teaspoon finely chopped fresh rosemary

1 to 2 fresh pretzel rolls (page 101), for serving

Add the olive oil to a small, fire-proof skillet (preferably cast iron) and then place on hot coals in the fire. Please do be careful. This can also be done on the stove top over medium-high heat.

When the oil is bubbly and hot, add the shallots and sauté using a long-handled spoon until soft, about 5 minutes. Add the tomatoes and cook until they release some of their juices, 3 to 4 minutes. Add the cheese. If the cheese starts to scorch around the edge, carefully remove the pan from the fire and allow the residual heat to melt the cheese. Stir well and frequently until all the cheese is melted. Finish with the lemon zest and fresh rosemary.

When the cheese cools, simply return to the fire or stove to rewarm. Serve with extra pretzel rolls for dipping. Any bread or cracker would do nicely as well.

German Pretzel Sandwiches

Last year, for Ivy's birthday, I set up a hot dog bar. The table was filled with dishes of pickles, jams, mustards, and onions so that everyone could craft their own combination. This flavorful sausage sandwich with mustard-spiked cream cheese and pickled peppers is what I devoured and then subsequently recommended to everyone at her party. It's been my favorite since. Bathe your sausages in beer before they hit the fire; the beer bath will add more flavor and speed up the roasting time.

SERVES 2

2 of your favorite high-quality sausages or hot dogs, fresh or smoked

2 Pretzel Rolls (recipe follows)

1½ tablespoons unsalted butter

1 recipe Mustard Cream Cheese (recipe follows)

½ cup pickled sweet peppers (page 21)

Roast your sausages over an open fire, grill them, or sear them in a skillet on your stove.

Halve, butter, and toast the pretzel buns (optional) on a grill, in a skillet, or under the broiler.

Spread them generously with mustard cream cheese, add your sausage, and top with pickled peppers.

Mustard Cream Cheese

MAKES ½ CUP

1 tablespoon Dijon mustard

1 tablespoon grainy mustard

4 ounces / 110 g cream cheese, at room
temperature

Mix the mustards and cream cheese together until
combined.

Pretzel Rolls

What makes something a pretzel is a dip in a baking
soda bath before it's baked; the baking soda gives the
pretzel that recognizable dark crust and tangy bite.
Think of all the pretzeling possibilities: crackers, bagels,
hamburger buns, etc. For delicate items such as crackers,
you can use a spray bottle or pastry brush to apply the
baking soda solution.

MAKES 4 PRETZEL ROLLS

1 recipe olive oil pizza dough (page 14)

Unsalted butter, for the pan

3 quarts / 2.8 L water

¾ cup / 180 g baking soda

⅓ cup / 70 g dark brown sugar

When ready to make the rolls, remove the dough
from the fridge and divide into four equal portions
(it's easiest to work with when it's cold).

Roll each piece of dough into a 9-inch-long
rope that is slightly tapered at the ends. If the
dough feels tight and no longer wants to stretch,
set it aside to rest while you work on another
portion. This allows the gluten to relax, and it
will be easier to work with after a few minutes.

Place the formed rolls on a well-greased or
Silpat-lined baking sheet and cover loosely with
plastic wrap.

Let rise until doubled, about 2 hours in a
warm spot.

Preheat the oven to 450°F. Set a wire cooling
rack over a dish towel on your counter.

For the pretzel solution, bring the water,
baking soda, and brown sugar to a boil in a large,
wide pot. Reduce to a simmer.

Carefully drop the rolls into the pretzel
solution and cook for 1 minute on each side; use
a large slotted spoon to turn. Remove them from
the liquid and place on the wire cooling rack set
over the dish towel to drain.

Use a very sharp knife to cut a ½-inch-deep
slit in the top along the length of each roll.

Return the rolls to the greased (or Silpat-
lined) baking sheet and bake for 15 to 17 minutes,
or until dark brown and cooked through.

Carefully remove the rolls from the baking
sheet and allow them to cool on a wire rack. If
the rolls stick, use a metal spatula to release.

These rolls are best eaten the day they are
baked.

Note: If you'd like to add salt or seeds (poppy,
sesame, or caraway), brush the rolls with an egg
wash (1 egg mixed with 1 teaspoon water) after
they've been boiled and cut and then top with
the seeds.

Smoky Potato Salad WITH Sour Cream AND Dill

When you are cooking over a fire, smoke becomes an ingredient. Here, smoky, fire-roasted potatoes are tossed, while warm, in a cool and creamy dill dressing. The salad is complex in flavor yet fresh and simple. When my only choice is to cook the potatoes indoors, I add a bit of natural hickory smoke to mimic the fire's smoky flavor.

SERVES 2

1 pound / 450 g baby red potatoes, cut into bite-size pieces

2 garlic cloves, roughly chopped

1½ tablespoons extra-virgin olive oil

¾ teaspoon kosher salt

¼ teaspoon freshly ground black pepper

⅓ cup / 40 g diced red onion

2 tablespoons sour cream

1½ tablespoons grainy mustard

¼ teaspoon liquid smoke (optional)

⅓ cup / 8 g chopped fresh dill

Flake salt, for finishing (optional)

Preheat the oven to 400°F.

Lay out two layers of aluminum foil about 18 inches long each.

In a large bowl, combine the potatoes, garlic, olive oil, salt, and pepper. Toss everything together to mix well. Set the potato mixture onto the double layer of aluminum foil. Fold over the sides of the foil to seal. Roast for 40 minutes, or until tender. Cool the potatoes in the packet for 10 minutes. Alternatively, roast the potatoes in a hot fire. Prepare the foil packet of potatoes as above and then place directly in the hottest part of the fire and roast until the potatoes are tender, about 20 minutes. After 10 minutes, flip the packet with long tongs so the potatoes roast evenly. Carefully remove roasted potatoes from the fire and set aside to cool in the packet.

In another bowl, combine the red onion, sour cream, grainy mustard, and liquid smoke, if using.

Toss the still-warm potatoes with the sour cream mixture and the fresh dill. Taste and finish with flake salt, if desired.

S'mores Terrine WITH Smoked Salt

I've often been a bit frustrated with my s'mores; I always want the chocolate to melt more than it does under the heat of my perfectly roasted marshmallow. For this terrine, you'll mix chocolate with cream, butter, marshmallows, graham crackers, and a whisper of smoked salt. On its own it's a decadent fudge. But when you use a wedge of this in place of solid chocolate on s'mores, you'll get an irresistibly soft chocolate that melts as easily as I always hoped it would.

MAKES ONE 9 X 5-INCH LOAF

12 ounces / 340 g dark chocolate, chopped (2¼ cups)

1¾ sticks / 200 g unsalted butter, plus more for the pan

¼ cup / 60 ml heavy whipping cream

1 teaspoon instant espresso powder

1 cup / 70 g mini marshmallows

1 cup / 85 g graham cracker crumbs

1 teaspoon smoked flake salt, divided

Butter and line a 9 x 5-inch loaf pan with parchment paper so that the parchment hangs over the sides.

Melt the chocolate and butter in a heavy-bottomed saucepan over low heat, stirring often so that it does not burn. Once completely melted, stir in the cream and espresso powder until combined. Add the marshmallows, graham cracker crumbs, and ½ teaspoon smoked salt.

Pour this into the prepared loaf pan and sprinkle with remaining ½ teaspoon smoked salt. Refrigerate 3 hours or overnight.

Remove the terrine from the pan by running a knife around the edge and lifting up on the parchment handles. Cut into thin slices. Serve chilled or at room temperature.

Leftovers will keep, well wrapped, in the refrigerator for up to 1 week or in the freezer for up to 1 month.

Too Hot to Cook

Thyme Lemonade

109

Assorted Meats, Cheeses, and Antipasti Salads

110

Roasted Tomato and Peach Panzanella

114

Gingered Peaches and Cream with
Browned-Butter Graham Crumbs

116

There were two chairs in the upper lounge of our dorm. Purple pleather covered chairs, if I remember correctly. They pointed toward each other, just slightly, in the corner of the room. Not long after Gabe and I started "hanging out," those became our chairs. People grew to expect to see us sitting there, especially between 9 p.m. and 3 a.m.

Due to the tight rules of the small liberal arts college we both attended, we couldn't be in each other's rooms past 9 p.m., so we moved our conversation to those purple chairs and stayed in them as long as we could, just to be near each other. At times we would sit and draw, casually do our homework, or read books while flirting over their covers. Later we'd find ourselves with our legs kicked over the sides, leaning in closer to the chairs and each other as the hours melted into midnight. Our words became a bit more scattered and incoherent as we both fought valiantly to stay awake. Gabe often lost that fight, which gave me time to notice how much I loved his dark eyebrows and the way his nose sloped perfectly down his face. I admired his sideburns that sometimes slid into a beard and wrapped around his lips to form a thin mustache; he longed for one that rivaled Tom Selleck's and dreamed of being able to form the ends into a sort of curl. I didn't even mind the drool that formed in the corner of his mouth as he finally succumbed to sleep. In fact, I'm pretty sure I found it endearing.

When we sit down to dinner tonight, just the two of us, it is the first time in two weeks. For one reason or another, date night got pushed aside and other things took its place. Consequently, during those two weeks, our relationship felt "off." I didn't feel like Gabe was excited to see me when I got home, cared to connect with me, or even liked me very much, and I think he felt the same from me. When one of us tried to reach out to the other, the other would pull away. There was distance and continued missed connections. We talked about feeling like we were missing each other but felt powerless to make a change: we needed a date.

I think the same is true for any couple: when your relationship is neglected, or pushed to the back burner while you "do life," reconnecting can feel forced or awkward; it's almost easier to let more time pass before you take yourselves in for a tune-up. But I always know when we need it, and, on this week's date-night prep, the tomatoes and peaches I smelled at the farmers' market made me eager for our dinner.

Tonight, Gabe steps into the kitchen with written instructions on how to start a couple of the recipes while I read about striped dragons and the mountains of made-up, far-away lands with the kids. He strips thyme leaves off their woody stems and squeezes fresh lemons, puckering when he tastes their juice. As I turn the last page, Gabe finishes cubing thick slices of soft, craggy bread.

After I finish tucking the kids into bed, I enter the kitchen to see Gabe squeezing the last few dregs of juice out of the lemons. I join him in the kitchen and heap finely chopped garlic onto the cubes of bread, coat them in olive oil, and put them in the oven. I grab a bowl and toss roasted tomatoes with fresh tomatoes and peaches, a bit of vinegar, garlic, and some olive oil to encourage the panzanella's flavors to connect, much as I hope Gabe and I will during dinner.

We sit down quietly. The conversation sputters awkwardly in the midst of thin slices of prosciutto and hot coppa. Ivy interrupts our silence with a request to come scratch "this arm and this arm and this back and this leg and this leg" and continually calling down the stairs, "Mama, whatcha doin'?"

"Dating your dad, sweetheart," I reply while plucking an olive from its orange and red chile bath.

By the time the house is quiet, we clean our plates and start to pick pieces of oil-soaked, garlicky bread cubes and creamy cheese straight off the platter, and soon our conversation starts to flow easily, as it did in the days of those purple pleather chairs.

Gabe talks about growing older and the gray hairs that are multiplying on his head. They stand out in stark contrast against his black hair

and catch the light in a way that I love.

"What do you think you'll look like when you're old?" I ask Gabe and imagine him with silver hair, a pair of sleek black glasses, and a few more wrinkles that tell the story of our life together.

"I'm not sure," he responds while deep in thought, "but I do know that I find you more beautiful now than when we met."

I smirk and roll my eyes, feeling loved and yet vulnerable. It's hard to believe Gabe is telling the truth as I glance at a picture of myself, nineteen and in Gabe's arms, that sits on the table beside us. My hair is long and bright and my face young and tight. But I allow myself to believe his words; I take them in and let them wrap around me like a gentle hug.

"I hope we don't long for our younger selves when we're old," I say. "Sure, our bodies will fade slowly, and we'll be wrinkly in places we didn't think could wrinkle, but we'll have more wisdom than we do in this moment and we'll have perspective."

I hope we'll still think it's important to date when we're old. Visions flash in my head: the older couples that I've noticed when we go out to restaurants, those who do almost everything they can to avoid eye contact. They eat their food, pay the bill, and push in their chairs without exchanging a word. Every time I see those couples, I beg Gabe to promise that that won't be us.

As we linger around the table together, I smile. Even after thirteen years of dating, we can spend hours sitting next to each other—this time not on purple pleather—and talk until we're both muttering nonsense. When we finally pull ourselves away from the table, I look down at my phone and notice that it's 1 a.m.

We still got it.

TIMELINE

1 TO 3 DAYS IN ADVANCE

Make thyme syrup

Make antipasti: lemony beans, marinated olives, red pepper salad

Make graham crumbs

DATE DAY

Assemble antipasto platter

Toast bread for panzanella

Prep peaches and cream for dessert

DINNER TIME

Make lemonade drinks

Caramelize figs and wrap in prosciutto

Assemble panzanella

Assemble dessert

PANTRY

Garlic

10 lemons

Granulated sugar

Dark brown sugar

Unsalted butter

Kosher salt

Freshly ground black pepper

Red pepper flakes

Extra-virgin olive oil

Red wine vinegar

Dried oregano

Soda water

Flake salt

GROCERY

Anchovy

1 package or small bunch fresh thyme

1 bunch fresh mint

1 bunch fresh basil

1 (15-ounce / 430 g) can cannellini beans

2 ounces / 60 g pecorino

1 sprig fresh rosemary

6 ounces / 170 g olives (such as Castelvetrano)

1 red onion

1 orange

1 small fresh red chile

1 (12-ounce / 340 g) jar fire-roasted red peppers, or 3 red peppers, roasted, seeded, and sliced (page 11)

2 tablespoons capers

3 fresh figs

3 slices prosciutto

3 ounces / 90 g artisan bread (a quarter of a loaf or so)

1 pint/ 280 g cherry tomatoes

2 peaches

1 cup / 30 g assorted herbs (I used basil, dill, mint, and tarragon)

1 cup / 30 g baby arugula

4 ounces / 110 g goat cheese

¾ teaspoon minced fresh ginger (from a 1-inch piece)

½ pint / 240 ml heavy whipping cream

Graham crackers

2 to 3 different types of salami/charcuterie, about 4 ounces / 110 g total

4 ounces / 110 g of your favorite cheese or an assortment

Thyme Lemonade

In summer, our little garden works overtime to provide us with a bounty of fresh herbs, and I'm always looking for new ways to use them. I love this lightly herbed lemonade on a hot day. It's also great with mint or tarragon or just on its own as thyme soda; it'll make all the necessary water drinking in the hot days of summer a bit more enjoyable.

SERVES 2

THYME SYRUP

2 tablespoons fresh thyme leaves, plus
   additional sprigs for garnish

½ cup / 100 g granulated sugar

½ cup / 120 ml water

THYME LEMONADE

½ cup / 120 ml thyme syrup

½ cup / 120 ml freshly squeezed lemon juice

1 cup / 240 ml soda water

For the syrup:

Combine the thyme, sugar, and water in a small saucepan over medium heat. Bring to a boil and then reduce to a simmer for 7 minutes. Remove from the heat and chill in the refrigerator to allow the thyme to infuse the syrup's flavor.

For the lemonade:

First, strain the thyme syrup in a fine-mesh sieve. Fill a pitcher half full with ice and then add ½ cup / 120 ml thyme syrup, lemon juice, and soda water. Pour into glasses and garnish each glass with a thyme sprig.

This sprightly little soda does nicely with vodka or gin as well.

Assembling the Antipasto Platter

The idea for this meal is simplicity, which might be odd because this chapter contains so many recipes. You could easily ignore the following recipes for simple antipasti salads and hit up your grocery store for a few marinated olives and roasted peppers, but with just a bit more effort, you can transform some pantry staples into a delightful array of salads. Even just one salad with a few assorted charcuterie would make a great start to this fresh meal.

A word about the charcuterie (a fancy word for cured meats): I like to have two or three options. Prosciutto is always good, and Gabe likes a bit of spice so I tend to grab a spicy coppa. My favorite charcuterie is Finocchiona, a fennel-flavored cured meat. A few crumbled pieces of aged Parmigiano work well on the plate too.

In fact, charcuterie and antipasti could easily be dinner. You could make a meal of assembled salads, thinly sliced meats, and chunks of salty cheese. It is, quite honestly, one of my favorite meals.

Lemony White Beans with Pecorino

A super simple little salad, bright with lemon and salty pecorino. I like to leave the beans whole and pick at them throughout the meal. I imagine you could easily whizz this up in a food processor for a light dip.

MAKES 2 CUPS / 340 G

Freshly grated zest and freshly squeezed juice of
    1 small lemon

¾ teaspoon kosher salt

1 teaspoon red pepper flakes

¼ teaspoon freshly ground black pepper

2 teaspoons chopped fresh rosemary

2 tablespoons extra-virgin olive oil

1 (15-ounce / 430 g) can cannellini beans,
    drained and rinsed

¼ cup / 10 g freshly grated pecorino, plus more
    for shaving on top

2 tablespoons chopped red onion

Whisk together the lemon zest, lemon juice, salt, red pepper flakes, black pepper, rosemary, and olive oil. Add the beans, grated pecorino, and red onions and then fold gently to combine. Allow to marinate at room temperature for a couple of hours or refrigerate overnight. Finish with shaved pecorino.

Bring to room temperature before serving.

Orange AND Red Chile—Marinated Olives

Store-bought olives on their own are just fine, but, with a few extra ingredients, they become something special. The longer these marinate, the more pronounced the orange and chile flavor will be.

Combine all the ingredients and let marinate for a couple of hours or refrigerate overnight.

Bring to room temperature before serving.

MAKES 1 CUP / 180 G

6 ounces / 170 g olives (such as Castelvetrano,) drained (about 1 cup)

3-inch piece orange rind, slivered

2 teaspoons fresh thyme leaves

1 small fresh red chile, thinly sliced

2 tablespoons extra-virgin olive oil

Roasted Red Peppers with Capers and Anchovy

An antipasto plate isn't complete without the bright red punch of roasted peppers. They add lovely color to the plate as a vibrant salad brimming with brine, spice, and fragrant basil.

MAKES 1½ CUPS / 340 G

1 anchovy, rinsed and finely chopped

2 tablespoons capers

1 garlic clove, finely chopped

1 tablespoon freshly squeezed lemon juice

2 tablespoons extra-virgin olive oil

1 (12-ounce / 340 g) jar fire-roasted red peppers, or 3 red peppers, roasted, seeded, and sliced (page 11)

¼ cup / 5 g thinly sliced fresh basil

Whisk together the anchovy, capers, garlic, lemon juice, and olive oil. Fold in the sliced peppers and basil. Let marinate for a couple of hours at room temperature or refrigerate overnight. Bring to room temperature before serving.

Caramelized Figs Wrapped in Prosciutto

I met my first fresh fig on a tree in Italy while taking a quick break during a long walk through the Umbria. How could one not fall in love when that is the setting of the first meet-up? When the prosciutto wraps around the warm fig, the thin layers of fat slowly melt into the fig, coating its sweetness with a punch of savory that makes these little bites nearly as unforgettable as that first meeting.

SERVES 2

1 tablespoon granulated sugar

1 tablespoon unsalted butter

3 fresh figs, halved

3 slices prosciutto, halved

Place the sugar in a small, shallow ramekin or saucer. Heat a cast-iron skillet over medium-high heat and add the butter. Once the butter is melted, dredge the fig halves flesh-side down in the sugar and then place in the hot pan. Let them sit, undisturbed, for 2 minutes or until deeply caramelized. Wrap each hot, caramelized fig half in half a slice of prosciutto. Serve warm.

Roasted Tomato AND Peach Panzanella

Everything I love about summer food is in this bowl.

SERVES 4

1 pint / 280 g cherry tomatoes, divided

½ teaspoon kosher salt, plus more as needed

¼ cup / 60 ml extra-virgin olive oil, divided

3 cups / 85 g ½-inch bread cubes from a rustic loaf

2 garlic cloves, minced, divided

1 peach, diced

1 tablespoon red wine vinegar

½ teaspoon dried oregano

1 cup chopped assorted herbs (I used basil, dill, mint, and tarragon)

1 cup baby arugula

⅓ cup / 60 g goat cheese, crumbled

Preheat the oven to 350°F. Line a baking sheet with parchment paper.

Place half the pint of cherry tomatoes on the prepared sheet and toss with a generous pinch of salt and 1 tablespoon olive oil. Roast for 45 minutes, gently stirring halfway through the cooking process. Cut the remaining cherry tomatoes in half and set aside.

Place the cubes of bread on a second parchment-lined baking sheet and toss with 2 tablespoons olive oil, a pinch of salt, and 1 minced garlic clove. Toast for 20 to 25 minutes, or until golden brown and completely crisp, stirring after 10 minutes. Remove and cool to room temperature.

In a large bowl, combine the roasted tomatoes, remaining minced garlic clove, diced peach, vinegar, oregano, ½ teaspoon salt, and remaining 1 tablespoon olive oil. Gently toss to combine and let sit at room temperature for 30 minutes.

Finish the panzanella by adding the crisped and cooled bread cubes to the bowl, along with the herbs, unroasted tomatoes, and arugula. Toss well and let sit for 10 minutes so that the juices start to soften the bread, still leaving a crunch. If you prefer the bread a bit softer, you can let it sit for longer.

Finish with crumbled goat cheese and serve.

Gingered Peaches AND Cream WITH Browned-Butter Graham Crumbs

I love it when simple things taste complex and perfectly balanced. Such is the case here. The peaches are the star, so the better quality your peaches, the better your dessert (or breakfast—it's fruit and cream, so why not?)

SERVES 2

1 peach, sliced

¾ teaspoon minced fresh ginger

1 tablespoon plus 2 teaspoons dark brown sugar, divided

1 tablespoon unsalted butter

3 graham crackers, roughly ground into small to medium crumbs (⅓ cup / 30 g crumbs)

Flake salt

½ cup / 120 ml heavy whipping cream

Few sprigs fresh mint (optional)

In a medium bowl, combine the sliced peach, ginger, and 1 tablespoon brown sugar and let sit for 15 minutes to a couple of hours so the juices begin to release.

In a small saucepan over medium heat, melt the butter and let it brown until it foams and smells nutty, about 4 minutes. Stir in the graham cracker crumbs and cook for 2 minutes. Remove the pan from the heat and set the crumbs aside to cool. Finish the crumbs with a pinch of flake salt. You can make the buttery graham cracker crumbs up to 3 days in advance and store them in a well-sealed container; if they soften, simply toast in a hot pan.

When almost ready to serve, whip the cream with the remaining 2 teaspoons brown sugar to form soft peaks. Whipped cream can be made earlier in the day and then refrigerated until ready to use.

Divide the macerated peaches between two small bowls and top with whipped cream and graham cracker crumbs. Garnish with fresh mint, if desired.

It Gets Him

I knew this meal would get him: when dinner is based around chips and pork, it's pretty easy to win his favor. Sometimes our dinners are multidish affairs with bright salads that highlight what's in season, cream-based sauces, and desserts heavy with bittersweet chocolate. While I think Gabe appreciates that food, he seems to react with more moans of satisfaction when I put a quesadilla in front of him. He's a sucker for cheese, tortillas, and hot sauce, so these chilaquiles had a pretty good shot of leaving him panting at his plate.

I let the pork bathe in citrus juices, herbs, garlic, and onions for most of the day. Outside, when I was playing with the kids, I could smell a sweet, meaty scent wafting through the air, and I felt sorry for those who were taunted by the scent but not invited over for date night.

In less than five minutes, we devoured a meal that took hours to prepare. Lingering at the table through spurts of conversation, I picked at bits of tender pork here and there, long after my stomach had said, "Enough!"

While I was distracted by my nibbling, Gabe handed me a little package wrapped in brown paper. I hastily grabbed it and ripped into the paper like a child. It was a children's book.

"Oh, thanks," I said somewhat flatly. "Is it really for me?"

"Read it," he said, and as I did I saw that this little book was more than just charming illustrations about utensils.

Pineapple Rosarita
121

Avocado Salad with Fresh Herbs and Pepitas
122

Braised Pork Chilaquiles with Roasted Tomatillo Salsa and Pickled Red Onions
123

Mexican Chocolate Sorbet with Red Wine–Poached Cherries
127

It's called *Spoon*, and it's about one in particular. This little spoon wants so badly to be a knife so that he can cut, or a fork so that he can be used everywhere, or even chopsticks because they are exotic. But he's a spoon, and he doesn't see why that's important.

Meanwhile, the knife and fork admire how children use Spoon to make music with pots and pans and how bakers use Spoon to measure. Chopsticks envy the fact that Spoon doesn't have to travel in pairs the way they do. Spoon's mom reminds him of the joys of dunking head first into ice cream; only spoons can do that. And at the end of it all, there's satisfaction and happy spooning, much like the end of a successful date.

Tucked inside the cover of the book, Gabe had written a little note, "You're such a beautiful spoon."

Gabe knows how much I struggle with

comparing myself to other forks and knives. I spend so much time lamenting over what I don't have, focusing on what others are doing, and then feeling bad that I'm not doing those very things. Meanwhile, I'm missing the fact that I'm a spoon. That I'm not created to do the things that forks, knives, and chopsticks can do but rather I'm created to do something else.

Sometimes I play the comparison game with my husband, wishing he were a knife. Which he loves, I'm sure. I long for him to be able to spread jam and to slice through thick loaves of crusty bread. I wish he were more interested in yard work so that I wouldn't have to remind him every week to mow the lawn. In the beginning of our marriage, I wanted and expected him to be more like my dad; I thought, "Why doesn't he spend his time reading, studying, and engaging me in interesting conversation?" It's so much easier for me to focus on who he is not, what he doesn't do, and what needs he's not meeting for me rather than loving him for who he is.

As I get older, and hopefully a little wiser, I find freedom in accepting my limitations and appreciating that I was created with a specific purpose. The more time I spend trying to reinvent the purpose, the more I'm wasting the life I was intended to live. I'm thrilled to be a spoon; after all, ice cream is my favorite food. I love that Gabe is a fork, and I'm in awe of his desire to serve the kids. I marvel at his joy, his humor, and his infectious laugh. I love that he is satisfied with simple things like melted cheese and tortillas and that he appreciates a meal made up of chips and pork.

There's a reason why he is a fork and I am a spoon. When I accept that about both of us, our marriage thrives. Marriage isn't about working to change the other person; it's about knowing them fully and loving them because of and in spite of your differences. Through that we are changed.

TIMELINE

1 TO 3 DAYS IN ADVANCE

Marinate pork

Braise pork

Make pickled red onions

Make tomatillo salsa (or you can purchase this)

Make chocolate sorbet base

Make red wine–poached cherries

DINNER TIME

Make cocktails

Make salad

Make chilaquiles

Assemble sorbet and poached cherries

GROCERY

1 large red onion

1 small red onion

1 large avocado

2 cups / 60 g chopped assorted fresh herbs (basil, cilantro, mint, dill)

3 tablespoons toasted pepitas

10 limes

1 bunch fresh cilantro

1 pound /450 g tomatillos (about 8 to 10)

1 cup / 240 ml chicken stock, homemade (page 18) or store-bought

1 jar pickled jalapeños

6 ounces / 170 g tortilla chips (Juanita's brand, ideally)

6 ounces / 170 g mix of grated melting cheeses (such as Beecher's Flagship, Gruyère, and Monterey Jack) (2½ cups)

Cotija

Mexican crema or sour cream

1 pint / 470 ml orange juice

3½ pounds / 1.6 kg bone-in pork shoulder (also called Boston butt), or 3 pounds / 1.3 kg boneless pork shoulder

12 ounces / 340 g bittersweet chocolate (about 60 to 70%)

2 cups / 225 g dark, sweet cherries (frozen will work too)

10 ounces / 280 g fresh pineapple, plus more for garnish

2 teaspoons fresh rosemary leaves, plus 2 sprigs for garnish

Red wine (something fruity like a Shiraz)

PANTRY

3 medium-size yellow onions

Garlic

1 lemon

1 ounce / 30 ml triple sec

4 ounces / 120 ml tequila

Apple cider vinegar

Cumin seeds

Dried bay leaves

Red pepper flakes

Allspice berries

Ground cumin

Kosher salt

Freshly ground black pepper

Flake salt or fleur de sel

Extra-virgin olive oil

Unsalted butter

Granulated sugar

Dark brown sugar

Ground cinnamon

Whole nutmeg

Cayenne pepper

Vanilla extract

Vanilla bean

Instant espresso powder

Pineapple Rosarita

I don't remember who or where, but I once heard someone mention the compatibility of rosemary and pineapple; from there my mind went to tequila, and then this riff on a margarita was born. Good things happen when you are thinking about tequila.

SERVES 2

Lime wedges, to rim glass (optional)

Kosher or flake salt, to rim glass (optional)

10 ounces / 280 g fresh pineapple, cubed (about 2 generous cups), plus more for garnish

2 teaspoons roughly chopped fresh rosemary leaves, plus more for garnish

2 tablespoons triple sec

½ cup / 120 ml tequila

¼ cup / 60 ml freshly squeezed lime juice

If desired, run a lime wedge along the edge of two rocks glasses and dip each glass into a shallow dish filled with kosher or flake salt.

Fill the glasses with crushed ice and set aside.

Place half the fresh pineapple and 1 teaspoon rosemary in a pint glass. Muddle fiercely with a muddler or the handle of a wooden spoon to release the juice of the pineapple and bruise the rosemary. The pineapple should be quite juicy and well mashed, about 30 seconds of muddling.

Next, add 1 tablespoon triple sec, ¼ cup / 60 ml tequila, and 2 tablespoons lime juice into the pint glass. Pour this into a cocktail shaker filled with ice. Shake vigorously for 30 seconds. Strain into one of the glasses. Garnish with a couple cubes of pineapple and a sprig of fresh rosemary. Repeat.

121

Avocado Salad WITH Fresh Herbs AND Pepitas

I like to think of this salad as a sort of deconstructed guacamole. The freshness of the herbs and the cool, creamy avocado is the perfect side for rich chilaquiles. This salad would do well next to simple grilled chicken or steak, and, if you like heat, feel free to include some thinly sliced jalapeño.

SERVES 2

1 large avocado

2 cups chopped assorted fresh herbs (basil, cilantro, mint, dill; save the cilantro stems for the salsa)

⅓ small red onion, finely diced

½ teaspoon cumin seeds, toasted (see technique on page 11)

2 tablespoons extra-virgin olive oil

½ teaspoon flake salt or fleur de sel

3 tablespoons toasted pepitas

½ a lime

Halve, pit, and peel the avocado. Place it flat-side down on a cutting board and slice thinly.

Place 1 cup fresh herbs on a serving platter. Then top with half of the sliced avocado, half of the red onion, ¼ teaspoon cumin seeds, a bit of olive oil, a sprinkle of salt, half of the pepitas, and a squeeze of lime. Add another layer in the same way. Serve immediately.

Braised Pork Chilaquiles WITH Roasted Tomatillo Salsa AND Pickled Red Onions

Classically, this dish uses stale tortillas as its base and is served for breakfast or brunch with a fried egg. I prefer tortilla chips as the base (Juanita's brand is my favorite) and love leftovers for breakfast with a sunny-side-up egg on top.

I use my 12-inch cast-iron skillet and the size is perfect. There are a number of steps in this recipe; you are welcome to buy the salsa and skip the pickled onions. But, of course, I recommend you make it as is and enjoy the leftovers for days.

SERVES 4 OR 2 WITH ENOUGH LEFTOVERS
FOR BREAKFAST

2 tablespoons unsalted butter

1 yellow onion, thinly sliced

½ recipe Roasted Tomatillo Salsa **(recipe follows)**, or 1 (8-ounce / 230 g) jar prepared salsa

1 cup / 240 ml chicken stock, homemade (page 18) or store-bought

6 ounces / 170 grams tortilla chips (8 cups)

8 ounces / 230 g mix of grated melting cheeses (such as Beecher's Flagship, Gruyère, and Monterey Jack) (2½ cups)

2 cups Citrus-Braised Pork **(recipe follows)**

Garnish with the following: Pickled Red Onions **(recipe follows)**, pickled jalapeños, crumbled Cotija, Mexican crema or sour cream, lime wedges, and chopped fresh cilantro (save the cilantro stems for the salsa)

In a 10- to 12-inch oven-safe skillet, heat the butter over low heat. Add the onion and cook, stirring often, until deeply caramelized, about 30 to 45 minutes.

Preheat the oven to 350°F.

Add the salsa and stock to the skillet with the onions and bring to a boil. Remove the pan from the heat and layer in half of the chips, cheese, and pork. Repeat with the remaining chips, cheese, and pork.

Place the entire skillet in the oven and bake until the cheese melts, about 5 minutes. Remove the skillet and garnish as desired.

Roasted Tomatillo Salsa

Store-bought salsa is perfectly fine here, but if you, like me, prefer getting your hand into every part of the meal, this is one of my favorite recipes for a simple, green salsa. It is an adaptation from a Rick Bayless recipe that I love. It's the perfect salsa for the chilaquiles—deeply flavored, not too spicy, and quick to make. You'll need 1 cup for the chilaquiles, but I like to keep another cup around for dipping my chips into while I'm cooking.

MAKES 2 CUPS

2 tablespoons extra-virgin olive oil

1 pound / 450 g tomatillos (about 8 to 10), husk removed, rinsed, and halved

6 large garlic cloves

½ cup / 10 g cilantro stems

¼ teaspoon kosher salt, plus more as needed

½ medium-size yellow onion, diced

1 tablespoon freshly squeezed lime juice

Add the oil to a large, heavy skillet over medium heat. Add the tomatillos and garlic and sear, turning them over in the pan every 3 to 4 minutes so they don't burn. Roast for 10 to 15 minutes in the pan until the vegetables are tender and charred and caramelized in parts. If the garlic starts to brown too quickly, remove it from the pan and then continue to roast the tomatillos until they are tender.

Transfer the roasted garlic and tomatillos to a food processor. Add the cilantro stems and salt and blend until smooth. Pulse in the onion and lime juice. Taste and adjust the seasonings; add some water if the salsa is too thick.

This salsa will keep for a week, covered and refrigerated.

Pickled Red Onions

Use this recipe as a guide; pickles are a great vehicle for adaptation. Don't feel the need to run to the store if your pantry is without allspice berries; just throw in some coriander seeds or fennel seeds instead. Even if you leave out the spices completely, the onion's pungent, fresh bite is a welcome taste when paired with the cheese and pork-laden chilaquiles. Save leftovers for tacos, an antipasto platter, or your next hamburger. I have a feeling that a little jar of these pink-tinted pickled onions will find a permanent place in your fridge.

MAKES ROUGHLY 2 CUPS / 460 G

½ cup / 120 ml water

1 cup / 240 ml apple cider vinegar

¼ cup / 50 g granulated sugar

1 teaspoon cumin seeds

½ teaspoon red pepper flakes

1 dried bay leaf

1 teaspoon allspice berries

1 teaspoon kosher salt

1 large red onion, halved and thinly sliced

Place a medium saucepan over medium-high heat. Add the water, vinegar, sugar, cumin seeds, red pepper flakes, bay leaf, allspice berries, and salt and bring to a boil. Add the onion slices and reduce the heat to low. Gently simmer for 30 seconds and then remove from the heat and let cool completely. Transfer the onions and the liquid into a jar or other lidded container. Refrigerate until ready to use.

The onions will keep for several months, covered and refrigerated.

Citrus Braised Pork

Whenever I go through the process of doing a long braise, I make extra and plan the rest of the week's dinners accordingly. Beyond the chilaquiles, this pungent pork makes ridiculous tacos, tostadas, and taco salads. Stir into soups, or tuck into white rolls with a tangy BBQ sauce—and nestle in some of those pickled onions while you're at it.

SERVES 6 TO 8

2 cups / 470 ml orange juice

2 teaspoons freshly grated lime zest

½ cup / 120 ml freshly squeezed lime juice

½ cup / 120 ml extra-virgin olive oil

10 garlic cloves, smashed

1 yellow onion, sliced

2 tablespoons dark brown sugar

1½ tablespoons kosher salt

2 teaspoons freshly ground black pepper

1 tablespoon dried oregano

1 tablespoon ground cumin

2 dried bay leaves

3½ pounds / 1.6 kg bone-in pork shoulder, or 3 pounds / 1.4 kg boneless pork shoulder

In a heavy Dutch oven or other oven-safe roasting pan with a lid, stir together the orange juice, lime zest, lime juice, olive oil, garlic, onion, brown sugar, salt, pepper, oregano, cumin, and bay leaves. Add the pork shoulder and turn to coat. Cover and refrigerate for at least 4 hours or overnight.

Preheat the oven to 325°F.

Cover the whole roasting pan tightly with aluminum foil. Roast, covered, for 1½ hours. Carefully flip the pork, cover again, and roast for another hour.

Remove the foil and roast for another 1½ to 2 hours, turning once halfway through. If the pork falls apart as you try to flip it over, it is done. If not, continue to roast until it falls apart and the marinade is reduced. For a shoulder of this size, the total cooking time is usually 4 to 5 hours, or an hour to an hour and a half per pound.

Remove from the oven and let rest for 20 minutes. Shred the pork in the pan with two forks and mix with the reduced marinade. Remove the bay leaves.

The pork can be fully prepared (marinated and braised) 1 to 2 days ahead and stored, covered, in the refrigerator. The flavor improves over time.

Mexican Chocolate Sorbet WITH Red Wine–Poached Cherries

I'm not one to say no to cream. But in the case of this sorbet, you will not miss the cream. The sorbet is rich, smooth, and gently warming with cinnamon, nutmeg, and a touch of cayenne.

MAKES 1 QUART

3 cups / 710 ml water

1½ cups / 300 g dark brown sugar

1 tablespoon instant espresso powder

1 teaspoon ground cinnamon

½ teaspoon freshly grated nutmeg

¼ teaspoon kosher salt

Pinch of cayenne pepper

12 ounces / 340 g bittersweet chocolate (about 60 to 70%), chopped

1 teaspoon vanilla extract

In a large saucepan over medium-high heat, bring the water, brown sugar, espresso powder, cinnamon, nutmeg, salt, and cayenne to a simmer. Stir until the sugar is dissolved.

Remove from the heat and add the chopped chocolate. Allow to sit for 1 minute. Vigorously whisk until the chocolate is completely melted, about 1 minute. Stir in the vanilla extract.

Transfer the sorbet base to a sealable container and chill completely.

Freeze in your ice cream machine according to manufacturer's instructions. Transfer the soft sorbet to a sealed container and freeze until firm, about 3 hours. The base for the sorbet can be made 1 to 3 days before the date. I recommend freezing the sorbet the day you plan to eat it.

Remove from the freezer about 20 minutes before serving. Serve with Red Wine–Poached Cherries **(recipe follows)**.

127

Red Wine–Poached Cherries

This is best when cherries are in season, but frozen cherries work too.

MAKES ABOUT 1½ CUPS,
EASILY DOUBLED FOR LEFTOVERS

2 cups / 225 g dark, sweet cherries, pitted

1 tablespoon granulated sugar

½ tablespoon freshly squeezed lemon juice

1-inch piece lemon peel

½ cup / 120 g red wine (such as Shiraz)

½ vanilla bean, split, or 1 teaspoon vanilla extract

⅛ teaspoon ground cinnamon

Combine the cherries, sugar, lemon juice, lemon peel, red wine, vanilla bean, and cinnamon in a small saucepan over medium heat. Bring to a simmer and reduce to low. Simmer on low for 8 to 10 minutes, or until the red wine is syrupy and reduced, about the consistency of warm maple syrup. Stir in the vanilla extract, if using.

Let cool to room temperature. The cherries can be made 1 to 3 days ahead and stored, covered, in the refrigerator. Remove the vanilla bean just before serving.

Serve at room temperature or chilled over the Mexican chocolate sorbet.

A Taste of Home

Sweet Plum Sangria

133

Tomato and Fennel Gazpacho
with Dungeness Crab

133

Salmon Cakes with Chile and Fresh Herbs

135

Braised Green Beans with
Smashed Tomato Vinaigrette

136

Fresh Raspberry Tart with
Lemon Cream Cheese Filling

138

"So about last night . . . " I say, reluctantly bringing up the argument that began the night before.

"Yeah," he says, both wanting and not wanting to talk about it.

"Mom!" Roman shouts.

"Well, I'm sorry . . . " I go on.

"MOM!!"

" . . . that I said . . . "

"MOM!! Mama!!! Mommy!!!!"

"Yes, Roman."

"I'm hungry."

"Okay, well Mama and Daddy are trying to talk. I'll get you a snack very soon."

I turn to Gabe, "So what I was trying to say is that I'm sorry . . . "

"Maaaaaamaaaaaa?!" Ivy charges in.

"Yes, baby. What is it?" Gabe says with a tone that is both tender and annoyed.

"I'mmmmm thuuuursty."

"Here you go," he replies, handing her a pink Hello Kitty cup filled with water.

"Tank you," she says.

"What were you saying?" Gabe asks, encouraging me to continue.

"Well, so, I don't know. What was I saying? Oh yeah, so I feel bad about the way I responded, and I just . . . "

"Hey, Mom!" Baron says, not realizing that he is about to get the mom glare that apparently just becomes a part of your arsenal the moment you pop a baby out.

"Buddy, Mom and Dad are trying to talk. Can you go play for a bit and then we can talk later?"

Gabe pulls me back to us, "Alright, sorry babe. You were saying?"

"Never mind. We can talk about it later." I say in defeat.

And this is why we need date nights.

When the kids finally stop asking us questions, all the water cups are filled, and the only sounds in the house are the sweet hums of little snores and the steam rattling the lid that sits on top a pot of beans, we cook, eat, and talk.

This time our conversation wraps around the food that is most abundantly in season.

Naturally, it's the food I crave as the warmth in the air brings up memories of plucking sweet and heavy raspberries off the thorn-covered vines. They taste softly of wind-blown dust

A person's heart withers if it does not answer another heart.

Pearl S. Buck

realize that they were actually onto something? Now I boil the hell out of my beans, but, instead of using water, they simmer in a flavorful broth and then get tossed in a tangy vinaigrette of smashed tomatoes and mint. Maybe growing up is more about taking bits and pieces of what you learned and then making them your own.

I think part of growing up is also about learning to like fish: at least for me it is. I have lived in the Pacific Northwest for nearly all of my life and am just now starting to appreciate salmon. It's been a source of shame, as salmon is practically the mascot of this region. But I realized that with enough red chile, fresh herbs, smoky paprika, cumin, and lemon, I really do like salmon.

Gabe and I steadily sip on sangria, dark red from the plums I crushed to make it. We dip our spoons into a lightly licorice-scented gazpacho, and I realize how comfortable we've gotten with the idea of dating at home. Once it felt strange; it felt as if we were admitting defeat on not being able to actually leave the house for a date. We used to be so tired and hungry by the time our date began that we wouldn't say a word throughout dinner, and sometimes that still happens. But mostly we've grown accustomed to our weekly late dinners.

I also realize that, with a weekly time on the calendar set aside just for us to connect, have a good conversation, and hang out, it makes the time in between our dates easier. Dates give us time to have the conversations that always get interrupted. I used to walk away from our attempted conversations feeling completely

and heat but mostly of what I think summer should. They are sweet and jammy until the last moment, when their tartness clenches the back of my mouth. I pucker, then instantly reach for another, trying to get my fill before their short season ends.

As the last of the berries nestle on top of the lemon-scented cream cheese filling, the green beans sputter on the stove. Grandma and my mom would always cook their beans until they were dull, saggy, tender, and sweet. As I began to find my own way in the kitchen, I judged those limp beans harshly while praising my flashy and crisp beans that, by contrast, spent just a moment in boiling water before I shocked them in ice. "This is how to cook green beans," I declared, while missing the soft, earthy beans of my childhood. Isn't that a sign of maturity? When you cast off what you learned as a child, seek your own answers, and then come around and defeated and seeing no possibility of Gabe and me actually having much of a relationship until the kids learned how to fill their own Hello Kitty cups or learned when to be quiet, neither of which will happen soon. I'd feel alone and disconnected from the one person I longed to be most connected to.

Date nights give Gabe and me the time to bond and—my favorite part—the longer we date, the more time we long to spend together when it's not date night. We unite in the random five-minute conversations throughout our day; we send more texts to each other and talk on the phone more often. In the evenings, we leave the TV off and spend time talking instead. The more I'm with Gabe, the more I want to be with him.

When he and I are connected, everything in life seems doable. I read in a book called *Hold Me Tight* that "[t]he more we can reach out to our partners, the more separate and independent we can be." I had to stop and reread the sentence several times. Doesn't it seem backward? The more you connect with someone, the more independent you can be? But the longer I thought about it, I realized that when my relationship with Gabe is going well—when we are honest, sharing regularly, and listening to each other—I feel known by him and more confident, empowered. I know that he will support me when I fall or in the moments when my independence fails me; I have a partner who is eager and willing to help me clean up my messes.

It's easy for me to think that life is made up of compartments. Kids are over here. Work is here. Friendships are here. Family is over there. Marriage is here. That is, until I realize that our marriage feels shitty and therefore everything else in life does too. Sometimes it feels so big, and I think I'm kidding myself that a simple meal around the table with my husband can fix all that. Then we sit down and eat, start to talk, listen to each other, and our connection builds. It might be small at first, but it's hope, and when there's hope there's possibility. One day you find yourself eager to connect in the little moments, during the times that aren't on the calendar, and you are able to really look into his eyes and remember why you chose to do life with that person and are eager to continue life with that person.

We don't bother with plates when I bring out the tart. I hand him a fork and, without holding anything back, we both confidently plunge into the creamy tart, the cinnamon-scented shell shattering underneath, and eat together until we've had our fill. Sometimes it's as easy as a tart piled high with raspberries and two eager forks.

TIMELINE

1 TO 3 DAYS IN ADVANCE

Make sangria

Make tart crust

Make salmon cakes

DATE DAY

Make tart filling and assemble tart

Make gazpacho, refrigerate

Braise green beans

Make smashed tomato vinaigrette

DINNER TIME

Toss beans with vinaigrette

Sear salmon cakes

GROCERY

6 plums

1 pound / 450 g tomatoes, plus more for garnish

1 medium-size fresh fennel bulb

1 bunch fresh basil

1 bunch fresh dill

1 bunch fresh mint

2 ounces / 60 g crab claw meat

¾ pound / 340 g green beans

½ cup / 80 g cherry tomatoes

1 scallion

8 ounces / 230 g salmon

1 small red onion

1 fresh red jalapeño pepper

1 (8-ounce / 230 g) package cream cheese

Crème fraîche or sour cream

2 pints raspberries / 480 g

1 bottle dry red wine (pinot noir, Sangiovese, or other light red works well)

PANTRY

3 lemons

Honey

Kosher salt

Flake salt

Freshly ground black pepper

Chicken stock, homemade (page 18) or store-bought

Garlic

Extra-virgin olive oil

Red wine vinegar

Capers

Mayonnaise

Dijon mustard

Ground coriander

Ground cumin

Smoked paprika

Ground cinnamon

Panko breadcrumbs

Egg

Unsalted butter

Granulated sugar

All-purpose flour

Dark brown sugar

Soda water

Brandy

Grand Marnier or Cointreau

Sweet Plum Sangria

Plums are second only to apricots in my ranking of favorite stone fruit. And yet I feel like they are overshadowed by their more popular cousins: the peach and the nectarine. While I really love apricots, it's quite possibly plum's nearly black color and vivid red flesh, their syrupy sweetness paired with a pleasant, piquant tartness that edges them to the top of the leaderboard. Here they soak in a fruity red wine in abundance, along with a touch of honey and different liquors for a refreshing and fitting way to start this Northwestern-inspired date.

SERVES 4

5 ripe plums, thinly sliced (about 3 cups)

¼ cup / 60 ml brandy

2 tablespoons Grand Marnier or Cointreau

2 tablespoons honey

1 bottle dry red wine (such as pinot noir or Sangiovese)

Soda water

In a large pitcher, add the plums, brandy, Grand Marnier, and honey. Stir well to combine.

Pour in the wine and stir once more.

Refrigerate for at least 4 hours or overnight.

Serve over ice with some of the plums and top with a splash of soda water.

The sangria will keep in the refrigerator for up to 3 days.

Tomato and Fennel Gazpacho WITH Dungeness Crab

The quality of this dish depends on your produce. In other words, use the best tomatoes you can find. If you're in the Northwest in early September, you'll use the jewel-toned and heavy heirloom varieties. The ones with almost purple flesh are my favorite.

SERVES 2

1 pound / 450 g tomatoes, roughly chopped, plus more for garnish

1 garlic clove

¼ medium-size fennel bulb

¼ cup / 5 g fresh basil, plus more for garnish

½ teaspoon kosher salt

½ teaspoon freshly ground black pepper

½ tablespoon freshly squeezed lemon juice

¼ cup / 60 ml extra-virgin olive oil

Flake salt, for finishing

2 ounces / 60 g crab claw meat

Add the tomatoes, garlic, fennel, basil, salt, pepper, and lemon juice to a food processor or blender and blend until completely smooth. Add the olive oil and mix just to combine.

Finish the gazpacho with thinly sliced basil, chopped tomatoes, flake salt, and a few pieces of crab claw meat per serving. The gazpacho can be made earlier in the day and then finished just before serving.

Salmon Cakes with Chile and Fresh Herbs

I'm very proud to call the Pacific Northwest my home, but I'm a bit ashamed to say that I'm a Seattleite who, until fairly recently, didn't like salmon; it's like saying you're from Hawaii and you don't like the sun. But these intensely flavored cakes make me want to change my mind.

MAKES EIGHT 2-INCH CAKES

8 ounces / 230 g salmon, skin removed

½ teaspoon kosher salt, plus more as needed

Freshly ground black pepper

½ cup / 55 g finely diced red onion

1 red jalapeño pepper, finely diced

¼ cup / 5 g chopped fresh basil

¼ cup / 5 g chopped fresh dill

1½ tablespoons chopped capers

¼ cup / 60 g mayonnaise

1 teaspoon freshly grated lemon zest

1 tablespoon freshly squeezed lemon juice

2 garlic cloves, minced

2 teaspoons Dijon mustard

½ teaspoon ground coriander

½ teaspoon ground cumin

1 teaspoon smoked paprika

½ cup / 30 g panko breadcrumbs

1 egg, lightly beaten

2 tablespoons olive oil

Crème fraîche or sour cream, for serving

Preheat the oven to 350°F. Line a baking sheet with parchment paper.

Place the salmon on the parchment and sprinkle both sides with salt and pepper. Roast for 10 minutes, or until just cooked or even slightly underdone, as it will be seared at the end.

When the salmon has cooled enough to handle, break into small flaky chunks and remove any bones. Let cool to room temperature.

While the salmon roasts, in a medium bowl, combine the red onion, red jalapeño, basil, dill, capers, mayonnaise, lemon zest, lemon juice, garlic, Dijon, coriander, cumin, smoked paprika, panko, salt, and egg. Fold in the cooled, flaked salmon.

Form a salmon cake by taking ⅓ cup / 70 g of the mixture in your hands and shaping it into a rough 2-inch-round cake. Continue to make the cakes with the remaining salmon mixture. You can store the formed salmon cakes, covered, in the refrigerator for up to 2 days.

Preheat the oven to 250°F.

Coat the bottom of a medium skillet with the olive oil and place over high heat. Once the oil is hot, sear the cakes in batches until deeply browned, 1 to 2 minutes per side.

Keep warm in the oven until you are ready to serve.

Serve with crème fraîche or sour cream, if desired.

Braised Green Beans WITH Smashed Tomato Vinaigrette

I went through an al dente bean phase because I thought those beans were more sophisticated than the beans that cook for 40 minutes or longer, the way my mom and grandma make them. But you know what I decided? Those pale and limp-looking beans taste so much better. Perfectly soft when you bite into them, these beans are braised with lemon and olive oil to give you flavor and sweetness. I'm bringing back Grandma's beans! To help what they lack in the beauty department, I've tossed them with a bright tomato vinaigrette, dappled with fresh mint. But I'd toss almost anything in this dressing, come to think of it; this dressing with grilled corn would be ridiculous.

For the green beans:

Combine the green beans, olive oil, lemon zest, lemon juice, garlic, salt, pepper, and stock in a large skillet set over medium-high heat.

Bring the mixture to a boil and then reduce to a simmer. Cover and cook for 30 minutes, or until soft.

Uncover and cook for 10 minutes more, over medium-low heat, stirring occasionally, until the liquid is reduced and coats the beans.

For the vinaigrette:

In a medium bowl, add the tomatoes and squish them between your fingers inside the bowl, so the juices don't splatter all over your kitchen; alternatively, you can smash them using the backside of a wooden spoon. The juices will help create the vinaigrette while the tomatoes still remain in large pieces.

Whisk in the red wine vinegar, lemon juice, olive oil, mint, and scallions.

Toss the warm or room-temperature green beans with the vinaigrette.

The dish can be served cold or at room temperature.

Before serving, finish with flake salt.

SERVES 2

GREEN BEANS

¾ pound / 340 g green beans, trimmed

1½ tablespoons olive oil

1 teaspoon freshly grated lemon zest

1½ tablespoons freshly squeezed lemon juice

1 garlic clove, roughly chopped

½ teaspoon kosher salt

¼ teaspoon freshly ground black pepper

1 cup / 240 ml low-sodium chicken or vegetable stock, homemade (page 18) or store-bought

VINAIGRETTE

½ cup / 80 g cherry tomatoes

2 teaspoons red wine vinegar

1 tablespoon freshly squeezed lemon juice

2 tablespoons olive oil

2 tablespoons chopped fresh mint

1 scallion, thinly sliced (white and green parts)

¼ teaspoon kosher salt

Flake salt, for finishing

Fresh Raspberry Tart WITH Lemon Cream Cheese Filling

My cousin grew up on a raspberry farm. One summer I went there to work and pick berries, but instead I ate berries and then, when I was too full to eat any more, I went inside and played with my cousin. I made $5 that year, and now that I think about it, I probably only made that much because my aunt felt bad for me. Regardless, I was perfectly content to nestle into the rows of those vines and eat my weight in sweet and tart berries. We really do grow them best around here (I may be biased), and this simple tart with a cinnamon-scented crust shows off the mighty raspberry quite nicely. The crust recipe is adapted from a recipe by the great Alice Medrich. I've used it both as tart crusts and as cookies hundreds of times.

MAKES ONE 9-INCH TART

CRUST

½ cup / 115 g unsalted butter, melted

2 tablespoons granulated sugar

¼ teaspoon kosher salt

¼ teaspoon ground cinnamon

1 cup / 130 g all-purpose flour

FILLING

1 (8-ounce / 230 g) package cream cheese, at room temperature

⅓ cup / 70 g dark brown sugar

1 teaspoon freshly grated lemon zest

1½ tablespoons freshly squeezed lemon juice

Pinch of kosher salt

2 pints raspberries

1 tablespoon honey

For the crust:

Preheat the oven to 350°F. Place a 9-inch tart pan on a baking sheet.

In a medium bowl, stir together the melted butter and sugar. Add the salt, cinnamon, and flour and stir just to combine. The dough will be quite soft.

Press the dough onto the sides and bottom of the tart pan and bake for 15 to 18 minutes, or until golden and completely set.

Let cool to room temperature on a wire rack.

Tart shell can be baked a day in advance; store wrapped in plastic wrap. You can also refrigerate the unbaked tart shell for up to 3 days before baking.

For the filling:

In a large bowl, combine the cream cheese, brown sugar, lemon zest, lemon juice, and salt and mix with an electric mixer on low speed. Scrape down the sides of the bowl and continue to mix on medium speed for 5 minutes.

To assemble, fill the cooled tart shell with the cream cheese filling. Spread evenly. Top with the fresh raspberries and drizzle with honey. This tart can be made the day of the date. Remove the tart from the refrigerator 30 minutes to 1 hour before you plan on serving.

A Sort-Of Fairy Tale

Hemingway Punch

143

Thyme and Parmesan Roasted Sweet Potatoes

144

Caribbean-Style BBQ Chicken Legs

145

Mango Miso Slaw

147

Caramelized Pineapple Sundaes
with Candied Coconut

148

"Movie night!" I say, and the kids cheer. I wonder at what age they'll realize that movie night often happens because Mom and Dad are too tired to entertain them any longer. Regardless, it's one of those activities that makes everyone happy. So, it happens.

Gabe is gone for the night, and I am left alone with the evening and the bedtime craziness in front of me. I make quick work of choosing a movie and we snuggle together, settling into the couch.

My plan is to read while the kids watch the movie, but I can't help watching, getting swept up in the story however predictable and flat it is.

When did I become one of those moms? I think, cringing, when I hear Cinderella proclaim, "He's the one. With him everything will be perfect. I want the perfect life and perfect this and perfect that," as a perfectly coifed Prince Charming sat in a dream bubble above her head. I'm not anti-princess; just as I did as a young girl, my daughter naturally gravitates toward that role. I remember tucking a tattered blanket into my underwear as I pranced down the stairs. Looking over my shoulder, I beamed as I saw what to me looked like a dress's grand train following behind me. I know that now we, as parents of little girls, are supposed to teach our girls that they don't need the prince and that they can rescue themselves. That's great and I agree, mostly, but I also want my daughter to see that she is worthy of having a young man

battle a dragon for her or climb an impossibly high tower and struggle with the thorns, the beasts, the raging waters, and whatever else stands in his way of winning her heart. Whatever it is, my princess is worth the fight.

What I can't stand about the princess movies is that they make love look so easy, natural, and instant. I watched those movies growing up, and I managed to become a strong, independent, and self-sufficient woman, but I did expect love and choosing "the one" to look like Cinderella and Prince Charming dancing at the ball, thinking every touch would be electric and that looking into each other's eyes would be enough. I thought I would "know" and there wouldn't be any doubt. And while I wasn't so naive to think that it really was happiness ever after, what I didn't know was how hard we would have to fight for our happily ever after.

Our date nights are part of our fighting for that happily ever after.

We were supposed to have our date the night before, but the evening got derailed when I stared a fish in the eye and decided to the close the refrigerator door and sulk on the couch instead. I had wanted to make the date special and treat Gabe, and so I bought a beautiful whole fish, a rarity in our house. But after a hectic day, I couldn't bring myself to deal with the fish. Feeling defeated, I went to bed at 8:30 instead of dating my husband.

When I woke up in the morning, I felt guilty. I could almost feel the fish's glassy eye watching me from its resting place in the fridge. Thus, when a little window appeared in our day when we already had our babysitter coming over with the intention of our using that time to work, we decided to use it to date.

Gabe, who plays the part of Prince Charming

brilliantly in all his tall, dark, and handsome glory, was working at the office while I, complete in frazzled hair and tattered apron set out to prep the fish, slice cabbage, roast potatoes, and bend sugar into submission as caramel.

I unwrap the fish from the white paper and stand there not knowing what to do next. Roman, who refused to go outside and play, stands next to me rattling off question after question about my plans for the fish. I answered his succession of questions as patiently as I could until I couldn't.

"Roman, Mama is trying to make some food for Daddy, and I can't really answer your questions when I'm doing that." He runs off crying. Good one, princess, I tell myself.

"What do I do with this thing?" I text a friend who is much more adept at fish cookery.

Standing over the fish, my eyes begin to well up with tears. I know, I know, it's just a fish, but I also have the slaw to make and the potatoes to finish, and my Prince Charming is still at work; he can't make me a cocktail. It all just feels so daunting. In light of everything, I don't really even want the date. Cranky, tired, and emotional, I think it would be best for Gabe not to be with me right now. "Stay away. Crazy lady here," I want to say. At the moment, it seems that the best option is for me to find a little corner to curl up in and cry, alone.

Just as I am about to run out of the kitchen and admit defeat, my fairy godmother shows up in the form of Julie, the fish-knowledgeable friend I had texted just a few moments before. She swoops in, praises my scale-scraping work, and reassures me that everything looks great. It would be nice if she'd turn my rags into a nice dress and do something with my hair, but she does something better: she nudges me to keep going, reminds me of why I was preparing this meal, and assures me that there will be other dates when it's not so hard.

So I push on with a vengeance, and, about fifteen minutes after she leaves, everything is ready.

Prince Charming shows up, not on a horse but with flowers in hand, and then quickly sets off to make us a cocktail. Who needs a white horse when you have a prince who knows his way around a cocktail shaker?

"What cup do you want yours in?" he asks, knowing me well enough to know that I'm particular about cups.

"A big one," I reply.

The table is cluttered with the paintings the kids and I had made earlier in the day, and the kitchen looks like the scene of a great battle; we take our date outside, out of the mess.

Whenever I'm not in the mood for a date, the food will often change my mind. Sure, the flowers Gabe brought me are lovely and the cocktail is the perfect mix of sweet and strong, but our meal, with its imperfect fish, red chiles, soft sweet mango, miso, and crisp cabbage, is what lifts the cloud hanging around me. Even though chicken would fare better than fish in my Caribbean-inspired sauce, I feel at peace with my full plate and this time with Gabe. Over and over, I dip my finger into the deeply amber pool of spiced caramel, tasting again and again to make sure that our dessert is still good; how can one sit down to a meal knowing that a sweet sundae of warm pineapple, toasted coconut, and caramel—that I know full well is delicious—will end the fanfare?

We sit, eat greedily, and talk as the sun warms our faces and the cocktail cools our throats. Before long Gabe goes back to work and I sort of clean up the aftermath of my kitchen battle.

I remember having watched Cinderella with the kids, and it reminds me of my very own fairy-tale scene: our dates.

"You know how Cinderella says Prince Charming is 'the one' and that their life would

now be perfect?" I ask the kids as I tuck them in later that night. "What do you think about that?"

I get some blank stares and off-subject comments before Baron says, "Nobody's perfect."

"That's right, and if we expect our lives to be perfect we are going to miss out on the beauty of the imperfection."

I have more I want to say, and I hope they will ask more questions so I can tell them about how their dad and I have to work hard for our marriage or how I'd take our fairy tale over Cinderella's any day. I want to tell them that, just before I said "I do" to their dad, I thought, "Ashley, is he the one?" but then responded to myself, "How the hell do I know? What I do know is that I'd be completely stupid if I didn't choose to spend the rest of my life with him."

I want to tell my kids that now he's my one but we had to work damn hard to get here. We've both battled our dragons, climbed the towering walls, and fought like hell for each other. But this story, our sweet, utterly imperfect fairy tale, is the sort of story worth telling and the one worth fighting for.

TIMELINE

1 TO 3 DAYS IN ADVANCE

Make brown sugar syrup

Make BBQ sauce

Season chicken legs

Make slaw dressing

Make candied coconut

Make spiced caramel

DATE DAY

Make slaw (but don't toss with dressing until just before serving)

Prep potatoes

DINNER TIME

Make punch

Roast potatoes

Toss slaw with dressing

Roast chicken legs

Sauté pineapple

Assemble sundaes

GROCERY

1 grapefruit

1 small mango

1 pineapple

4 limes

2 large sweet potatoes

1 package or small bunch fresh thyme

1 bunch fresh cilantro

2 red jalapeño peppers

1 small red cabbage

1 red onion

Thumb-size piece fresh ginger

Whole-milk yogurt

½ cup / 120 ml heavy whipping cream

½ cup / 10 g finely grated Parmesan

1½ pounds / 680 g chicken legs / drumsticks (about 6 legs)

2 tablespoons shiro (white) miso paste

1 (6-ounce / 170 g) can tomato paste

¾ cup / 110 g whole roasted, salted peanuts

Unsweetened flaked coconut

1 pint / 450 g vanilla ice cream

Luxardo maraschino liqueur

PANTRY

Garlic

½ large yellow onion

Unsalted butter

Kosher salt

Freshly ground black pepper

Extra-virgin olive oil

Olive oil

Apple cider vinegar

Soy sauce

Molasses

Honey

Ground ginger

Ground cumin

Ground coriander

Ground allspice

Ground cinnamon

Whole nutmeg

Dark brown sugar

Granulated sugar

1½ tablespoons cornstarch

Vanilla bean

Liquid smoke (optional)

Rice wine vinegar

Toasted sesame oil

Rum

Hemingway Punch

Ernest Hemingway liked his daiquiris with a bit of grapefruit juice and Luxardo, a maraschino liqueur, but I think he would have also appreciated our version that uses a deep, almost molasses–like simple syrup and a touch of freshly grated nutmeg.

SERVES 2

GRAPEFRUIT SUGAR

¼ cup / 50 g granulated sugar

1 teaspoon freshly grated grapefruit zest

Lime wedge, for rimming the glass

PUNCH

3 ounces / 90 ml rum

½ ounce / 10 ml Luxardo maraschino liqueur

¼ cup / 60 ml freshly squeezed grapefruit juice

¼ cup / 60 ml freshly squeezed lime juice

1½ ounces / 40 ml Brown Sugar Syrup (recipe follows)

Pinch of freshly grated nutmeg

Lime wedges, for serving

For the grapefruit sugar:
Combine the sugar and zest in a shallow bowl.

Rim the edge of two highball glasses with a lime wedge and then dip into the grapefruit sugar. Whatever sugar is left over can be stored in an airtight container or a resealable plastic bag.

For the punch:

Fill the highball glasses with crushed ice. Combine the rum, Luxardo, grapefruit juice, lime juice, and syrup in a cocktail shaker with ice. Shake and then pour into the prepared glasses.

Finish each cocktail with freshly grated nutmeg and a wedge of lime.

Brown Sugar Syrup

1 cup / 215 g dark brown sugar

½ cup / 120 ml water

In a small saucepan over medium heat, bring the brown sugar and water to a boil. Reduce to a simmer and stir until the brown sugar is dissolved. Cool to room temperature.

Leftover syrup can be stored in the fridge for up to 1 month.

Thyme AND Parmesan Roasted Sweet Potatoes

The cornstarch in this recipe helps to crisp the sweet potatoes and give them a light, shattering crust.

SERVES 2

1½ tablespoons cornstarch

2 sweet potatoes, peeled and sliced into ¼-inch rounds

2 tablespoons olive oil

2 tablespoons fresh thyme leaves

½ cup / 10 g finely grated Parmesan

¾ teaspoon kosher salt

¼ teaspoon freshly ground black pepper

Preheat the oven to 450°F. Line a baking sheet with parchment paper.

Place the cornstarch in a large resealable plastic bag and add the sweet potatoes. Seal the bag and toss to coat.

Place the coated sweet potatoes in a large bowl and then add the olive oil. Toss to ensure that all of the potatoes are covered in olive oil.

Add the thyme leaves, Parmesan, salt, and pepper and toss once more to coat.

Lay the sweet potatoes on the baking sheet in a single layer and then place on the middle rack of the oven.

Roast for 50 minutes, flipping the rounds halfway through, until the potatoes are fully cooked, crisp on the outside, and deeply golden in parts. Serve warm with extra BBQ sauce (**recipe follows**) for dipping.

Caribbean-Style BBQ Chicken Legs

You know the whole roasted fish I mentioned earlier? It really wasn't that bad, but these sweet, tangy, spicy chicken legs are so much better. They are loosely called "Caribbean-style" because there's rum in the sauce, lots of citrus, fresh ginger, and a bit of allspice.

MAKES 6 CHICKEN LEGS

DRY BRINE

2 teaspoons kosher salt

1 teaspoon freshly ground black pepper

1½ pounds / 680 g chicken legs/drumsticks
(about 6 legs)

BBQ SAUCE

½ large yellow onion, diced

2 garlic cloves, roughly chopped

2 tablespoons extra-virgin olive oil

¼ teaspoon kosher salt, plus more as needed

1 red jalapeño pepper, finely diced (more or less
depending on desired amount of heat)

¼ cup / 60 ml rum

1 (6-ounce / 170 g) can tomato paste

½ cup / 120 ml apple cider vinegar

¼ cup / 60 ml soy sauce

¼ cup / 60 ml molasses

3 tablespoons honey

2 teaspoons minced fresh ginger

1 teaspoon ground cumin

½ teaspoon ground coriander

½ teaspoon ground allspice

½ teaspoon freshly grated nutmeg

¼ cup / 60 ml water

1 teaspoon freshly grated lime zest

1 tablespoon freshly squeezed lime juice

⅛ teaspoon liquid smoke (optional)

2 tablespoons olive oil, for frying

For the dry brine:

A day or two before you plan on having the date, salt and pepper the chicken and then cover and refrigerate.

For the BBQ sauce:

Sauté the onions and garlic with the olive oil and a pinch of salt over medium-low heat for 10 to 15 minutes, or until translucent and just starting to caramelize. Stir occasionally. Add the jalapeño and sauté for an additional 2 minutes. Add the rum and scrape up any browned bits from the onions and garlic. Simmer until reduced to a glaze, 1 to 2 minutes.

Whisk in the tomato paste, cider vinegar, soy sauce, molasses, honey, ginger, cumin, coriander, allspice, nutmeg, salt, and water and then simmer for 15 minutes.

Stir in the lime zest, lime juice, and liquid smoke, if using. This should yield 1½ cups / 360 g.

The BBQ sauce can be made up to 1 week in advance. Cover and store in the refrigerator until ready to use.

To cook the chicken:

Preheat the oven to 400°F. Move a rack to the top third of the oven.

Heat 2 tablespoons olive oil in a cast-iron skillet on high. Sear the chicken legs for 2 minutes per side, or until the skin is crisp and golden brown, 4 minutes total.

Add ½ cup / 120 g BBQ sauce to a medium bowl and toss the hot chicken legs in the sauce. Place the chicken legs back in the skillet and spoon any additional sauce from the bowl on top.

Place the skillet into the oven and roast for 20 minutes. Turn the broiler on high.

Broil the chicken legs for 3 to 5 minutes, or until crisp and nearly blackened on top.

Let the chicken rest in the pan for 10 minutes before serving. Serve with extra BBQ sauce on the side.

Mango Miso Slaw

Since this date, this slaw has been my lunch on many occasions. It is vibrant, salty, and sweet, and I can't help picking out the peanuts and eating them, one by one.

SERVES 2

2 tablespoons shiro (white) miso paste

2 tablespoons freshly squeezed lime juice

2 teaspoons rice wine vinegar

1 teaspoon toasted sesame oil

1 teaspoon minced fresh ginger

1 teaspoon honey

¼ teaspoon kosher salt

⅓ cup / 80 g whole-milk yogurt

1 small red cabbage, shredded (4 cups / 225 g)

¼ medium-size red onion, sliced

1 cup / 20 g roughly chopped fresh cilantro

1 small mango, peeled, pitted, and diced

1 red jalapeño pepper, seeded and finely diced

½ cup / 70 g whole roasted, salted peanuts, plus more for garnish

Whisk together the miso, lime juice, rice vinegar, sesame oil, ginger, honey, salt, and yogurt. The dressing can be made a day or two ahead and stored, covered, in the refrigerator.

In a large bowl, combine the shredded cabbage, onion, cilantro, mango, jalapeño, and peanuts. Toss with the dressing, transfer to a serving dish, and then top with more peanuts. Serve immediately.

A SORT-OF FAIRY TALE

Caramelized Pineapple Sundaes with Candied Coconut

This started out as a light dessert: roasted pineapple with a bit of golden-toasted coconut flakes. But then I thought that caramel would be nice—a spiced caramel, aromatic and copper in color. So I made caramel. Then I thought that this would make a killer ice cream sundae: cold ice cream melting under caramelized pineapple, some golden-toasted and candied coconut flakes for garnish, and then more caramel to cover it all. And there went the idea for a light dessert.

SERVES 2

¼ cup / 25 g unsweetened flaked coconut

1 teaspoon granulated sugar

⅛ teaspoon kosher salt

1 tablespoon unsalted butter

1 tablespoon Spiced Caramel Sauce (recipe follows), plus more for serving

1 generous cup / 230 g fresh pineapple, cut into 1-inch cubes

1 pint / 450 g vanilla ice cream

Preheat the oven to 350°F. Line a baking sheet with parchment paper.

Spread the coconut on the parchment and sprinkle with sugar and salt. Bake for 5 to 7 minutes, or until golden.

Cool to room temperature and store in an airtight container until ready to use. This can be made up to 1 week in advance.

In a sauté pan over medium heat, melt the butter and caramel. Add the pineapple and sauté, stirring often, for about 5 minutes, or until the pineapple is soft and coated with caramel.

Scoop the vanilla ice cream into two bowls and top with the caramelized pineapple and its sauce and garnish with candied coconut flakes.

Spiced Caramel Sauce

MAKES 1 CUP

¼ cup / 60 ml water

½ cup / 100 g granulated sugar

½ vanilla bean, split

½ cup / 120 ml heavy whipping cream

¼ teaspoon kosher salt

¼ teaspoon ground cinnamon

¼ teaspoon ground ginger

Pinch of allspice

Pinch of freshly grated nutmeg

Add the water, sugar, and vanilla bean to a small saucepan. Stir well to combine. Cover and set on medium-high heat. Cook for 4 minutes. Remove the lid and cook for another 3 to 5 minutes, but don't stir; gently swirl the pan if it's not cooking evenly.

The caramel is ready when the sugar is a deep, dark amber color and is smoking.

Remove from the heat and carefully pour in the cream. It will sputter and seize up at first, but just wait for it to calm down and then stir slowly; it will come back together. Stir in the salt, cinnamon, ginger, allspice, and nutmeg.

This caramel is best served warm. Store whatever you don't use during date night in the refrigerator, covered, for up to 2 weeks.

Our Burger

Oven-Baked Onion Rings

153

Our Perfect Burger with Special Sauce

154

Bittersweet Chocolate Malted Shakes

156

At different points in our marriage, burgers have been a sort of buoy, keeping us afloat and providing grace and goodness in difficult seasons. I don't solely credit burgers for saving and sustaining us throughout those periods, but they do make me smile. To Gabe and me, a good, classic burger gave us a bit of hope when we needed it.

There have been other burgers—the fancy kind with bacon, various types of cheese, sometimes even Kobe beef—but when I'm craving a burger, it's bound to be one of two that have entered our lives at times when we needed something to help us put one foot in front of the other.

We moved to California just weeks after our second anniversary. We wanted to seal ourselves off as husband and wife, to separate ourselves from our everyday comforts, including our families, and to become a little family of our own. Just the two of us. It was either L.A. or New York, until we looked at the cost of living in New York. We decided to go to L.A., and our fate was sealed when I got a pastry cook job at Spago in Beverly Hills, Wolfgang Puck's flagship restaurant.

Spago would be my first real restaurant experience; I had no idea what I was getting myself into. We packed our red Oldsmobile Achieva and drove away from all we knew; we were young, naive, and eager for an adventure.

I left Seattle with six months' experience at a bakery, with a passion for making chocolates at home, and about 30 pounds less than what I should have weighed. While I was falling more and more in love with food and the world around it, I was massively struggling to control myself and what I was eating. What started as "I 'need' to lose some of the weight I put on while spending months living off gelato in Italy" turned into, "Well, just a little more." No matter how thin I was, I still found things that I didn't like about my body. I was exercising too much, counting every single calorie that was going into my mouth, and feeling incredibly alone in a new marriage. And yet I was hopeful about our new adventure.

Reality hit quickly; to say that the job at Spago was difficult in the beginning would not be saying enough. In the midst of the yelling, the demands, and the need to master my position, I lost sight of myself. Food became my comfort when everything else felt unstable. I allowed myself to be free and to eat. It wasn't even really a conscious decision. It was just me giving myself some grace.

We'd eat dinner at 2 a.m. when I got home

and go to In-N-Out Burger on our days off. We'd sit on the benches in the sun, share a milk shake, and take in the moment when life didn't seem so hard. The rattling of the ticket machines from work grew to a soft murmur in my head while I bit into a juicy burger and the pile of crumpled, special sauce–covered napkins grew around me.

It's not hard to put on weight when you feed yourself lots of burgers; burgers aren't exactly health food, but for me in that season they were. Now, I've found more balance and eat a burger on special occasions, with no guilt and complete pleasure.

By the time we left L.A., I was healthy and had fallen in love with the job, but we were leaving because we were starting a family and a new adventure—a family we didn't think we could have because of complicated health issues induced by my previous undereating.

Shortly after our move back to Seattle, we discovered Burger Master. This Seattle staple has been around since 1952, and most locations allow you to drive up, roll down your window, and be served by a friendly staff. Unfortunately, they don't wear roller skates, but they do use local beef and give out Dum Dums with the kids' meals, so everyone is happy. It became a quick, easy meal that satisfied us more than traditional fast food. After all, if we went to Burger Master, I wouldn't have to do the dishes or spend time scraping up dried bits of food off the floor long after dinner was over. Sure, there may be little nubs of fries in the car, but for the sake of dinner made easy, it was worth it. When the day had been particularly long and filled with incessant whining and pointless arguments, Gabe and I would bring the iPad and prop it on baby Ivy's lap so he and I could have 10 minutes of quiet to connect over our burgers. Sometimes you just do what you have to do to make the time.

One date night, I made burgers. They weren't fancy burgers, but they were just right. The patty was thin and well salted and had a good amount of grit and gristle on the outside. A hefty handful of fresh, crisp vegetables balanced the burger's juicy ground beef. I used the leaves found on the inside of a head of lettuce; they were tender, almost sweet, and so crisp that they balanced each bite. Two slices of thick, but not too thick, tomatoes and a couple rings of raw, biting, hot onion helped enliven and balance our burgers too. Pickle slices— dill, never sweet—adorned as well, and burger sauce smothered the top and bottom of the buttered and toasted sesame bun. Then there was the cheese. American cheese. So, really not actually *cheese*. I realized I was running the risk of losing my food cred as I unwrapped the orange squares from their cellophane wrappers, but I was willing to take that chance for the sake of my perfect burger. American cheese wouldn't steal the show. Instead, it would melt perfectly under a slightly warm, well-rested patty and add nostalgia to the burger more than any other cheese ever would.

We ate our burgers with crisp baked onion rings and the promise of a bittersweet chocolate shake. The meal woke us up to some joy in an otherwise tiring and normal day. Somehow, our classic burger sauce, bright and slightly sweet, heirloom tomato slices, and homemade buttered, crisped sesame buns made the day's exhaustion and frustration fade, even if only just a bit. It was enough.

151

TIMELINE

1 TO 3 DAYS IN ADVANCE

Make special sauce

Make chocolate ganache

Make hamburger patties

Make hamburger buns

DATE DAY

Prep onion rings

Make whipped cream and chocolate
shavings to garnish milk shakes

Prep burger toppings

DINNER TIME

Assemble onion rings and bake

Cook and assemble burgers

Blend shakes

GROCERY

1 head iceberg lettuce

1 tomato

2 slices cheese (American or Cheddar)

½ cup / 120 ml buttermilk

½ pint / 240 ml heavy whipping cream

12 ounces / 340 g ground beef (15 to 20%
fat)

2 tablespoons dill relish

Thinly sliced dill pickles

1 (8.5-ounce / 240 g) bag kettle-fried
potato chips

Panko breadcrumbs

5 ounces / 140 g bittersweet chocolate

Instant espresso powder

1 pint / 450 g vanilla ice cream

2 tablespoons malted milk powder

2 tablespoons sesame seeds (optional)

PANTRY

1 large yellow onion

Garlic

Unsalted butter

Kosher salt

Freshly ground black pepper

Cayenne pepper

Garlic powder

Neutral oil (such as canola or vegetable)

Ketchup

Soy sauce

Yellow mustard

Mayonnaise

All-purpose flour

Baking powder

Honey

Olive oil

Whole milk

Active dry yeast

Eggs

Bread flour

Oven-Baked Onion Rings

I'm not saying that because they are baked in the oven, these onion rings are healthy. But I will say that they are incredibly crisp, better than many of their fried counterparts, and totally worth the inevitable mess that comes with the process. The best way to keep the mess to a minimum, and this goes for any sort of breading, is to keep one hand for plunging into the dry mix and the other hand for working with the wet mix. Pack on the chip and breadcrumbs well before you bake them and be sure to serve with plenty of "special sauce."

SERVES 2

3 tablespoons neutral oil (such as canola or vegetable)

2 generous cups / 60 g kettle-fried potato chips

½ cup / 30 g panko breadcrumbs

½ cup / 70 g all-purpose flour, divided

½ teaspoon kosher salt

¼ teaspoon freshly ground black pepper

¼ teaspoon cayenne pepper

¼ teaspoon garlic powder

½ cup / 120 ml buttermilk

½ teaspoon baking powder

½ large yellow onion, sliced and then separated into 8 to 10 onion rings

Line a baking sheet with parchment paper and drizzle with the oil. Set out a wire rack.

Blend the potato chips in a food processor until finely ground.

In a shallow bowl, combine the chip crumbs and panko. In a second shallow bowl, combine ¼ cup / 35 g flour, salt, pepper, cayenne, and garlic powder. In a third shallow bowl, whisk together the buttermilk, remaining ¼ cup / 35 g flour, and baking powder.

With one hand for dry ingredients and the other for wet, dip the sliced onions into the flour mixture, then the buttermilk mixture, and finally the chip and panko mixture. Press the crumbs onto the ring so they adhere well; each ring should be thickly coated. Set the rings on the wire rack. Breaded onion rings can sit at room temperature for up to 1 hour.

Preheat the oven to 450°F.

Thirty minutes before you are ready to eat, place the oiled baking sheet into the preheated oven. After 8 minutes, carefully remove the hot baking sheet from the oven and fill with breaded onion rings. Place the pan back in the oven and bake for 8 minutes. Remove the pan, flip the rings, and bake for an additional 8 minutes.

Once the rings are golden all over, remove them from the oven and carefully set them onto the wire rack to cool slightly before serving. Serve with the burger sauce for dipping (**recipe follows**).

Our Perfect Burger WITH Special Sauce

When I'm hungry, which is quite often, a classic burger ALWAYS sounds good. I'm pretty particular about my burgers, but not in a fancy, gourmet way. I want the lettuce crisp, the tomato sweet, the pickles to make my mouth pucker, and the cheese to be American. We all have our vices, and plastic-like cheese is apparently mine (and Cool Ranch Doritos). This burger is the best version of the classic burger, in my not-so-humble opinion.

Into the ground beef I mix in a bit of butter. I mean, butter might be a bit excessive here, but I figure we're going all out tonight and what's a little more butter going to hurt? The beef and the butter happened to be next to each other on the counter, and the next thing I knew I was combining the two. The beef is as you would expect when you add butter to it: buttery. It is incredibly juicy and has a sort of nutty, caramelized taste that makes this already over-the-top burger even more ridiculous.

MAKES 2 GENEROUS BURGERS

BEEF PATTIES

12 ounces / 340 g ground beef (15 to 20% fat)

1½ teaspoons kosher salt

½ teaspoon freshly ground black pepper

1 tablespoon unsalted butter, at room temperature

BURGERS

1 tablespoon olive oil

2 slices cheese (American or Cheddar)

1 tablespoon unsalted butter

2 burger buns (page 15), split

1 recipe Special Sauce (**recipe follows**)

Small, inner iceberg lettuce leaves

Tomato slices

Yellow onion slices

Thinly sliced dill pickles

For the beef patties:

Gently combine the beef, salt, pepper, and butter in a bowl and then let rest on the counter for 30 minutes or, to get the best results, let rest covered in the fridge for a couple hours or overnight. Form into 2 large patties. Refrigerate until ready to use.

For the burgers:

In a very hot cast-iron skillet or on the grill, place the oil and then cook the burgers to your desired doneness (see note below). I find that about 3 to 4 minutes on each side gives me just the right amount of pink. Lay the cheese on the patty for the last minute of cooking. Set aside to rest for a few minutes before building your burger.

While the pan that you just cooked your burger in is still hot, throw in the butter and add the bun halves to the pan. Toast until golden and crisp.

Build your burger by slathering special sauce on BOTH sides of the bun. Add the patty and lettuce, tomatoes, thinly sliced rings of raw onion, and LOTS of pickles and top with the other crisped and sauce-smeared bun.

Note: For medium-rare, cook the burger to 130°F to 135°F; medium 140°F to 145°F; medium-well 150°F to 155°F; and well-done 160°F or higher.

Special Sauce

I have thought of just scrapping everything and bottling and selling this sauce for a living. It's all the condiments you'd want on a burger in a convenient little sauce. It's tangy, slightly sweet, a touch spicy from raw garlic, and made incredibly savory with soy sauce, which is what puts the "special" in this sauce.

SERVES 2

2 tablespoons dill relish

2 teaspoons yellow mustard

⅓ cup / 80 g mayonnaise

1 garlic clove, minced

2 tablespoons ketchup

½ teaspoon soy sauce

½ teaspoon honey

Whisk all the ingredients together. The burger sauce can be made up to 1 week in advance. Store, covered, in the refrigerator.

Bittersweet Chocolate Malted Shakes

Most chocolate shake recipes call for chocolate ice cream. It makes sense, but, if you start with a ganache base, you'll get a richer and more intense chocolate flavor. If you are a serious chocolate fanatic, you can make a double chocolate shake by using chocolate ice cream and the ganache. Whoa.

I use Carnation's Malted Milk Powder, which I find in my local grocery store in the coffee and tea section. If you can't find it, bourbon makes a fine substitute.

SERVES 2

CHOCOLATE GANACHE

½ cup / 120 ml heavy whipping cream

4 ounces / 110 g chopped bittersweet chocolate

Small pinch of kosher salt

1 teaspoon instant espresso powder

SHAKE

1 pint / 450 g vanilla ice cream

1 recipe chocolate ganache

2 tablespoons malted milk powder (substitute bourbon)

½ cup / 120 ml heavy whipping cream

1 ounce / 30 g bittersweet chocolate, finely chopped, for garnish

For the chocolate ganache:

Place the cream in a heavy-bottomed saucepan and bring to a simmer over medium heat. Remove from the heat and add the chopped chocolate, pinch of salt, and espresso powder. Allow to sit for 1 minute and then whisk to combine. Cool to room temperature if using the same day, or, if making ahead, cover and refrigerate. The chocolate ganache can be made up to 1 week in advance.

For the shake:

In a blender, combine the ice cream, chocolate ganache, and malted milk powder. Pour into serving glasses (or make it one with two straws).

Whip the cream until soft peaks form. Garnish the shakes with whipped cream and the chocolate.

Note: Ganache is one of those things that everybody should know how to make. With ganache in the fridge, you are steps away from the best cup of hot chocolate you've ever had. You have a quick and easy tart filling in your reach and can dress up a simple scoop of vanilla ice cream in a matter of seconds. It also makes a mean mocha. So, what I'm saying is you better make a double batch.

Eat with Your Hands

Homemade Cream Soda

162

Salad of Apples, Grapes, and
Blue Cheese on Endive

163

Bacon and Leek Tart with Ricotta Custard

164

Bittersweet Brownies with
Salted Peanut Butter Frosting

166

"Got any games to play?" I ask as we each devour two slices of the bacon-heavy tart, saying very little between each smoky, salty bite. The tart's richness is cut with a piece of bitter endive, its leaf forming a sort of taco shell around crisp grapes, tart apples, and pungent blue cheese: briny and "farm-y" in Gabe's words. Buttery toasted walnuts soften the salad and prepare us for another bite of ricotta tart.

"We used to play Twenty Questions," I tell Gabe coyly before we open up the dusty Rummikub box.

His tilted smile and awkward squirming tell me he doesn't really remember.

"Do you remember that day?" I ask, feeling a bit prideful because I am about to out-romance him. This doesn't usually happen.

"I remember we were driving in your mom's car heading to Seattle," he says, squinting his eyes as if trying to see the image of us more clearly.

"Nope. It was your beat-up Honda, and we were driving to my parents' house," I blurt out. "You really don't remember?"

"I do. We drove down to Chuckanut, and I played you a song I wrote."

"No. That was for our first anniversary," I reply. See what I mean? He's usually the out-romancer who forgets nothing. "We were playing Twenty Questions, and I was trying to use the last of my questions to get you to admit that you liked me."

He smirks.

"You told me that you liked me, sort of. I don't remember the actual words, just that I felt relief in that my little ploy had worked. Do you remember what you did next?"

He sits in silence.

I start to tell him, but then I remember the photo I found earlier in the week.

"Hold on," I say while running down the stairs to retrieve the photo.

After a few minutes, Gabe joins me downstairs and starts to flip through the box of photographs with me; he laughs when he finds a picture of himself and Chuck Mangione. He quickly takes a photo of the picture, posting it on Facebook before I find the image I am looking for.

After he had told me that he had feelings for me in the car, I had asked, "Now what?" Gabe had pulled the car into one of the viewpoints that dotted the road overlooking the bay.

159

Without saying a word, he asked me to get out of the car while he set up his camera on the car's wrinkled hood.

Standing next to each other, we had taken the photo and then gotten back in the car and said nothing else about what had happened.

The picture is us, standing on a rock with the bay and sun behind us so our faces are almost too dark to see our expressions. But I see a soft smile on my face, slightly awkward but filled with excitement. He has his arm gently around me, almost touching me.

It's taken me over ten years to realize that it was the perfect thing to do in that moment. Sometimes I can muddy up moments with too many words or see conversation as our sole means of connection. Of course, that's wildly important, especially for me, but sometimes you don't need to say anything else. Sometimes the best thing is to stop and take a photo, so that on a date night thirteen years later you remember the moment when you first confessed, "I like you."

It's easier for me to focus on building the memories—to dream of the memories to come without stopping to remember the memories we've made. To take note of our past joys and allow them to inform our present joy. My memories are best triggered with photos. I can see our joy, remember the way the trees shaded us from the sun, the way the water sparkled behind us, and even experience again the surge of excitement I felt when Gabe's hand brushed against my back.

We had no idea as we stood there on that rock that like would turn to love, which would then turn to me standing next to him in front of a blazing fireplace on a cold day in December, when we said "I do."

"I do" led us to moves across a couple of states, a dog, three kids, a few more moves, and now this: date nights in the quiet of our home while the kids sleep and dishes remain in the sink.

"I do" led us to a table that often seats five but one night a week is for two.

When we think we can't eat any more tart or ruffly endive, I grab the pan of brownies along with two forks and place it in front of us. Somehow we each manage a few bites of brownie and the creamy, slightly salty peanut butter frosting. We eat from the pan freely and smile at the other; there's no need for formalities and plates when it's just the two of us at the table. This time, I snap a picture before we clear the table, turn the lights off in our messy kitchen, and head upstairs.

TIMELINE

1 TO 3 DAYS IN ADVANCE

Make vanilla syrup

Make brownies

Make ricotta

Make tart crust

DATE DAY

Prep salad

Make tart filling

DINNER TIME

Mix cream sodas

Bake tart

Make salad

GROCERY

1 large head endive

2 ounces / 60 g red grapes

1 small apple (I like something good
   and tart here, such as Granny Smith,
   Gravenstein, or Pink Lady)

1 large or 2 small leeks

1 package or small bunch fresh thyme

1 package or small bunch fresh chives

2 ounces / 60 g crumbled blue cheese
   (about ¼ cup)

5-ounce / 140 g wedge Parmesan

1 cup / 230 g whole-milk ricotta (page 17)
   or store-bought

Heavy whipping cream

4 strips regular-cut bacon

3 ounces / 90 g bittersweet chocolate

¼ cup / 30 g walnuts

PANTRY

Garlic

Freshly ground black pepper

Flake salt

Kosher salt

Extra-virgin olive oil

Unsalted butter

Eggs

Vanilla bean

Vanilla extract

Granulated sugar

Confectioners' sugar

All-purpose flour

Whole nutmeg

Instant espresso powder

Cocoa powder, sifted if lumpy

Smooth peanut butter

Soda water

Homemade Cream Soda

This is the sort of recipe that does wonders for your kitchen cred. "You make your own cream soda?" they'll say.

"Sure I do," you respond casually while you finish the soda with a splash of heavy cream. What they don't need to know is that all you did was flavor sugar water with a vanilla bean.

SERVES 2

¼ cup / 60 g Vanilla Syrup (recipe follows)

1 cup / 240 ml soda water

2 tablespoons heavy whipping cream, plus more to taste

Fill two glasses with ice. Divide the vanilla syrup and soda water between the glasses. Finish with 1 tablespoon of cream per glass, or more to taste. Gabe prefers a bit more cream; you may too.

Vanilla Syrup

Don't let the simple process overshadow the complexity of this syrup. Our fridge is rarely without it, as I love to use it in coffee, tea, and anywhere else that needs a sweet and heady vanilla flavor. Feel free to throw in an additional vanilla bean.

MAKES 2½ CUPS / 650 ML

1 vanilla bean

1 cup / 200 g granulated sugar

2 cups / 470 ml water

Carefully run the knife down the center of the vanilla bean and scrape out the seeds. Add the bean, seeds, sugar, and water to a medium saucepan over medium-high heat. Bring to a boil and then reduce to a simmer for 5 minutes. Remove the pan from the heat and let cool while the vanilla bean steeps in the syrup.

This syrup can be stored, covered, in the fridge for up to 2 weeks.

Salad of Apples, Grapes, AND Blue Cheese ON Endive

In this salad I like the grapes dark and sweet, the apples tart and crisp, the endive chartreuse and lightly bitter, the cheese good and stinky, and the walnuts deeply toasted. If you can't find endive, use arugula or butter lettuce.

SERVES 2

1 large head endive

⅓ cup / 60 g halved red grapes

⅓ cup / 60 g diced apples (I like something good and tart here, such as Granny Smith, Gravenstein, or Pink Lady)

2 ounces / 60 g crumbled blue cheese (about ¼ cup)

¼ cup / 30 g walnuts, toasted (see technique on page 11) and roughly chopped

1 to 2 tablespoons extra-virgin olive oil

Flake salt, for finishing

Cut off the root end of the endive to release the leaves. Arrange the leaves on a plate.

Scatter grapes, apples, blue cheese, and walnuts evenly onto the endive. You can perfectly arrange each leaf if you'd like, but I like to leave it rough and arrange our own perfect bites while at the table.

Drizzle the entire plate with extra-virgin olive oil and finish with flake salt.

Note: This salad can easily be prepared for a group dinner as well by simply cutting all of the endive in small ribbons and doing more of a tossed salad.

Bacon AND Leek Tart WITH Ricotta Custard

This is a hefty tart loaded with great flavor. Beyond date night, it makes a wonderful brunch dish. I love to finish the tart with a bit of fresh arugula for a nice peppery, crisp bite.

MAKES ONE 9-INCH TART

CRUST

1 cup / 140 g all-purpose flour

¼ teaspoon kosher salt

3 ounces / 90 g Parmesan, freshly grated (about ¾ cup packed)

½ cup / 115 g unsalted butter, cubed and chilled

3 tablespoons ice-cold water

FILLING

1 cup / 230 g whole-milk ricotta (page 17)

1 egg

2 garlic cloves, minced

1 teaspoon chopped fresh thyme leaves

½ teaspoon freshly ground black pepper

½ teaspoon kosher salt, plus more as needed

2 ounces / 60 g Parmesan, freshly grated (about ½ cup packed)

Pinch of freshly grated nutmeg

4 strips regular-cut bacon, roughly chopped

1 large or 2 small leeks, sliced ⅛ inch thick (white and light green parts only)

1 tablespoon chopped fresh chives

For the crust:

Preheat the oven to 375°F.

Combine the flour, salt, and Parmesan in a food processor and pulse a few times to combine. Add the butter and then pulse quickly about 20 times, or until the mixture is a sandy texture.

With a few more pulses, blend in the ice-cold water. The dough should stick together when you pinch it between two fingers.

Pour the crumbly dough into a 14 x 4-inch rectangular pan or 9-inch round tart pan with a removable bottom. Press the dough firmly up the sides of the pan. Then press the bottom to form a uniform base.

Chill for 15 minutes.

Remove the tart shell from the refrigerator and poke a few times with a fork. Place on a baking sheet and slide the tart pan onto the oven's middle rack. Bake for 15 minutes and then use a fork to poke any areas that may be bubbling up. Bake for an additional 10 minutes. Remove from the oven and set aside.

For the filling:

While the crust chills, prepare the filling. Stir together the ricotta, egg, garlic, thyme, pepper, salt, Parmesan, and nutmeg until well combined.

While the crust bakes, sauté the bacon on medium heat in a medium skillet; stir often, until brown around the edges and just starting to crisp, 5 to 7 minutes. Remove all but 2 tablespoons bacon fat. Reduce the heat to low. Add the leeks to the pan with the cooked bacon and a pinch of salt. Sauté for 10 minutes, stirring often and separating the leeks, until they are soft and lightly browned in parts.

Pour the filling into the par-baked tart crust. Top with the bacon and leek mixture. Return to the oven and bake for 20 minutes, or until the custard is slightly puffed and golden around the edges.

Let the tart cool in the pan for 15 minutes before unmolding. Garnish with chives and serve warm or at room temperature.

Crust can be made ahead, baked or unbaked, and frozen for up to 1 month.

Note: In the summer, I love using this fully baked crust for a fresh tomato tart. The filling is whipped goat cheese with fresh herbs like tarragon or chives, and then it's topped with gorgeous heirloom and cherry tomatoes. It's literally a blue ribbon recipe; it took first place in a tomato recipe contest.

EAT WITH YOUR HANDS

Bittersweet Brownies WITH Salted Peanut Butter Frosting

When it comes to brownies, I like them chewy, fudgy, and so rich with dark chocolate that all you need is a little piece to satisfy the inevitable desire for something sweet after a rich meal.

These brownies use browned butter to give them a soft toffee flavor and contain both unsweetened chocolate and cocoa powder to reinforce their richness.

I could have just let them be that, but I decided to add a rich peanut butter frosting. Watch out.

BROWNIES

¾ cup / 170 g unsalted butter, plus more for the pan

3 ounces / 90 g unsweetened chocolate, chopped

1½ cups / 300 g granulated sugar

1 tablespoon vanilla extract

3 eggs

¾ teaspoon kosher salt

½ teaspoon instant espresso powder (optional)

½ cup / 40 g cocoa powder

½ cup / 70 g all-purpose flour

FROSTING

6 tablespoons / 85 g unsalted butter, at room temperature

¾ cup / 100 g smooth peanut butter

⅓ cup / 40 g confectioners' sugar

½ teaspoon flake salt

Note: That light, wrinkled, and crackly top on a brownie is one of my favorite parts of a brownie. I realize though that some people like a more cake-like top. So, here's a way to please both with this one recipe. If you like the crackly top, follow the recipe above; if you prefer your brownies without the crackly top, simply add the eggs when you add the sugar. The crackly top comes when the sugar has a chance to melt before it bakes.

Also, if you are partial to an even fudgier brownie, bake these brownies with 2 eggs instead of 3.

For the brownies:

Preheat the oven to 325°F.

Grease an 8-inch square pan. Line the pan with parchment paper so that a couple inches hang over the edge. Then grease the parchment.

Place the butter in a medium saucepan and melt over medium-high heat. Allow the butter to cook until the milk solids bubble up and then settle into the pan and caramelize. Swirl the butter in the pan in order to see the color of the little bits on the bottom. As soon as the milk solids are golden and the butter smells nutty, 3 to 5 minutes, remove the pan from the heat.

Pour the browned butter into a medium bowl and add the chopped chocolate. Let stand for 1 minute to melt and then whisk together. Whisk in the sugar and vanilla while the butter mixture is still warm. Stir in the eggs, salt, and espresso powder, if using, until well blended.

Over the bowl with the chocolate mixture, sift in the cocoa powder and flour. Fold the ingredients together until just combined using a spatula.

Pour the batter into the prepared pan and bake for 25 to 30 minutes, or until a toothpick inserted in the middle pulls out clean. Let cool to room temperature.

For the frosting:

With an electric mixer, whip together the butter, peanut butter, and confectioners' sugar in a large bowl. Continue to mix until everything is well combined and the frosting has lightened in color.

Frost the cooled brownies and finish with the flake salt.

If the brownies are too fudgy to cut, refrigerate for 30 minutes and then cut. Let the brownies sit at room temperature for 10 minutes before serving. Brownies can be made 1 to 3 days in advance. The frosting can be made up to 1 week in advance.

Wooed by Fried Chicken

Basil Mint Jubilee
171

Fried Chicken Sandwiches
on Black Pepper Biscuits
173

Pickled Vegetable Salad
175

Chocolate Pecan Ice Cream Pie with
Bourbon Butterscotch and Pretzel Crust
176

This date wooed me before it even began. The promise of a quiet evening with my husband is plenty romantic, but I couldn't help being hopelessly enchanted by the anticipation of fried chicken.

Don't get me wrong: I will love sitting next to him on the couch after we lick our fingers of herb-scented grease, but it's the thought of that deeply browned crust outside a tender and flavorful chicken thigh that has me wishing the kids would rush off to bed so I can be alone with a bit of bourbon and a cast-iron skillet filled with oil.

Fried chicken isn't the sort of food we usually eat. Most often our weekday meals are heavy with vegetables rather than grease. They come together quickly, are rarely given much thought before the kids start moaning, "I'm huuuuuungry," and often are made up of whatever I can find in the back of the crisper drawer along with some pasta from the pantry. All these factors make our date night dinners highly anticipated, and also envied by the kids.

Because of the nature of the food on our date nights, I find myself spending more time in the kitchen than I normally would for one meal. Sometimes I have to drag myself there; other times, like with fried chicken, I'm eager to start cooking. Whatever my mood is when I begin cooking, I always find that at the end of it I'm more relaxed, feeling grateful and happy. Which is the perfect way to start a date.

I've talked to a lot of people about our date nights, and quite often people think I'm a little mad to make such elaborate food at the end of a long day. They, like me, only have enough energy to turn the pages of a good book or raise a glass of wine to their lips. I get it, I do. And this is the very reason why I sometimes need fried chicken to date my husband.

That sounds terrible, doesn't it? But quite frankly, it's the truth. And the fact that that truth no longer makes me question my marriage shows me that I've come a long way in understanding the complexities of maintaining a relationship. When we were dating, I didn't care that anyone else existed except for Gabe. I paid very little attention to other relationships; it was as if I knew from the beginning that he was to be the one I walked through life with, so no one else seemed to matter much.

This continued well into our marriage, and it wasn't until we had kids that I discovered how truly selfish I was, thinking that the time when they all were finally quiet and in bed belonged to me. During the day, I had played Legos when I wanted to read, changed diapers when I had just sat down to eat, given hard lessons about sharing when I really just wanted to sink into the couch and let my mind think of nothing. So when late evening's quiet finally came, I wanted nothing more than to answer only to myself. Soon, however, I realized my desires overshadowed my marriage and that I had selfishly ignored the person I cared for the most.

These days, I use a bit of my own desires—cooking and eating indulgent foods—to encourage us to nurture our marriage. For some people, motivation comes from somewhere other than the kitchen; I have a good friend who loves long walks, and she's kind enough to invite her husband along. She loves the exercise but also uses that time to hold hands with her husband, ask him about his day, and catch up on the things that get set aside until you finally have time to talk. Another friend and her husband keep it simple by just committing to connect for at least 15 minutes a day; it doesn't sound like much, but Gabe and I have had too many days when we were lucky if we acknowledged each other's presence for 30 seconds.

Some people, like me, need the encouragement of a good meal to woo them to the table and to connect with their partner, while others might need a walk or an intentional 15 minutes with their partner. The point is to connect; whatever gets you there is more than good enough.

TIMELINE

1 TO 3 DAYS IN ADVANCE
Make honey syrup
Season chicken with spice mix
Make biscuit dough
Make ice cream pie

DATE DAY
Bake biscuits
Pickle vegetables for salad

DINNER TIME
Make jubilees
Fry chicken and assemble sandwiches
Toss salad

GROCERY

1 package or 1 small bunch fresh mint
1 package or 1 small bunch fresh basil
1 bunch fresh flat-leaf parsley
1 small beet
1 carrot
1 red onion
1 ear fresh corn, or ¾ cup / 90 g frozen kernels
1 head frisée or other bitter green, such as arugula
Dill pickle slices
3 ounces / 90 g goat cheese
½ gallon of your favorite vanilla bean ice cream
1 cup/ 240 ml buttermilk
1 pint / 470 ml heavy whipping cream
4 boneless, skinless chicken thighs (about 1 pound)
¼ cup / 30 g raw almonds
1¼ cups / 125 g raw pecan halves
3 cups / 100 g tiny pretzel twists
3½ ounces / 100 g bittersweet chocolate

PANTRY

1 lemon
Garlic
1 egg
Unsalted butter
Honey
Grainy mustard
Smoked paprika
Dried oregano
Dried thyme
Dried marjoram
Garlic powder
Freshly ground black pepper
Kosher salt
Smoked flake salt
All-purpose flour
Dark brown sugar
Granulated sugar
Turbinado sugar
Cornstarch
Baking powder
Fennel seeds
5 whole cloves
Mustard seeds
Peppercorns
1 cup / 240 ml apple cider vinegar
Extra-virgin olive oil
Vegetable, canola, or peanut oil, for frying
Bourbon

Basil Mint Jubilee

Gabe titled this recipe a "jubilee," and I thought it appropriate. After all, the jubilee, with its honey syrup and basil, is a bit different from a conventional julep. I like to let a bit of the ice melt into the bourbon before I really start drinking it.

SERVES 2

16 fresh mint leaves, plus 2 sprigs for garnish

8 fresh basil leaves

1 ounce / 30 ml Honey Syrup (**recipe follows**)

4 ounces / 120 ml bourbon

Squeeze of fresh lemon juice

Muddle the mint and basil leaves in two julep or highball glasses until they are lightly bruised and fragrant. Divide the honey syrup between the glasses and then fill the cups with crushed ice.

Pour half the bourbon into each, top with a squeeze of fresh lemon juice, and then stir well to combine.

Finish with more crushed ice to fill the cup and then garnish with mint sprigs.

Honey Syrup

¼ cup / 80 g honey

¼ cup / 60 ml water

Combine the honey and water in a small saucepan over medium-high heat. Bring to a boil and then simmer for 1 minute. Remove from the heat.

Let cool to room temperature and then refrigerate. Will keep for up to 2 weeks in the refrigerator, covered.

Fried Chicken Sandwiches ON Black Pepper Biscuits

This sandwich is over-the-top craziness. It is inspired by Pine State Biscuits in Portland, where I enjoyed a similar biscuit sandwich with honey, pickles, and mustard. The black pepper biscuits bring warming heat to perfectly balance these salty, sweet, tangy, and ridiculous sandwiches.

SERVES 4

BLACK PEPPER BISCUITS

1 recipe shortcakes (page 20)

1½ teaspoons freshly ground black pepper

SANDWICHES

4 black pepper biscuits

2 tablespoons grainy mustard

Dill pickle slices

4 fried chicken thighs **(recipe follows)**

1 tablespoon honey

For the biscuits:

Preheat the oven to 400°F. Follow the recipe for the basic shortcakes, adding in the black pepper with the flour.

Form the dough into a round or rectangle 1 inch thick and then use a 3-inch biscuit cutter to cut out four biscuits. You can squish the scraps together to get the fourth biscuit; alternatively, cut the biscuits into 3-inch squares. Biscuit dough can be made and refrigerated 1 day in advance or frozen for up to 1 month. They are best served the day they are baked.

Brush the tops with heavy whipping cream and then bake for 20 minutes, or until golden around the edges and the biscuit it set.

For the sandwiches:

Split the black pepper biscuits and spread one side with grainy mustard. Top with pickle slices and hot fried chicken and drizzle with honey. Serve immediately.

Fried Chicken

I'm not Southern, but I must say that I am quite proud of this fried chicken. The chicken's overnight marinade in salt and spices brings intense flavor, and a double dip in both spiced flour and buttermilk gives it a thick and crisp exterior. Cornstarch in the flour mixture makes the crust crisper and more tender, while baking powder helps to make the crust airy and light.

Gabe suggests not eating this in front of someone you've been dating for less than six months. It's a good judge of true love to watch your partner devour a fried chicken sandwich: there's no graceful way of doing it. It's really a sandwich that needs the aid of a knife and a fork.

MAKES ENOUGH FOR 4 SANDWICHES

4 boneless, skinless chicken thighs (about 1 pound)

Vegetable, canola, or peanut oil, for frying (about 4 cups)

SPICE MIX

1 teaspoon smoked paprika

1 teaspoon dried oregano

1 teaspoon dried thyme

1 teaspoon dried marjoram

1 teaspoon garlic powder

½ teaspoon freshly ground black pepper

2 teaspoons kosher salt

FLOUR DREDGE

1 cup / 140 g all-purpose flour

1 tablespoon cornstarch

½ teaspoon baking powder

BUTTERMILK DREDGE

1 cup / 240 ml buttermilk

1 egg

The day before you plan on frying the chicken, whisk together the paprika, oregano, thyme, marjoram, garlic powder, pepper, and salt to form the spice mix. Set aside 1 tablespoon of the spice mix and sprinkle the rest all over the chicken thighs. Cover the chicken with plastic wrap and refrigerate overnight.

To fry the chicken, mix together the flour, cornstarch, baking powder, and reserved spice mix in a pie plate or shallow dish.

Mix together the buttermilk and egg in another pie plate or shallow dish.

Set up a wire rack over a sheet tray. Fill a large, heavy skillet (I use my 12-inch cast-iron pan) with ¾ inch of oil. Set on high heat and bring to 360°F. Preheat the oven to 375°F.

Dredge the chicken in the buttermilk mixture, then the flour mixture, then the buttermilk mixture again and finally back into the flour. Set on the rack over the sheet tray.

Fry the chicken for 3 minutes per side until deep golden brown. Return the chicken to the wire rack and bake for 8 to 10 minutes, or until just done inside.

Pickled Vegetable Salad

Nothing cuts through the richness of fried food like a good pickle, and here I've made an entire salad of them. The pickles will keep for a few weeks in the fridge, so they can be done well in advance. Their flavor will intensify as they sit.

Once you've made the salad, you can use the pickling liquid as a base for future salad dressings or throw in some more vegetables or fruit to make more pickles. Have you ever had a pickled peach? It's a beautiful thing on a cheese platter or over a bed of arugula with goat cheese.

SERVES 2

1 cup / 240 ml water

1 cup / 240 ml apple cider vinegar

¼ cup / 50 g granulated sugar

1 teaspoon fennel seeds

1 teaspoon mustard seeds

2 garlic cloves, smashed

1 teaspoon kosher salt

5 whole cloves

½ teaspoon peppercorns

1 small beet

1 carrot

¼ red onion

¾ cup corn kernels (from 1 ear), fresh or frozen

2 cups roughly chopped frisée or other bitter green such as arugula

¼ cup/ 30 g almonds, toasted and roughly chopped (see technique on page 11)

3 ounces / 90 g goat cheese, crumbled

¼ cup / 5 g roughly chopped fresh flat-leaf parsley

2 tablespoons extra-virgin olive oil

Freshly ground black pepper

The day or morning before you plan to eat the salad (or even a few weeks in advance), combine the water, vinegar, sugar, fennel seeds, mustard seeds, garlic, and salt in a small saucepan set over medium heat. Combine the cloves and peppercorns and then tie them in a bit of cheesecloth so that they are easy to fish out later. Add the little sachet to the pickling solution. Bring the mixture to a boil and simmer for 3 minutes.

While the vinegar mixture cooks, slice the beet, carrot, and red onion into very thin (⅛-inch) slices with a mandoline or sharp knife.

Combine the beets and red onions in a small bowl or jar and the carrots and corn in another bowl or jar to keep the beets from dyeing the other vegetables.

Pour the hot vinegar mixture over the vegetables so that they are completely submerged. Cover each container with plastic wrap or a lid and let sit at room temperature until cool. Then refrigerate until ready to serve.

Drain the pickled vegetables, reserving the pickling liquid if you plan to make another batch of pickles soon.

On a platter or two salad plates, add the chopped frisée. Arrange the pickled vegetables on top. Finish with almonds, crumbled goat cheese, and parsley, drizzle with extra-virgin olive oil, and grind some black pepper on top.

Chocolate Pecan Ice Cream Pie WITH Bourbon Butterscotch AND Pretzel Crust

After a name like that, I've nearly run out of space to say anything else about this dessert. I could have called this Bourbon Butterscotch Ice Cream Pie with a Browned-Butter Pretzel Crust and Chocolate-Covered Toasted Pecans with Smoked Salt. I could have, but I didn't. Regardless of the name, do me a favor and make this pie. It's an instant classic.

MAKES ONE 9-INCH PIE

CRUST

3 cups / 100 g tiny pretzel twists

½ cup / 115 g unsalted butter

⅓ cup / 60 g dark brown sugar

FILLING

1 recipe Bourbon Butterscotch Sauce (**recipe follows**)

½ gallon of your favorite vanilla bean ice cream, slightly softened at room temperature

1 recipe Chocolate-Coated Pecans with Smoked Salt (**recipe follows**)

For the crust:

Preheat the oven to 350°F.

Process the pretzels in a food processor until you have mostly fine crumbs, about 1 minute (a few bigger pieces here and there are fine). In a medium skillet over medium heat, melt the butter and then continue to heat until the butter smells nutty and the milk solids have caramelized (you'll see little golden bits on the bottom of the pan).

Stir together the pretzel crumbs and brown sugar in a bowl. Stir in the brown butter. Add the crumb mixture to a standard pie plate and press up the sides and onto the bottom.

Bake for 10 minutes. Remove from the oven and allow to cool to room temperature. Crust can be made up to 3 days ahead and stored in an airtight container.

For the filling:

Pour ½ cup / 120 ml of bourbon butterscotch into the baked piecrust. Freeze for 1 hour. Spread vanilla ice cream over the butterscotch. Top with chopped chocolate pecans. Freeze for 1 hour before serving.

Serve pie slices with the remaining bourbon butterscotch. This pie can be made ahead and stored, covered, in the freezer for up to 1 week.

Bourbon Butterscotch Sauce

Butterscotch is essentially a caramel made from brown sugar. You may have noticed that I'm a big fan of brown sugar: regular granulated sugar pales in comparison to its deep molasses flavor. So it's no surprise that butterscotch is one of my favorite flavors. This sauce gets a boost from bourbon and comes together quickly and with very little fuss. Once refrigerated, the sauce looks a bit cloudy, but, when rewarmed, it softens and turns smooth and pourable.

MAKES 1½ CUPS / 360 G

1 cup / 200 g dark brown sugar

1 cup / 240 ml heavy whipping cream

4 tablespoons / 60 g unsalted butter

3 tablespoons bourbon

½ teaspoon kosher salt

Add the brown sugar, cream, and butter to a small saucepan. Stir to combine. Bring to a full boil over high heat. Reduce the heat to medium and then boil for 5 minutes. Remove from the heat and carefully whisk in the bourbon and salt. Let cool to room temperature before adding to the crust.

The sauce can be made up to 1 week ahead and stored, covered, in the refrigerator.

Note: If the sauce separates after refrigerating, simply whisk while rewarming on the stove, and it will blend together beautifully.

Chocolate-Coated Pecans with Smoked Salt

I have to admit that melting chocolate is one of my least favorite kitchen tasks. So when I had the idea of letting the warmth of the just-toasted pecans do the melting for me, well, I thought it quite genius. If you don't have smoked salt, regular sea salt or flake salt is fine.

MAKES 1¼ CUPS (ENOUGH FOR 1 PIE)

1¼ cups / 125 g raw pecan halves

3½ ounces / 100 g bittersweet chocolate, chopped

½ teaspoon smoked flake salt

Preheat the oven to 350°F. Line a baking sheet with parchment paper.

Place the pecans on the baking sheet and roast for 7 to 9 minutes, or until fragrant and golden throughout.

In a medium bowl, combine the chocolate and hot pecans. Stir until the chocolate melts and coats the pecans. Pour the mix out onto the parchment-lined baking sheet and then sprinkle with smoked flake salt. Refrigerate until the chocolate sets, about 10 minutes. Break or chop into small pieces before topping the pie.

Store in an airtight container for up to 1 week or freeze for up to 1 month.

Breakfast for Dinner

Blood Orange Screwdrivers
182

Homemade Sausage Patties with Roasted Apples
183

Baked Eggs with Spinach and Gruyère
185

Croissant French Toast with
Brown-Butter Maple Syrup
186

I set down my keys in their usual spot as I opened the door to our office. Something black caught my eye as I tossed my keys on the windowsill. A whistle? I remember seeing this whistle and hearing its shrill call shortly after it arrived in the mail.

"It's the loudest one made," Gabe proclaimed, as I questioned its arrival into our house the moment the kids got a hold of it.

"Great," I think, while they set out to prove the validity of the whistle's claim.

Now that whistle is on my key chain. He didn't order it to aid the kids in driving Mama crazy: he bought it for my key chain. For me, in the off-chance I'm alone and happen to have my keys in hand and am in need of the world's loudest whistle. He bought it to keep me safe. Apparently, he likes having me around and wants to protect and care for me even when he's not there.

Standing in the office, staring at my keys, I let this whistle and the man who put it there woo me with its unconventional sort of romance that could have easily gone unnoticed.

This morning, the little black whistle has made me cry.

When Gabe and I had just started dating, we both went to great lengths to show our love to each other. Once, he made reservations at a restaurant that I had fallen in love with through a cookbook. I had dreamed and gushed about how wonderful it would be to go to this restaurant, but, since it was in San Francisco and we were in Seattle, it seemed just that: a dream. Then one day, Gabe walked in the door with a paper airplane. He launched it with the flick of his wrist, and it landed right in my lap. I looked at him, puzzled, before he urged me to open up the paper. It was a reservation confirmation for the restaurant in San Francisco.

"We're going this weekend," Gabe beamed. I sat there silently as it all sank in.

While we were dating, Gabe and I spent five months apart while I lived in Italy. In the midst of finals, packing, and preparing myself to leave my family and Gabe for that long, I wrote him a letter to open for every day that I would be gone. Some of the letters were quite short, and some gushed on and on about how much I'd miss him and how I hoped this was the last time in our lives that we'd be apart.

I'm a sucker for a good airport scene in a movie. You know the ones: at the very last minute, the girl or guy decides to rush to the airport to tell the other, "Don't leave! I love you." They kiss in an airport full of people, while I wipe the rivers of tears from my cheeks. And sometimes, I wish Gabe and I could bust out in song and choreographed flirtation the way that Marius and Cosette do just after meeting, "A heart full of love, I do not even know your name."

Yes, I'm a romantic, but I find that the longer I'm in this relationship, the less important the grand romantic gestures seem, and, in their place, the romance in the everyday wins out. Like the black whistle on my key chain, or the cup of tea he made for me this afternoon without my even asking, or when he folds the laundry, tucks in the kids, and makes them oatmeal in the morning.

Later that night, he sits at the table next to me, with a smile on his face, asking me how my day was and handing me a cocktail: red, sweet, and floral with just a splash of orange blossom water.

When I practically lick my plate clean of the nutty, sticky syrup that drenched the buttery cracks and crags of my custard-soaked croissant, I raise the white flag and retire to the couch while he clears the table of our dishes. It's not that he enjoys doing the dishes; in fact, I know just the opposite is true. But he loves me, so he does the dishes.

Google "What is romance?" and you'll find "fancy sparkly things," not "doing the dishes for each other," and "flair and flourishes," not "commitment and longevity." There probably isn't a definition that describes how heart-stopping, frighteningly honest, and yet sometimes even mundane romance really is. True romance is to put the desires of your partner before yours; it's to unload the dishwasher for the third time that day and to make him a special extra sausage patty flecked with crackly fennel seeds.

I adore the romance in our reality. He still longs to wrap his arms around me even though what he's wrapping is a bit softer and marked with the stretching of three pregnancies. Rather than getting frustrated with me on the mornings when I linger in bed longer than I should, he brings me coffee. And nothing is more romantic to me than to see him twirl around the living room with our little girl in hand as he teaches her that she is worthy of great love and everyday romance.

While I wouldn't say no to a bouquet of flowers or a sweet card tucked between my napkin and plate, I won't let their absence keep me from seeing the romance that happens when we continue to wake up next to each other and promise to live out our love and commitment each day.

TIMELINE

1 TO 3 DAYS IN ADVANCE
Make sausage
Make brown-butter maple syrup

DATE DAY
Make custard for French toast
Roast apples
Juice oranges for screwdrivers

DINNER TIME
Make screwdrivers
Make baked eggs
Cook sausages
Make French toast

GROCERY

1 bunch or small package fresh sage
1 package or small bunch fresh thyme
4 blood oranges
1 apple
1 small tomato
3 cups / 90 g spinach
1 ounce / 30 g Gruyère
Heavy whipping cream
2 croissants
8 ounces / 230 g ground pork (20% fat
    recommended)
Orange blossom water (optional)

PANTRY

Garlic
Eggs
Unsalted butter
Whole milk
Kosher salt
Freshly ground black pepper
Fennel seeds
Red pepper flakes (optional)
Dried oregano
Maple syrup
Vanilla extract
1 vanilla bean
Dark brown sugar
Ground cinnamon
Whole nutmeg
Dijon mustard
Olive oil
Vodka

BREAKFAST FOR DINNER

Blood Orange Screwdrivers

When I see blood oranges in the store, I can't resist. I always get a strange thrill when I cut past their seemingly normal, orange exterior to reveal a shockingly blood-red interior. I think their flavor is more floral than regular oranges, but it's probably mostly just the color I love; you are welcome to use regular oranges in this screwdriver if you can't find the blood orange variety. And the same goes for the orange blossom water. I love the floral, almost perfume taste it adds to this simple cocktail, but it's totally optional. You can purchase it online and use it in cocktails, over fruit salads, and sprinkled on vanilla ice cream alongside some cardamom and toasted pistachios. (I have my friend Sara to thank for that last idea.)

SERVES 2

4 ounces / 120 ml vodka

10 ounces / 300 ml freshly squeezed blood orange juice (from 4 oranges; may substitute regular oranges)

2 teaspoons orange blossom water (optional)

Orange peel, for garnish

Divide the ingredients into two highball glasses. Stir together and then finish with ice. Garnish each with a twist of orange peel.

Homemade Sausage Patties WITH Roasted Apples

For very little work, you can have flavorful sausage patties that make a hearty addition to breakfast for dinner. We serve them as patties here, but you can easily crumble and sauté them and then fold into a frittata or quiche. Avoid using extra-lean pork here, as you'll end up with dry pucks. In fact, if you can find it, use sausage-grade ground pork, which contains extra fat ground in with the meat. Be sure not to overbake, and feel free to mix a little olive oil or softened butter into the meat for moisture if you feel that yours might be on the dry side.

SERVES 2

8 ounces / 230 g ground pork (20% fat recommended)

½ teaspoon kosher salt

¾ teaspoon freshly ground black pepper

1 teaspoon fennel seeds, toasted (see technique on page 11)

2 garlic cloves, minced

1 teaspoon minced fresh sage

1 teaspoon fresh thyme leaves

2 teaspoons Dijon mustard

Pinch of red pepper flakes (optional)

Combine the pork, salt, pepper, fennel seeds, garlic, sage, thyme, Dijon, and red pepper flakes, if using, in a bowl and mix well; I find my hands are best for this job. Cover and let stand for at least 30 minutes, but overnight in the refrigerator is best.

Divide the meat into four equal portions. In a hot, dry skillet, sear the patties on both sides for 2 to 3 minutes, or until deeply browned and the internal temperature reaches 165°F.

Let the sausage patties rest for 10 minutes. Serve with Roasted Apples (**recipe follows**).

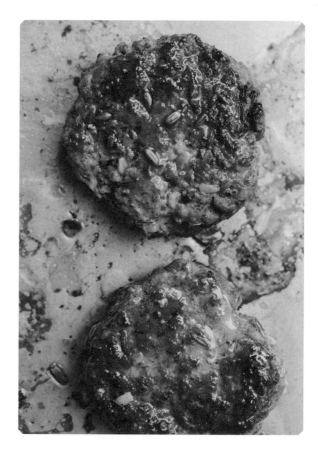

Roasted Apples

Pork and apples—such a classic pair. These sweet, soft roasted apples make a great side dish for all sorts of pork recipes and are even fantastic over ice cream for dessert.

SERVES 2

1 apple, peeled and cut into ½-inch dice

1 tablespoon olive oil

½ teaspoon fresh thyme leaves

Preheat the oven to 400°F. Line a baking sheet with parchment paper.

Toss the apples with olive oil and thyme. Bake for 20 minutes, or until golden in parts and tender but not mushy.

Baked Eggs WITH Spinach AND Gruyère

These eggs make a great, quick weeknight dinner for the family. Simply double the recipe and bake in a skillet or cast-iron pan.

SERVES 2

1 tablespoon plus 1 teaspoon olive oil, divided

1 small tomato, chopped (⅔ cup)

1 garlic clove, minced

½ teaspoon dried oregano

½ teaspoon kosher salt

3 cups / 90 g spinach

Pinch of freshly grated nutmeg

2 tablespoons heavy whipping cream

¼ cup / 30 g grated Gruyère

2 eggs

Place an oven rack 6 inches below the broiler and preheat the broiler. Grease two 4-ounce ramekins with ½ teaspoon olive oil each.

Add 1 tablespoon olive oil to a medium sauté pan on medium heat. Once hot, add the tomato, garlic, oregano, and salt. Sauté for 3 to 4 minutes, or until the tomatoes are soft. Add the spinach and sauté until wilted, another 2 to 3 minutes. Turn off the heat. Stir in the nutmeg and cream.

Divide the vegetable mixture in half and add to the greased ramekins. Top each ramekin with half of the Gruyère and then finish by cracking an egg over the top.

Place the ramekins on a baking sheet. Broil until the egg white is just set, 2 to 5 minutes, depending on your broiler. Watch your eggs closely, as you want the yolk to remain runny.

Let sit for 5 minutes before serving.

Croissant French Toast WITH Brown-Butter Maple Syrup

We happen to live down the street from one of the best bakeries in Seattle, Honoré. The smell of the bakery's buttery croissants often makes its way to my kitchen, and it inspired this decadent dessert (or breakfast) hit. I'm particularly pleased with the syrup that adorns these custard-soaked croissants.

SERVES 2

BROWN-BUTTER MAPLE SYRUP

3 tablespoons unsalted butter

¼ cup / 60 ml maple syrup

Pinch of kosher salt

FRENCH TOAST

¼ cup / 60 ml whole milk

¼ cup / 60 ml heavy whipping cream

1 egg

1 teaspoon vanilla extract

1 vanilla bean, split and seeds removed (optional)

1 tablespoon dark brown sugar

¼ teaspoon kosher salt

¼ teaspoon ground cinnamon

2 tablespoons unsalted butter

2 croissants, split in half

For the syrup:

In a medium skillet over medium heat, brown the butter (see the technique on page 11). Let sit for 5 minutes before stirring in the maple syrup. The mixture will bubble up. Stir in the maple syrup and salt to combine and then pour into a heat-safe container to cool. You can make the syrup up to 3 days ahead and store, covered, in the refrigerator. Warm for 15 seconds in the microwave and whisk together before serving.

For the French toast:

Whisk together the milk, cream, egg, vanilla extract, vanilla seeds (if using), brown sugar, salt, and cinnamon. This step can be done earlier in the day and then refrigerated until ready to use.

Heat the butter in a large skillet over medium-high heat. Give one croissant half a quick dip in the custard and then place in the hot skillet. Repeat with the remaining croissant halves. Cook for about 2 minutes per side, until golden brown. Serve with the syrup.

An Elegant Classic

Apple Flip

191

Fall Crudités with Creamy Olive Tapenade

193

Roasted Red Onions with
Golden Raisin Gremolata

194

Chanterelle Pot Pie

196

Poached Pears in Muscat

197

Sometimes I don't want to cook. There are days I want to eat a package of stale ramen noodles with their clenching, salty broth or a simple peanut butter and jelly sandwich. And, yes, when I make boxed macaroni and cheese for my kids, I often take a bowl for myself.

When I feel the urge to curl up with a meal that came from a box, I worry. I think, "Is this the end? I've built a large part of my life around food, and now even setting a pot of water to boil sounds like too much effort." In her book, *An Everlasting Meal*, Tamar Adler writes, "I think that cooking must be allowed to swell to contemptible proportions when it seems contemptible, just like other disproportionately terrible annoyances, and then allowed to shrink when it is time." She goes on to explain how we fall back in love with food. "My answer is to anchor food to somewhere deep inside you, or deep in your past, or deep in the wonders of what you love."

After many cycles of waning interest, I have found that it's okay to admit that there are days when we order takeout, go get a burger, or boil some pasta and then cover it with butter and Parmesan and call that dinner. Then, I'll flip through a cookbook and see a recipe I've made before. I'll remember using those ingredients for the first time and the way their foreign taste excited my tongue. Or I'll walk to the farmers' market and spot the first frilly ribbed edges of chanterelles; I'll pick one up and bring it close

to my nose, remembering what it was like the first time I eyed a patch of the vivid yellow mushrooms in the woods. I had filled my basket full and then came home to sauté them in butter and garlic.

Standing over the stove now, I watch the yellow coats of chanterelles turn to bronze, caramelized and sweet. Their scent swells inside me, and I'm charmed by the transformation. I breathe it in, knowing that chanterelle season lasts only a few short weeks, and I am grateful for any time with them. I will mourn their passing briefly before I'm delighted with something new coming into its peak season.

All of life is marked by seasons and this continual swelling and shrinking. When I was first married to Gabe, some of the feelings that had felt like butterfly wings flapping incessantly in my stomach began to fade. What I once marked as an asset in him became an annoyance.

"Why must he always be tapping?" I thought, when not long before I had marveled at his ability to make music anywhere. What was once, "I love that he is so cheerful" became, "Why must he be so damn happy all the time?"

I panicked at those thoughts, terrified that I was falling out of love, but what I've since learned is that just as winter's gray soon produces sprouts that turn into spring, and then into the brilliance of summer, followed by the buttery-colored fall, our relationship has its own seasons. We steady ourselves in the hard seasons and celebrate those that are lighter. Over time, even the hard seasons are marked with celebration because we stood together during them. Our date nights have been our anchor, stabilizing us through it all. I used to fear the hard seasons, but now I recognize that they leave us wiser and are necessary for us to be able to recognize the joy on the other side.

Tonight, we sit down to a dinner that boasts the best of this season. Chanterelles tucked in a bit of cream and capped with a buttery crust towering with golden, wispy layers. Beets, carrots, fennel, and endive sit crisp and raw, revealing their natural sweetness, bitterness, and crunch while we drink a cocktail scented softly with apples and wait eagerly for a pear poached in Muscat to end the feast. Tonight, I am grateful to be anchored in my love for the food of this season and for my husband, sitting across from me, offering his stabilizing presence in my life.

AN ELEGANT CLASSIC

TIMELINE

1 TO 3 DAYS IN ADVANCE

Make creamy tapenade

Prep crudités and store in fridge, covered

Prep onion dish

Make pot pie filling

Poach pears

DATE DAY

Roast onions and make gremolata

DINNER TIME

Make flips

Bake pot pie

GROCERY

1 small beet

½ fennel bulb

3 carrots

1 head endive

1 large red onion

1 celery stalk

1 medium-size potato

1 orange

2 ripe pears

Sprig fresh rosemary

1 bunch fresh flat-leaf parsley

1 package or small bunch fresh thyme

3 cups / 225 g chanterelles

Crème fraîche

¼ cup/ 60 ml heavy whipping cream

¼ cup/ 40 g pitted Kalamata olives

Capers

¼ cup /40 g golden raisins

1 cup / 130 g frozen peas

Puff pastry, homemade (page 19) or store-bought

Apple brandy (such as Calvados)

Benedictine liqueur

1 (375 ml) bottle Muscat wine (such as Muscat de Beaumes de Venise)

Dry red wine

1 tablespoon dry sherry wine

PANTRY

Lemons

Garlic

1 yellow onion

Eggs

Unsalted butter

Freshly ground black pepper

Kosher salt

Flake salt

Red pepper flakes

Dijon mustard

Mayonnaise

1 cup / 240 ml vegetable stock, homemade (page 18) or store-bought

Extra-virgin olive oil

Honey

Maple syrup

Red wine vinegar

Granulated sugar

Whole nutmeg

1 star anise

1 vanilla bean (optional)

Apple Flip

Sometimes I like to go wander the aisles at liquor stores, examining bottles that are new to me and envisioning them in future cocktails. One such recent trip led me to Benedictine, an aromatic and herbal liqueur with a soft medicinal taste. The original recipe is said to be invented by Alexandre Le Grand, with a bit of help from a chemist. I was sad to hear that the connection to Benedictine monks was only a ploy to increase sales, although the Benedictine website claims that the recipe was created by Dom Bernardo Vincelli in 1510. It is interesting to note, however, that this recipe is so closely guarded that, at any time, only three people know it. Still, I prefer to imagine monks having a hand in my cocktail.

Please choose only the best and freshest eggs for this cocktail, as there is some risk involved with consuming a raw egg white. If the raw egg scares you, feel free to leave it out. It is still a delicious cocktail.

SERVES 2

3 ounces / 90 ml apple brandy (such as Calvados)

1½ ounces / 40 ml Benedictine liqueur

2 teaspoons maple syrup

2 teaspoons freshly squeezed lemon juice

2 very fresh egg whites

Freshly grated nutmeg or ground cinnamon, for finishing

Add the apple brandy, Benedictine, maple syrup, lemon juice, and egg whites to a cocktail shaker. Shake vigorously for 30 seconds. Now, fill the cocktail shaker with ice and shake again for 15 seconds.

Strain into two coupe or martini glasses. Finish with a sprinkle of freshly grated nutmeg.

AN ELEGANT CLASSIC

Fall Crudités WITH Creamy Olive Tapenade

When I know a heavy, buttery pot pie is in our future, I want something light to snack on while I cook. Thinly sliced striped beets, carrots, fennel, and endive look beautiful arranged on a platter; in fact, it's so striking that I can't resist snapping a picture before I dip the raw vegetables into the creamy dip of olives and capers. Perhaps mayonnaise defeats the intention of lightness, but I don't mind one bit.

SERVES 2

TAPENADE

1 garlic clove, peeled

⅛ teaspoon kosher salt

¼ cup / 40 g pitted Kalamata olives

1 teaspoon capers, rinsed

1 teaspoon Dijon mustard

⅓ cup / 80 g best-quality mayonnaise

⅛ teaspoon freshly ground black pepper

VEGETABLE CRUDITÉS

1 small beet, peeled and thinly sliced

½ fennel bulb, thinly sliced

2 carrots, peeled and thinly sliced

1 head endive, root removed and leaves separated

For the tapenade:

Mince the garlic with the salt. Chop the olives and capers on top of the garlic and continue to chop until a thick paste forms.

Add the olive paste to a small bowl and then whisk in the Dijon, mayonnaise, and pepper. Taste and adjust the seasonings to your liking. This dip can be made up to 3 days in advance.

For the crudités:

Prep the vegetables and arrange on a platter. Serve with the dip. The vegetables can be cut and refrigerated up to 3 days in advance.

AN ELEGANT CLASSIC

Roasted Red Onions WITH Golden Raisin Gremolata

In the oven, red onions soften, sweeten, and lighten in flavor. Gremolata is a pungent, finely chopped garnish classically made up of garlic, parsley, and lemon zest. I've replaced the lemon with orange to complement the onions and added plump golden raisins for a nice contrast.

This simple and healthy dish has graced many of our Thanksgiving tables.

SERVES 4

ONIONS

1 large red onion

¼ cup / 60 ml freshly squeezed orange juice (zest the orange first, as you'll need it for the gremolata)

1 tablespoon extra-virgin olive oil

1 tablespoon honey

1 tablespoon red wine vinegar

2 teaspoons minced fresh rosemary

¾ teaspoon kosher salt

¼ teaspoon freshly ground black pepper

Pinch of red pepper flakes

GREMOLATA

½ garlic clove or 1 small clove, minced

¼ teaspoon finishing salt (like Maldon or fleur de sel)

1 tablespoon chopped fresh flat-leaf parsley

1 teaspoon freshly grated orange zest

¼ cup / 40 g golden raisins, roughly chopped

For the onions:

Position a rack in the center of the oven and preheat to 400°F.

Remove the top of the onion and the outer papery layer. Cut into eight equal wedges, leaving the root attached so that the onion wedges remain intact. Place the onions in a single layer in a small roasting dish. You don't want the onions to overlap.

Whisk together the orange juice, olive oil, honey, vinegar, rosemary, salt, pepper, and red pepper flakes in a small bowl. Pour over the onions in the roasting dish. Cover with foil.

Roast for 60 minutes. Remove the foil and baste the onions with the liquid. Then continue to roast 30 minutes longer, uncovered, until the juices have reduced to a slightly thickened glaze.

The onions can be made 3 hours ahead. Let stand in the roasting dish at room temperature. Rewarm in a 350°F oven before serving, if desired. Place the onions on a serving plate.

For the gremolata:

Mince the garlic and salt on a cutting board until a paste forms. Roughly chop the parsley, orange zest, and raisins on top of the garlic salt.

Sprinkle the gremolata over the top of the onions just before serving.

Chanterelle Pot Pie

Autumn in the Pacific Northwest means chanterelle mushrooms bursting from wooden crates in every grocery store and market; we make pot pie to celebrate the bounty. Lucky for me, chanterelles are my favorite, but really any mushroom works here.

SERVES 2

5 tablespoons / 70 g unsalted butter, divided

3 cups / 225 g chopped chanterelle mushrooms

1½ teaspoons kosher salt, divided

2 teaspoons fresh thyme leaves

3 garlic cloves, finely chopped

⅓ cup / 80 ml dry red wine

½ medium-size yellow onion, diced

1 carrot, diced

1 celery stalk, diced

1 medium-size potato, peeled and cut into ½-inch dice

1 cup / 240 ml vegetable stock, homemade (page 18) or store-bought

¼ cup / 60 ml heavy whipping cream, plus more for brushing

1 cup / 130 g frozen peas

¼ teaspoon freshly ground black pepper

1 tablespoon dry sherry wine

1 sheet puff pastry, homemade (page 19) or store-bought

Preheat the oven to 400°F.

In a large, wide pan or Dutch oven, melt 3 tablespoons butter over medium-high heat. Add the chanterelles, ¼ teaspoon salt, thyme, and garlic in an even layer. Sauté until the mushrooms soften and begin to caramelize, about 10 minutes. Don't stir too often at this point; you want the mushrooms to brown. Deglaze the pan with red wine and cook until the mushrooms absorb the wine, about 1 minute, stirring often. Remove the mushrooms from the pan and set aside.

Melt the remaining 2 tablespoons butter in the pan. Add the onion, carrot, and celery along with ½ teaspoon salt. Sauté until the onions are translucent, 5 to 7 minutes. Add the potatoes, mushrooms, ½ teaspoon salt, and vegetable stock. Bring to a simmer, cover, and cook until the potatoes are tender and the stock has reduced, about 20 minutes.

Stir in the cream, peas, pepper, remaining ¼ teaspoon salt, and sherry wine. Simmer on low for an additional 5 minutes, or until the mixture has thickened. Taste and add more sherry, salt, and pepper, if desired. Cool to room temperature. At this point, you can cover and refrigerate the filling for up to 3 days.

An hour before serving, set out a 16-ounce baking dish or two 8-ounce ramekins. Cut a round of puff pastry 1 inch larger than the diameter of your roasting dish or dishes.

Pour the pot pie mixture into your dish and top with puff pastry. Tuck the edges of the puff pastry under and into the baking dish. Cut a few slits on top, brush with cream, and bake for 30 to 35 minutes, or until the top is golden and cooked through and the interior bubbles.

Poached Pears IN Muscat

This dinner begs for a simple, light dessert. Muscat fills each bite with a floral and delicate citrus scent and gives poached pears the perfect amount of sweetness. And yet, to me, it isn't dessert without some sort of cream; you can leave it off, but you know I won't

SERVES 2

1 (375 ml) bottle Muscat wine (such as Muscat Beaumes de Venise)

¼ cup / 50 g granulated sugar

2 ripe pears, peeled

1 star anise

1 vanilla bean, split (optional)

1-inch piece lemon peel

1 tablespoon freshly squeezed lemon juice

¼ cup / 60 g crème fraîche, for serving

Combine the Muscat, sugar, pears, star anise, vanilla bean (if using), lemon peel, and lemon juice in a saucepan. Bring to a simmer over medium heat and then reduce the heat to low, cover, and simmer gently for 30 minutes, turning the pears halfway through.

Remove the pan from the heat and let cool for 30 minutes with the lid on. If making ahead, cover and refrigerate at this point for up to 2 days. Rewarm before serving.

To serve, place one pear in a bowl along with some of the warm poaching liquid. Float a small amount of crème fraîche alongside the pear. Serve without hesitation.

AN ELEGANT CLASSIC

Fall Comfort

Spiced Cider Toddy
201

Brussels Sprouts Slaw with Grapes and Feta
202

White Bean and Pumpkin Gratin with Crispy
Shallot Crumbs
204

Grandma's Apple Cake with Maple Cream
206

"Is there a couple in our lives whose marriage we admire?" I ask Gabe. "I mean, like an older couple and not our parents."

He sat and thought for a while and then replied, "No."

I wanted this to change. I wanted us to be able to learn from a couple that had stood firm through more perilous storms than we have so we could learn from their mistakes. And I wanted to be encouraged by a marriage that had maintained joy throughout decades of being together. So I wrote a few awkward emails, and soon we had a date on the calendar to have dinner with an older couple we'd never met. They were friends of friends, and we all went to the same church but had never seen one another. In a matter of a few short days, they were to join us for date night.

At 5:30 p.m. on the night of our double date, I rushed through the door, eager to start cooking dinner for us and the guests, who were coming at 7:00. There was still a cake to bake, cream to whip, squash to roast, Brussels sprouts to shred, and, well, basically everything else to do. Luckily, our dinner was simple: a fresh slaw of Brussels sprouts, feta, and grapes alongside a warming gratin of squash and white beans, with plenty of nutty Gruyère and heavy cream.

I had enough time to sit down with the kids, see the day's drawings and doodles, talk about recess, and listen to Baron read to me before I began to peel apples and chop onions. Gabe poured us each some wine and tried to stay out of my way while we talked about each other's day.

Our guests arrived just as the cake emerged from the oven with a crackly sugar top and a sweet perfume of cinnamon and nutmeg. We all sat down at the table and quickly started into the sort of conversation that you have with people with whom you've been friends for years. There was a lot of laughter, and all of us gushing over our kids and their grandkids. All throughout the evening, I watched how they still caught the other's eye and that there was light and joy on their faces. They spoke excitedly of their first apartment together, recalling the charm of its 700 square feet. They laughed about the price they had paid for rent and how much of a stretch it was on them and their marriage. And as our kids continued to ignore our pleas to stay upstairs so the adults could talk, they welcomed

> If we commit ourselves to one person for life, this is not, as many people think, a rejection of freedom; rather, it demands the courage to move into all the risks of freedom, and the risk of love which is permanent; into that love which is not possession but participation.
>
> Madeleine L'Engle

them to the table with grace and excitement.

Finally, when we had nearly licked our plates clean of the dense cake dotted with large bites of tart apple, I asked them their secret. I don't remember exactly how I asked or what I said, but basically it was, "How do you do it?" And I meant, "By what miracle or magic powers do you maintain a growing relationship for so long, still have things to talk about, and still like and desire and want to be around each other?"

"Commitment," he replied simply. "It's what gets you through the bumps."

Perhaps it was the quickness or simplicity of his answer that unraveled me so deeply; they said many other things that night that reminded me of the wisdom that comes when you've been in a relationship for so long, but this really stuck with me.

It makes complete sense. Commitment. Somehow, I fear we've gotten commitment all wrong. These days it is seen as restrictive, binding, and confining, when in fact its presence is what gives freedom in marriage.

I trust Gabe's commitment so completely that I'm not afraid for him to see who I really am. I was never worried that he'd run once he smelled my morning breath or saw how careless I am about hanging up my clothes. I can allow myself to be completely and utterly broken in front of him because he has said, "Yes, in all things, I am here to stay." I am free to be completely and wholly Ashley because he is committed to me and to us.

There is comfort in our commitment but not complacency. It's not, "I'm stuck with him"; it's, "How can we love each other better because you're my person and I'm yours?" The commitment keeps us bound together in the times when we are tempted to quit. Because of commitment we are able to come out on the other side to experience how incredible it is when you are completely known and still loved.

We cleared the table, and I couldn't help feeling grateful, as I have many times in our marriage, to the young twenty-one-year-old me for being brave enough to say yes to Gabe. I knew then that I was committing to forever: I just didn't know how freeing and life-giving that commitment would prove to be.

TIMELINE

1 TO 3 DAYS IN ADVANCE

Bake apple cake

Make spiced cider

Make slaw dressing

DATE DAY

Prep slaw components

Roast squash

Make gratin

DINNER TIME

Make toddies

Bake gratin

Make crispy shallot crumbs

Toss slaw

Make maple cream

GROCERY

2 cups / 470 ml apple cider

1 small piece fresh ginger

4 ounces / 110 g Brussels sprouts

1 small leek

2 ounces / 60 g grapes (I use concord)

8 ounces / 230 g cubed butternut squash or pumpkin

1 medium-size shallot

2 medium-size tart apples (such as Granny Smith or Gravenstein)

1 bunch or small package fresh sage

2 ounces / 60 g sheep's milk feta

2 ounces / 60 g Gruyère

½ cup / 120 ml heavy whipping cream

½ cup / 120 g crème fraîche (page 17) or whipped cream

½ cup / 25 g panko breadcrumbs

1 (15-ounce / 430 g) can cannellini beans

PANTRY

Lemons

1 large yellow onion

Garlic

Unsalted butter

Eggs

Honey

Dijon mustard

Champagne vinegar

Extra-virgin olive oil

Canola or walnut oil

Kosher salt

Flake salt

Freshly ground black pepper

Whole nutmeg

1 stick cinnamon

Ground cinnamon

4 whole cloves

Granulated sugar

All-purpose flour

Baking soda

Vanilla extract

Maple syrup

Whiskey, bourbon, or apple brandy (such as Calvados)

Spiced Cider Toddy

A large batch of spiced apple cider simmering on the stove serves two purposes. First of all, it promises a comforting fall drink, and, second, it scents the home with a smell that is quintessentially fall. My grown-up version is pleasantly spiced with fresh ginger, cinnamon, and cloves and adds a shot of whiskey, bourbon, or Calvados on those nights when a little extra warmth is needed.

SERVES 2

SPICED CIDER

2 cups / 470 ml apple cider

1 stick cinnamon

4 whole cloves

2-inch piece fresh ginger, thinly sliced

2 tablespoons honey

TODDY

4 ounces / 120 ml whiskey, bourbon, or apple brandy (such as Calvados)

Ground cinnamon or toasted cinnamon sticks, for garnish

For the spiced cider:

Bring the apple cider, cinnamon stick, cloves, ginger, and honey to a simmer in a small saucepan. Let simmer for 5 minutes. Remove the pan from the heat. This can be made up to 3 days before you plan on enjoying the cocktail and stored, covered, in the refrigerator.

For the toddy:

Warm the spiced cider in a small saucepan over medium heat, if needed. Divide the spiced cider between two warm mugs. Stir in half of the whiskey to each and then garnish with freshly ground cinnamon or a toasted cinnamon stick.

Brussels Sprouts Slaw WITH Grapes AND Feta

I use a slaw much like this one to convert Brussels sprouts haters to lovers or, at the very least, appreciators. A mandoline makes quick work of shredding the little sprouts. This version is laced with creamy and salty feta and sweet, crunchy grapes.

I used concord grapes on our date. They have a short season, but, if you can find them, use them. While halving and removing the seeds from each grape, I told Gabe, "This is love."

"You don't have to do that. I can eat the seeds," he said.

"No. This is me loving you. Let me do this. It makes me happy." They were just grape seeds, but it's the little things.

SERVES 2

4 ounces / 110 g finely shredded Brussels sprouts (about 1½ cups)

1 small leek, thinly sliced (white and light green parts only)

2 ounces / 60 g halved red or black grapes (about ⅓ cup)

1½ teaspoons Dijon mustard

¼ teaspoon granulated sugar

1½ teaspoons Champagne vinegar

1½ teaspoons freshly squeezed lemon juice, plus more to taste

4 to 5 tablespoons / 60 to 70 ml extra-virgin olive oil

Kosher salt and freshly ground black pepper

2 ounces / 60 g sheep's milk feta

In a medium bowl, combine the shredded Brussels sprouts, leeks, and grapes.

In another bowl, whisk together the Dijon, sugar, Champagne vinegar, lemon juice, and olive oil. Add salt and pepper to taste. The dressing can be made up to 3 days in advance.

Toss the salad with the dressing. Finish with crumbled feta.

White Bean AND Pumpkin Gratin WITH Crispy Shallot Crumbs

This is the edible equivalent of a warm, pillowy blanket on a cold day—comfortable. It's easy, unpretentious, and deeply satisfying. This gratin sits beautifully on the holiday table, as the flavors are reminiscent of a green bean casserole (minus the green beans).

SERVES 4

GRATIN

8 ounces / 230 g butternut squash or pumpkin, peeled and cut into ½-inch cubes (about 2 cups)

1 tablespoon extra-virgin olive oil

Kosher salt and freshly ground black pepper

½ large yellow onion, diced

1 tablespoon unsalted butter, plus more for the pan

3 garlic cloves, chopped

1 teaspoon chopped fresh sage

1 (15-ounce / 430 g) can cannellini beans, drained and rinsed

½ cup / 120 ml heavy whipping cream

1 cup / 60 g grated Gruyère

⅛ teaspoon freshly grated nutmeg

Flake salt (optional)

CRISPY SHALLOT CRUMBS

2 tablespoons unsalted butter

¼ cup / 40 g chopped shallot (from 1 medium-size shallot)

1 garlic clove, finely chopped

½ cup / 25 g panko breadcrumbs

Kosher salt and freshly ground black pepper

Preheat the oven to 425°F.

Line a baking sheet with parchment paper.

Combine the squash, olive oil, and a pinch of salt and pepper on the baking sheet and toss well to coat. Roast for 15 to 20 minutes, or until just tender and golden in parts. Set aside.

While the squash roasts, make the crispy shallot crumbs. Melt the butter in a 12-inch skillet (cast iron is best). Add the shallots and garlic and sauté over medium heat until fragrant and the butter bubbles, 2 to 3 minutes.

Stir in the panko and continue to cook until the breadcrumbs just start to turn golden. Add a hefty pinch of salt and a few turns of freshly ground black pepper.

Transfer the crispy crumbs to a small bowl and set aside.

If it's not still on, preheat the oven to 425°F.

In a medium skillet over medium-high heat, sauté the onions in butter with a pinch of salt until translucent, 5 to 7 minutes. Add the garlic and sage and cook for 2 minutes more. Stir in the roasted squash and the white beans. Add the cream and bring the mixture just to a simmer.

Remove the pan from the heat and stir in the cheese, nutmeg, and a scant ½ teaspoon kosher salt and freshly ground black pepper. Taste and adjust the seasonings to your liking.

Pour the bean and squash mixture into a small buttered roasting dish. Top with the crispy crumbs. At this point you can cool the gratin to room temperature, then cover and refrigerate until ready to bake (up to 1 day in advance).

Bake for 10 minutes, or until the top is crisp and the edges are bubbling.

I like mine with a touch of flake salt on top. Gabe likes his as is.

Note: The shallot crumbs can be made in bulk and scattered liberally over roasted vegetables, soups, and pasta dishes. They'll keep for up to 1 week, covered.

Grandma's Apple Cake with Maple Cream

Can I tell you a little secret? Sometimes I like to make cakes like this one—hearty, full of spice and soft fruit—with breakfast in mind. Of course, I did think it a perfect way to end a heavy, fall-centric meal, and it was, but I was also thinking about a thick slice alongside a cup of coffee and a good book in the morning.

I found this recipe tucked into a wooden recipe box my grandmother gave me. Since then it's been a favorite of ours, for dessert and breakfast.

MAKES ONE 8-INCH CAKE

APPLE CAKE

Unsalted butter, for the pan

1½ cups / 210 g all-purpose flour

¾ teaspoon baking soda

½ teaspoon kosher salt

1 teaspoon ground cinnamon

½ teaspoon freshly grated nutmeg

¾ cup / 150 g granulated sugar

¾ cup / 180 ml mild-flavored oil (I use canola or walnut)

2 eggs

½ teaspoon vanilla extract

2 medium-size tart apples (such as Granny Smith or Gravenstein), peeled and cut into ½-inch cubes

MAPLE CREAM

½ cup / 120 g crème fraîche (page 17) or whipped cream

1 tablespoon maple syrup

For the apple cake:

Preheat the oven to 350°F.

Butter or spray an 8-inch round cake pan. Line the bottom with parchment paper and butter the parchment.

Combine the flour, baking soda, salt, cinnamon, nutmeg, and sugar in a medium bowl.

In another bowl, whisk together the oil, eggs, and vanilla.

Add the wet ingredients to the dry, along with the apples. Use a rubber spatula to fold all the ingredients together until combined. The batter will be very thick.

Scrape the batter into the prepared pan, spread until level, and place in the middle of the oven. Bake until a toothpick inserted comes out clean, 45 to 50 minutes.

Cool for 10 minutes on a wire rack before inverting and then cooling completely. This cake is best the day after it's been baked. Wrap well in plastic wrap and leave on the counter overnight.

For the maple cream:

Whisk together the crème fraîche and maple syrup in a small bowl. Serve with the cooled cake.

Note: I like to sprinkle a bit of turbinado sugar on top just before baking to give the cake a sweet, crunchy cap.

Kale WITH Apples, Currants, AND Warm Pancetta Vinaigrette

The warmth of this vinaigrette softens the kale just enough to make it a bit more pleasant to chew, while still being a bright, fresh salad.

SERVES 2

4 ounces / 110 g pancetta, cut into ¼-inch cubes

1 small bunch Lacinato kale

2 tablespoons olive oil, divided

1 small shallot, finely minced (¼ cup / 40 g)

1 teaspoon Dijon mustard

2 teaspoons red wine vinegar

½ apple, unpeeled and diced (I like something tart and crisp, like Pink Lady or Granny Smith)

¼ cup / 35 g dried currants

2 teaspoons freshly squeezed lemon juice (from ½ a small lemon)

Shaved Parmesan, for finishing

Add the pancetta to a large sauté pan set over medium-low heat. Cook until brown and most of the fat has rendered, about 10 minutes.

While the pancetta cooks, wash the kale, remove the tough inner ribs, and cut into 1-inch ribbons.

Once the pancetta is brown, add 1 tablespoon olive oil and the shallots and cook 5 to 7 minutes, or until the shallots are golden around the edges and cooked through.

Remove the pan from the heat and whisk in the remaining 1 tablespoon olive oil, mustard, and red wine vinegar.

Pour the warm vinaigrette over the kale. Add the apples, currants, and lemon juice. Toss to combine. Use a vegetable peeler to shave large, thin wisps of Parmesan over the salad to finish.

Cacio e Pepe WITH Parmesan Frico

This dish shows the power of simplicity. Take care when choosing your ingredients; quality counts.

SERVES 2

8 ounces / 230 g dried bucatini or spaghetti

3 tablespoons unsalted butter

1 teaspoon freshly ground black pepper, plus more for finishing

1 cup / 45 g finely grated pecorino, divided

2 Parmesan Frico (recipe follows), for serving

Heat a large stockpot of water that tastes of the sea (heavily salted). Add the pasta and cook according to package directions.

While the pasta cooks, melt the butter with 1 teaspoon pepper in a large sauté pan set over medium-low heat. Let the pepper infuse for 1 minute and then turn off the heat.

When the pasta is al dente, before draining, remove a scant ½ cup / 120 ml pasta water and add to the butter. Simmer for 2 minutes over low heat.

Drain the pasta and add to the sauté pan, along with ¾ cup /30 g pecorino. Toss the pasta in the sauce with tongs until the cheese has melted and created a creamy sauce that coats the pasta. If the sauce is still wet, continue to simmer until the water has reduced and clings to the pasta.

Place a Parmesan frico at the bottom of two bowls and divide the pasta between them. Finish with the remaining pecorino and more freshly ground black pepper.

Parmesan Frico

Think of this as the best cheese cracker you've ever had. The pasta is fine without it, but, with it, it's an unforgettable dish. I use a microplane to grate fine wisps of Parmesan.

SERVES 2

1⅓ cups / 120 g packed, freshly grated Parmesan

Preheat the oven to 400°F. Line a baking sheet with parchment paper.

Using ⅔ cup / 60 g Parmesan, form a thick, even 6-inch circle of cheese on the parchment.

Bake for 6 to 8 minutes, until the cheese melts and is golden.

Carefully remove the parchment from the tray and flip over onto an inverted bowl. Peel off the parchment and gently press the Parmesan circle around the inverted bowl. Cool for 30 seconds and then remove. Repeat with the remaining cheese.

Frico can be made up to 3 days in advance and stored in an airtight container.

Nutella Semifreddo

A *semifreddo* is essentially a rich ice cream that doesn't require an ice cream maker for churning. I love this because, inevitably when I go to make ice cream, I've forgotten to freeze the bowl. This dessert comes together quickly, can be made well in advance, and satisfies in the same way all those many helpings of gelato did back when I lived in Italy.

SERVES 6

4 large eggs

¼ cup / 50 g granulated sugar

¾ cup / 230 g Nutella

1 cup / 240 ml heavy whipping cream, plus more for serving

Chopped toasted hazelnuts

Whipped cream, for serving

Line a loaf pan with plastic wrap, leaving an overhang on all sides to use to remove the semifreddo later.

In a large bowl, add the eggs and whip with an electric mixer on medium speed until frothy, about 2 minutes. While the eggs whip, slowly add the sugar and then beat on high speed until the eggs are light and tripled in volume, 5 to 7 minutes.

Decrease the mixer speed to low and then add the Nutella to the bowl. Mix for 15 seconds. Turn off the mixer and scrape down the sides of the bowl. Finish whisking the Nutella and eggs together by hand. The eggs will lose a lot of volume once the Nutella is added. This is fine, I assure you.

In a separate bowl and with clean beaters, whip the cream to medium peaks. Whisk together the egg and Nutella mixture with the cream.

Pour the mixture into the prepared loaf pan and freeze for 8 hours or overnight. When ready to serve, lift the semifreddo out of the pan using the plastic wrap and slice into thick slices.

Serve with toasted hazelnuts and softly whipped cream.

A Winter BBQ

BBQ Pulled Pork Sandwiches with Apple and Radicchio Slaw
221

Baked Beans
224

Oranges with Avocado, Olives, and Mint
225

Milk Punch and Ritz Cracker Mendiants
226

If I could speak to myself on the day of my wedding, this is what I would say . . .

I understand you're a bit scared. You're young and you are about to make a decision that will affect the rest of your life. You think it's the right choice; you think you love him. But what really is love? I know that is what you are thinking because I am you.

For months leading up to the wedding day, you've been asking everyone who would listen to help you understand what love really is. Sure he gives you butterflies, and you can't imagine not spending every day with this man. You've lost countless hours of sleep just clinging to his presence and not wanting to waste a moment with him. But is that really love? Is that enough to sustain a marriage that will survive moves across state lines, financial stress, young children, loss, and much more that we have yet to experience?

In case you do read this, you should know that you are making the right decision. But you don't really know love. The love you feel, anxiously awaiting that glimmer in his eyes when he sees you for the first time in your wedding dress and for the last time you aren't his wife, that love is just the start.

There will be days when the butterflies don't flutter as rapidly as you think they should and you will question love. You will resent him for shining light on parts of you that are selfish or unflattering. He won't complete you in the way you expect. But love isn't simply about how he makes you feel; love is a choice and love is action.

Love is him warming up the espresso machine for you in the morning so it's ready when you wander sleepily down the stairs. Love is how he saves the last scoop of ice cream for you, every time. Love is the way he wrestles with your sons (you have two, and I can't wait for you to meet them) after a long day of work. Love is the way he dances with your daughter (she'll make you melt with each glance into her big brown eyes).

You'll slowly start to understand that when your dad told you, "Love is a choice," he wasn't being as unromantic as you first thought. You'll realize that each day you have a choice. You can either choose to love Gabe and allow your feelings and actions to reflect that love, or you can choose to allow the daily difficulties and his imperfections (yes, I know you can't see it now, but he's not perfect, and neither are you) ruin your marriage.

Some days are better than others, but over

217

time you'll realize that praying for him and encouraging him is more useful than resenting him. You'll start to see all the things he does for you and your family rather than focusing on what he doesn't do. And you'll realize that on the day you married him, you really had no idea what love was and that, ten years later, you love him in a way that you never thought possible.

It's going to be hard. You'll find out things about yourself that you really wish could have stayed hidden, and yet, through it all, you'll slowly become a better person. One that really knows and understands love—at least I hope that's what happens; I'm not quite there yet.

What I do know is that no matter how tired you are, no matter how much you would just rather curl up on the couch and tune out the noise of the day, every once in a while you'll need to put the kids to bed a bit earlier and ask your husband out on a date, even if that date happens at home.

You'll plan the meal with great excitement and get inspired staring at the vibrant produce at the store while Ivy (that's your daughter) tries her best to pull everything off the shelves and into the cart. You'll spend the next seven hours, on and off, preparing for a meal that you and your husband will devour in ten minutes. He'll appreciate every minute of your effort, and you'll love mincing each clove of garlic. You'll remind yourself of this moment and of how many times you've learned the same lesson before; you'll choose him over your own selfish desires and realize it is what love is all about.

TIMELINE

1 TO 3 DAYS IN ADVANCE

Marinate and cook pork

Make barbecue sauce

Make baked beans

Make milk punch

Make mendiants

DINNER TIME

Make orange and avocado salad

Make slaw

Assemble sandwiches

Warm beans

GROCERY

1 tart apple (such as Granny Smith)

1 head radicchio

1 bunch fresh cilantro

1 package or small bunch fresh mint

1 scallion

1 shallot

1 large orange

1 avocado

Sour cream

Heavy whipping cream

5 strips bacon

1 (3-pound / 1.4 kg) bone-in pork shoulder roast, or 2½ pounds / 1.1 kg boneless pork shoulder

Kalamata olives

2 (14.5-ounce / 410 g) cans navy or kidney beans

Sturdy rolls or burger buns (page 15)

10 to 15 Ritz crackers

Roasted, salted cashews

Dried cherries

Cocoa nibs

Bittersweet or semisweet chocolate chips (about 6 ounces / 170 g)

PANTRY

1 lemon

Garlic

Unsalted butter

Whole milk

Kosher salt

Freshly ground black pepper

Flake salt

Ground cumin

Cayenne pepper

Hot smoked paprika

Yellow mustard

Ketchup

Natural hickory liquid smoke (optional)

Mayonnaise

Maple syrup

Apple cider vinegar

Canola oil

Extra-virgin olive oil

Confectioners' sugar

Muscovado sugar or dark brown sugar

Ground cinnamon

Vanilla extract

Bourbon

BBQ Pulled Pork Sandwiches WITH Apple AND Radicchio Slaw

Every so often (or every quite often), I get a powerful craving for a BBQ pulled pork sandwich. There is something about the flavor that's both sweet and savory, with a bright vinegary pop that has me longing for it again and again. Apple and radicchio slaw offers a great freshness in this hearty sandwich.

I prefer a good, substantial roll for this sandwich: something with a bit of chew yet something that yields easily so that dinner doesn't feel like a wrestling match. The bun recipe on page 15 works well here, as does a store-bought potato roll or something similar.

SERVES 2

BBQ PULLED PORK

3 garlic cloves, minced

¼ teaspoon cayenne pepper

2 tablespoons hot smoked paprika

1 tablespoon kosher salt

1 tablespoon dark brown sugar or muscovado sugar

2 teaspoons ground cumin

3 tablespoons yellow mustard

1 (3-pound / 1,360 g) bone-in pork shoulder roast, or 2½ pounds / 1,115 g boneless pork shoulder

1 cup / 240 ml water or chicken stock (page 18)

1 recipe Tangy Muscovado Barbecue Sauce (recipe follows)

SANDWICHES

2 large rolls or burger buns (page 15)

1 tablespoon unsalted butter

1⅓ cups / 215 g pulled pork

1 cup / 100 g Apple and Radicchio Slaw (recipe follows)

For the pork:

In a small bowl, combine the garlic, cayenne, paprika, salt, brown sugar, cumin, and yellow mustard. Stir well to combine. Rub over the pork and let sit for at least 1 hour or overnight in the fridge.

Preheat the oven to 325°F.

Place the pork shoulder in a large Dutch oven or roasting pan with the water. Wrap the pan tightly in foil. Roast, completely covered, for 4 to 5 hours, or until the meat easily falls apart when prodded with a fork. Add more water or stock while the pork roasts if it looks dry.

Let the pork rest 10 minutes. Add ⅔ cup / 175 g barbecue sauce to the roasting pan and scrape up any crusted-on bits on the bottom.

Use two forks to pull apart the pork into bite-size shreds. If there are any tough or fatty pieces, pull those out as you shred the meat.

Taste and add more sauce if needed or reserve the remaining barbecue sauce to serve on the sandwiches.

For the sandwiches:

Slice and butter the buns and then toast them in a hot skillet or pan. Add roughly ⅔ cup / 105 g pulled pork to each bottom bun and top with ½ cup / 50 g slaw. Finish with top buns and serve with a little extra sauce on the side.

Tangy Muscovado Barbecue Sauce

Sweet, tangy, bright, and rich, this sauce has it all. A few drops of natural hickory smoke gives the impression that this sauce has smoked all day.

MAKES 1 CUP / 270 G

½ cup / 120 ml apple cider vinegar

2 tablespoons yellow mustard

½ cup / 130 g ketchup

¼ teaspoon cayenne pepper, plus more to taste

1 teaspoon kosher salt

½ teaspoon freshly ground black pepper

½ cup / 100 g muscovado sugar or dark brown sugar

3 garlic cloves, minced

Few drops natural hickory liquid smoke (optional)

In a medium saucepan over medium-low heat, whisk together the apple cider vinegar, mustard, ketchup, cayenne, salt, black pepper, muscovado sugar, garlic, and liquid smoke, if using. Bring to a simmer and cook on medium low for 10 minutes to reduce slightly and bring the flavors together.

Sauce can be made ahead and stored in the refrigerator for up to 1 week.

Apple AND Radicchio Slaw

A meaty sandwich needs something fresh for balance. This slaw resembles the classic only in that it is bound together by a tangy and creamy dressing. There's apple for sweetness, radicchio for a bitter bite, and cilantro for freshness and flavor; it's just what this sandwich needs.

SERVES 4

2 tablespoons sour cream

1 tablespoon mayonnaise

1 teaspoon apple cider vinegar

½ tablespoon freshly squeezed lemon juice

⅛ teaspoon kosher salt, plus more as needed

½ tart apple (such as Granny Smith), julienned

1 cup / 30 g thinly sliced radicchio

1 cup / 20 g chopped fresh cilantro

1 scallion, thinly sliced (white and green parts)

Freshly ground black pepper

In a large bowl, whisk together the sour cream, mayonnaise, vinegar, lemon juice, and salt. Add the apple, radicchio, cilantro, and scallion and toss to combine. Finish with more salt, if desired, and freshly ground black pepper.

Baked Beans

Nothing fancy here, just a classic.

SERVES 4

5 strips bacon, roughly chopped

2 garlic cloves, sliced

½ cup / 70 g sliced shallot (1 large)

¼ cup / 60 ml maple syrup

1 tablespoon dark brown sugar

1 teaspoon kosher salt

¼ teaspoon freshly ground black pepper

2 tablespoons yellow mustard

¼ cup / 65 g ketchup

2 tablespoons apple cider vinegar

2 (14.5-ounce / 410 g) cans navy or kidney beans, drained and rinsed

In a medium saucepan, sauté the bacon over medium heat until golden, about 10 minutes. Reduce the heat to medium low and add the garlic and shallots and sauté until just starting to brown, another 8 minutes or so.

Stir in the maple syrup, brown sugar, salt, pepper, mustard, ketchup, cider vinegar, and beans. Bring to a simmer and then reduce the heat to medium low. Cover and cook for 45 minutes, stirring occasionally. The beans can be made up to 3 days in advance and then warmed just before serving.

Note: If time allows, I love to slowly braise these beans in the oven alongside the pork. I use dry navy beans instead of canned beans; I don't bother to soak the beans and instead let the sweet, tangy juices make incredibly tender and richly flavored baked beans. Place all the baked bean ingredients in a Dutch oven, substituting 2 cups dry navy beans for the canned beans, and then cover everything with at least 2 inches of water. Place a lid on the roasting dish and bake at 325°F for about 6 hours, or until the beans are tender. Check the pot every now and again, as you may need to add more water.

Oranges WITH Avocado, Olives, AND Mint

This salad, I find, is perfect for ending this hefty meal. It's bright, refreshing, and simple.

SERVES 2

1 large orange

½ avocado, diced

¼ cup / 40 g roughly chopped, pitted Kalamata olives

¼ cup / 10 g fresh mint leaves

1 tablespoon extra-virgin olive oil

Flake salt, for finishing

Using a sharp knife, slice off the top and bottom of the orange and remove the peel including the pith. Slice into ¼-inch-thick rounds.

Arrange the orange slices on a platter and add the diced avocado, Kalamata olives, and mint leaves. Drizzle with extra-virgin olive oil and sprinkle with flake salt.

Milk Punch

I only recently became aware of such a thing as milk punch, but once I did I was not quick to forget it. These two words evoke warmth and comfort and, although it's traditionally served over ice or just out of the freezer as a slushy, I take my milk punch hot. A bit of freshly grated nutmeg on top is a nice touch too. You can do no wrong here.

SERVES 2

1 cup / 240 ml whole milk

½ cup / 120 ml heavy whipping cream

¼ cup / 30 g confectioners' sugar

⅛ teaspoon ground cinnamon

¼ teaspoon vanilla extract

2 to 3 ounces / 60 to 90 ml bourbon

Whisk together the whole milk, cream, sugar, cinnamon, and vanilla extract. Finish with bourbon and ice and drink as is.

On cold nights, however, throw everything but the bourbon into a small saucepan, bring to a simmer, and stir until the sugar dissolves. Remove from the heat, pour into a deep mug, top with bourbon, and enjoy with something sweet. The milk punch base can be made up to 3 days in advance. Cover and refrigerate. Serve cold with ice or warm before adding the bourbon.

I like mine with ½ ounce / 10 ml bourbon, milk, and more cinnamon on top; Gabe prefers 1 to 1½ ounces / 30 to 40 ml of bourbon.

Ritz Cracker Mendiants

Mendiants are an elegant chocolate candy made with melted chocolate that is poured into a round circle just a bit larger than a quarter, or like the size of a small cracker, and then topped with various nuts and dried fruits. These mendiants seem elegant, until you bite into the cracker and realize it's just plain delicious.

MAKES 10 TO 15 MENDIANTS

1 cup / 170 g bittersweet or semisweet chocolate chips

½ teaspoon canola oil

10 to 15 Ritz crackers

¼ cup / 30 g roasted, salted cashews

2 tablespoons dried cherries

1 tablespoon cocoa nibs

Flake salt

Line a baking sheet with parchment paper.

In a small bowl, combine the chocolate chips and oil. Melt over a double-boiler or in a microwave at 20-second intervals, stirring well in between.

Gently drop a cracker into the melted chocolate. Use a fork to flip the cracker to coat the other side and then flip again. Lift the cracker out of the chocolate with the fork and carefully tap any excess chocolate off on the side of the bowl.

Lay the chocolate-covered cracker on the prepared baking sheet. Top with a cashew, a dried cherry, a few cocoa nibs, and some flakes of salt.

Repeat until all the crackers have been covered and adorned.

Refrigerate until set.

These will keep, well sealed, for up to 2 weeks.

227

All Over the Mediterranean

Gordon's Cup with Caraway

231

Fresh Carrot Salad

233

Mediterranean Lamb Tostadas

234

Stewed Apricots with Cardamom Yogurt and Marcona Almonds

237

I know why I love food. I think I figured it out right around the time I tasted truffles for the first time. Not the chocolate—the fungus. My first truffle tasted like earth and perfume and nothing I'd ever had before. With every bite of my shaved truffle pasta, the little black, unassuming, wrinkled, and rotten-looking nub released an intoxicating flavor, maddeningly difficult to describe. I wasted no time devouring it all and, once finished, concluded that I was crazy about truffles.

"Food doesn't have to taste this good," I thought. Sure, we need to eat to survive, but the fact that we get pleasure from it made me feel more loved than I had ever let myself feel.

I've felt loved like that several times since then; I feel it with a purple and deeply red tomato just hours off the vine. Melted cheese poured over a simple plate of potatoes and a few cornichons on the side makes me swoon. Briny oysters with just a bit of lemon leave me feeling refreshed, as if I have just swum in the ocean. And my heart always skips a beat when I taste chocolate so smooth and bitter it's nearly savory.

I chase after these feelings every time I eat, and my desire for myself and for others to feel loved is why I cook.

"What do you feel when you eat?" I ask Gabe while we drink wine and savor an octopus terrine drenched in a light and grassy olive oil. He eats in silence while I want to jump up on the counter of the restaurant bar and pronounce my excitement of the simple dish's beauty.

"Well, I don't think I get as excited as you do," he says. "I like it, but mostly I like watching you enjoy it."

I wonder if he knows that, when I slice an onion, I'm loving him. That I taste dressing again and again to make sure that the acidity and the sweetness are perfectly balanced because I want him to taste the salad and feel inexplicably loved. That I try five types of feta at the cheese counter because I want it to be salty and creamy, to crumble well and yet melt on his tongue. And that I cram into a tiny parking spot at Pike Place so I can buy the Greek yogurt I've been telling him about: the one that is softly sweet and so creamy it tastes as rich as gelato, but with a subtle tang.

I realize that I'm the one who cries over a dish so perfectly mastered it tastes like all things good in the world in one simple bite, but that

Gabe is happy with melted cheese in between two store-bought tortillas. I'm the one who reads about fermentation and sourdough on a Saturday night and who sits in front of the oven watching the buttery layers of puff pastry rise to triple their original height. And while he'll take a picture of me doing so, he doesn't have the same fascination. But that will not stop me from sautéing, roasting, baking, and shaking a cocktail to say I love you because I do love him deeply, and sometimes this is the best I can do to show it.

Other people use words, some reach for a hand to hold, and still others love by spending time with a person. I feed people.

I'll never stop loving Gabe in this way. He will always be the first one I want to share the perfect bite with. I'll always look to him eagerly while he chews, hoping that he feels it. He may not ever be brought to tears by food, or have the desire to jump up on the table to scream the merits of a dish, or watch the puff pastry at the oven window, but I'll never stop trying. I'll hunch over our kitchen counter, brushing wisps of silver hair out of my wrinkled eyes, carefully slicing the onions and thinking of him with each pungent ring that falls to the cutting board, happy to still be feeding and loving the both of us, well. Then he'll reach for my hand and join me at the table, loving me the way he knows best.

ALL OVER THE MEDITERRANEAN

TIMELINE

1 TO 3 DAYS IN ADVANCE

Make caraway syrup

Make dressing for carrot salad

Grate carrots

Season lamb

Make apricots and cardamom yogurt

Make carrot salad (reserve the cilantro until just before serving)

Make tzatziki

DINNER TIME

Make cocktails

Cook lamb, toast pitas, and assemble tostadas

PANTRY

4 lemons

Garlic

Kosher salt

Freshly ground black pepper

Ground coriander

Sweet paprika (smoked or regular)

Ground cumin

Dried oregano

Red pepper flakes

Caraway seeds

Extra-virgin olive oil

Champagne vinegar

Honey

Granulated sugar

1 stick cinnamon

Ground cinnamon

Ground cardamom

½ vanilla bean

Gin

GROCERY

1 cucumber

1 lime

8 ounces / 230 g carrots

½ fresh red jalapeño pepper

1 bunch fresh flat-leaf parsley

1 package or small bunch fresh dill

1 bunch fresh cilantro

1 package or small bunch fresh mint

1 head romaine

1 small tomato

1 hothouse cucumber

½ cup / 60 g crumbled feta

1 pint plain whole-milk Greek yogurt

8 ounces / 230 g ground lamb

2 pita breads (preferably without pockets)

¼ cup / 40 g pitted Kalamata olives

8 ounces / 230 g dried apricots

¼ cup / 30 g Marcona (or regular) almonds

1 cup / 240 ml dry white wine

Gordon's Cup WITH Caraway

This cocktail came about when I had cucumbers, limes, and gin in the house and knew I wanted them together. But the drink needed something else to elevate it without making it fussy: caraway. Caraway syrup adds a bit of warmth to this bright, simple drink.

SERVES 2

CARAWAY SYRUP

1 tablespoon caraway seeds

½ cup / 120 ml water

½ cup / 100 g granulated sugar

GORDON'S CUP

10 to 12 thin slices cucumber

1 ounce / 30 ml caraway simple syrup

2 tablespoons freshly squeezed lime juice (from ½ large lime)

3 ounces / 90 ml gin (Hendrick's is lovely here)

Pinch of kosher salt

For the caraway syrup:

Toast the seeds in a saucepan over medium heat. Once fragrant, after about 2 to 3 minutes, add the water and sugar. Bring to a boil and cook for 1 minute. Remove the pan from the heat and let cool. Once cool, strain the caraway seeds from the syrup. Syrup will keep in the fridge for up to 2 weeks.

For the Gordon's Cup:

Divide the cucumber and caraway syrup between two glasses. Muddle them gently until fragrant and the cucumber is broken. Stir half the lime juice and gin into each glass.

Top with ice and a pinch of salt.

Fresh Carrot Salad

I know picnics and winter aren't synonymous, but I do tend to think of picnicking when I eat this salad. I'm particularly fond of the gentle wisp of cinnamon in the salad that's warming without making the carrots taste too sweet. Add more jalapeño if you like heat.

SERVES 2

2 tablespoons extra-virgin olive oil

2 tablespoons freshly squeezed lemon juice

1 garlic clove, minced

¾ teaspoon ground coriander

⅛ teaspoon ground cinnamon

½ teaspoon sweet paprika (smoked or regular)

½ fresh red jalapeño pepper, seeded and very thinly sliced

½ teaspoon kosher salt

8 ounces / 230 g carrots, grated (2 to 2½ cups)

½ cup / 15 g chopped fresh cilantro

Whisk together the olive oil, lemon juice, garlic, coriander, cinnamon, paprika, red jalapeño, and salt. Toss the dressing with grated carrots and cilantro.

This salad can be made 1 day in advance; I'd advise adding the cilantro just before serving to keep it fresh looking.

Mediterranean Lamb Tostadas

I'm not sure what to call these. The tostada has Mexican roots, while the lamb nods toward Morocco and the rest feels Greek. It's a confused tostada, but it is satisfying without being heavy. Use pita chips instead to make confused nachos.

SERVES 2

SEASONED LAMB

½ teaspoon freshly grated lemon zest

1½ teaspoons ground cumin

½ teaspoon ground coriander

¾ teaspoon kosher salt

¼ teaspoon freshly ground black pepper

½ teaspoon dried oregano

⅛ teaspoon ground cinnamon

1 tablespoon chopped fresh mint

1 garlic clove, minced

Pinch of red pepper flakes

8 ounces / 230 g ground lamb

2 tablespoons extra-virgin olive oil

TOSTADAS

2 tablespoons extra-virgin olive oil, divided

2 pita breads (preferably without pockets)

2 cups / 60 g shredded romaine

1 small tomato, diced

¼ hothouse cucumber, diced

½ cup / 60 g crumbled feta

¼ cup / 40 g chopped, pitted Kalamata olives

¼ cup / 5 g chopped fresh mint

¼ cup / 5 g chopped fresh flat-leaf parsley

1 recipe Tzatziki Dressing **(recipe follows)**

For the seasoned lamb:

One to 2 days before you plan to eat, mix together the lemon zest, cumin, coriander, salt, pepper, oregano, cinnamon, mint, garlic, and red pepper flakes in a medium bowl. Add the lamb and gently combine with clean hands. Store, covered, in the refrigerator until ready to cook.

Coat the bottom of a medium skillet with the olive oil and place over medium-high heat. Add the lamb, breaking it up as it cooks. Sauté until cooked through, about 8 minutes.

For the tostadas:

In a large skillet on medium-high heat, add 1 tablespoon oil. Add 1 pita and fry on both sides until crisp, about 1 to 2 minutes per side, watching closely. Repeat with the remaining 1 tablespoon oil and the second pita.

Place each crisp pita on a dinner plate and top with half each of the lamb, romaine, tomato, cucumber, feta, olives, mint, and parsley. Serve with a generous topping of tzatziki.

Tzatziki Dressing

Because I can't get enough of Tzatziki, I decided to turn it into a dressing so I could could pour it on everything. Any leftover dressing can be served over grilled chicken or steak or used as a dip for fresh vegetables. That is, IF there are leftovers.

MAKES 1½ CUPS / 360 G

1 cup / 230 g plain whole-milk Greek yogurt

1 cup / 115 g finely diced hothouse cucumber

½ tablespoon Champagne vinegar

1 tablespoon freshly squeezed lemon juice

2 tablespoons extra-virgin olive oil

1 garlic clove, minced

2 tablespoons chopped fresh dill

2 tablespoons chopped fresh mint

¼ teaspoon honey

¼ teaspoon kosher salt

Pinch of freshly ground black pepper

Whisk together the yogurt, cucumber, Champagne vinegar, lemon juice, olive oil, garlic, dill, mint, honey, salt, and freshly ground black pepper. Taste and adjust the seasonings if you'd like.

Tzatziki can be made up to 2 days ahead and stored, covered, in the refrigerator.

Stewed Apricots WITH Cardamom Yogurt AND Marcona Almonds

Just because you are opting to eat a lighter dinner does not mean you must miss out on something sweet. This dessert, which I also happen to love for breakfast, is deceptively satisfying and decadent.

SERVES 2

STEWED APRICOTS

1 stick cinnamon

1 cup / 240 ml dry white wine

2 tablespoons freshly squeezed lemon juice

1 tablespoon honey

½ vanilla bean, split

8 ounces / 230 g dried apricots

CARDAMOM YOGURT

1 cup / 230 g plain whole-milk Greek yogurt

1 tablespoon honey

⅛ teaspoon ground cardamom

TO SERVE

¼ cup / 35 g Marcona (or regular) almonds, toasted (see technique on page 11)

For the stewed apricots:

In a medium saucepan over medium heat, toast the cinnamon stick until fragrant, about 2 minutes. Carefully add the wine, lemon juice, honey, vanilla bean, and apricots. Bring to a boil and then reduce the heat. Cover and simmer on low for 30 minutes, or until the apricots are tender and falling apart.

Let the apricots cool in the pan, covered. Serve while the apricots are slightly warm or at room temperature, or store, covered, for up to 1 week once the apricots have come to room temperature.

For the cardamom yogurt:

Whisk together the yogurt, honey, and ground cardamom. The yogurt can be made up to 3 days ahead and stored, covered, in the refrigerator.

To serve:

Divide the yogurt between two dishes. Top with stewed apricots and finish with almonds.

Dinner and a Movie

Sun-Dried Tomato Caesar
with Parmesan Croutons

241

White Pizza with Sausage
and Pickled Peppers

243

Salted Peanut Toffee Popcorn

244

I was in college and dating Gabe when I noticed, for the first time, my parents holding hands. Gabe and I had just started dating, and each touch felt electric; even an accidental brush of the arm had me longing for more. But I wondered, if Gabe and I were to get married, what would holding his hand feel like thirty years from then, well into our marriage as my parents were?

When I asked them, my dad replied, "It feels more of gratitude and comfort than electricity. Although it still feels that way too at times." He gazed sweetly at my mom. "Gratitude?" I thought. It seemed a very lovely answer, but I didn't really get it.

And I don't get it until I am curled up with my husband on the couch thirteen years later.

We relegate this date night as movie night, and the casualness of the date determines the food. The salad sits on the table just briefly before we descend upon it; we intended to wait for the pizza, but the pungent sun-dried tomato dressing weakens us.

"I don't think we'll be making out tonight," I joke as the dressing's intense garlic flavor fills my mouth.

"A little garlic never scared me," he said with a flirtatious smile.

Later, full from the creamy white pizza, studded with more garlic, we settle into the couch with our beer and the sweet and salty crunch of toffee-covered popcorn.

I try to focus, but I feel guilty for using our date night to watch a movie. We can watch a movie any night; shouldn't we use our date nights for deep conversation that builds our marriage rather than mindlessly watching a movie? But all those feelings of guilt fade when I tuck deep into Gabe as the movie begins. My head falls into position in the crevice of his arm and chest and, like a favorite chair, the more I find rest in its comfort, the more it molds to the shape of my body.

I think of my dad's response all those years ago: gratitude. Yes, I totally get it.

As the movie continues, I feel grateful that he is the one who sits next to me on the couch.

When we were dating, we both set out to prove something to the other. In the beginning especially, I rarely saw him without my makeup on and smelling as if I had just walked through a field of wild flowers. I wasn't trying to be something I wasn't, but I definitely wasn't showing him the not-so-pretty parts that you can't hide in a marriage. Then, everything about the other person was exciting, especially touch.

While a kiss from Gabe doesn't always leave me numb now, it's marked with something deeper, better. He's smelled my morning breath, and yet he's still here. He's loved me in spite of my defunct skills of keeping the laundry pile from towering. He has watched my belly expand and (mostly) contract through three pregnancies, and yet he is still here.

In Timothy Keller's book *The Meaning of Marriage*, he writes, "Only when you maintain love for someone when it is not thrilling can you be said to be actually loving a person." Marriage reveals an often unthrilling reality. But actions maintain love, not feelings; we work through the seasons when we feel we have to fight for our love, and we rejoice in the times when it comes easy.

After many years of riding the waves of marriage, our love feels more real, deeper, and more sustaining. I love Gabe in spite of his flaws, and he loves me in spite of mine. And although those sparks in the early days were nice, I'd take his touch, the gratitude it induces in me, and the love we now have over the fireworks any day.

TIMELINE

1 TO 3 DAYS IN ADVANCE

Make salad dressing

Make ricotta (if desired)

Make pickled peppers

Make pizza dough

Make popcorn

DATE DAY

Make croutons

Brown sausage and prep
pizza ingredients

DINNER TIME

Place dough ball out to rise

Toss salad

Bake pizza

GROCERY

1 head romaine

8 ounces / 230 g Italian roasting peppers
or colorful mini peppers

1 red jalapeño pepper

3 ounces / 90 g fresh mozzarella

Whole milk for ricotta (page 17) or use
store-bought ricotta

2 ounces / 60 g Parmesan

Heavy whipping cream for ricotta (page
17) or use store-bought ricotta

1 (6-ounce / 170 g) hot Italian sausage link

½ cup / 130 g sun-dried tomatoes

¼ cup / 40 g pickled sweet peppers,
homemade (page 21) or store-bought

Fresh good-quality rustic loaf

1 (8-ounce / 230 g) ball (½ recipe) olive oil
pizza dough (page 14) or store-bought
dough

¼ cup / 65 g popcorn kernels

1 cup / 140 g roasted, salted peanuts

PANTRY

2 lemons

Garlic

Unsalted butter

Kosher salt

Freshly ground black pepper

Flake salt or smoked flake salt

Dried oregano

Extra-virgin olive oil

Olive oil

Canola oil

Apple cider vinegar

Dark brown sugar

Corn syrup

Maple syrup

All-purpose flour

Active dry yeast

Granulated sugar

Sun-Dried Tomato Caesar WITH Parmesan Croutons

I love a bright and tangy salad with my pizza. This is a riff on a classic. Even though Gabe is not a fan of tomatoes (or salad), he approves of this recipe.

SERVES 2

DRESSING

¼ cup / 65 g roughly chopped sun-dried tomatoes

½ cup / 10 g freshly grated Parmesan

2 tablespoons / 30 g freshly squeezed lemon juice

1 garlic clove

Pinch of kosher salt

2 tablespoons water

½ cup / 120 ml extra-virgin olive oil

Freshly ground black pepper

CROUTONS

3 tablespoons olive oil

½ cup / 10 g freshly grated Parmesan

½ teaspoon kosher salt

2 cups ½-inch cubes rustic bread

SALAD

½ head romaine, left whole or chopped

Parmesan shavings

¼ cup / 65 g sun-dried tomatoes

For the dressing:

In a food processor, combine the sun-dried tomatoes, Parmesan, lemon juice, garlic, pinch of salt, and water. Process for 1 minute. Stream in the olive oil and blend for 10 seconds. It won't be homogenous, but it will be delicious.

Taste and add more salt and pepper, if desired. Makes 1 cup / 240 ml of dressing, which will keep in the refrigerator for up to 1 week. Whisk vigorously before using if it separates.

For the croutons:

Preheat the oven to 400°F and position a rack in the top of the oven. Line a baking sheet with parchment paper.

Mix the oil, Parmesan, and salt in a large mixing bowl until a paste is formed. Add the cubed bread and mix well with a spatula, until all the bread is well coated with the sticky Parmesan paste.

Turn the bread onto the prepared baking sheet.

Bake for 10 minutes, stir, and rotate the pan. Bake for another 10 to 12 minutes, or until golden brown and crisp.

To assemble the salad:

Toss the lettuce with the dressing or drizzle over the top. Finish with shaved Parmesan, sun-dried tomatoes, and croutons.

White Pizza with Sausage and Pickled Peppers

We live down the street from Delancey, the epic pizza restaurant owned by Molly Wizenberg (Orangette.com) and her husband, Brandon. We are lucky to call those two friends, and even luckier to eat their pizza on a regular occasion. This is my version of my favorite pizza at Delancey. They don't always have the pickled peppers, but when they do you can be sure they go on top of my pie. At home, I also love adding fresh arugula after the pizza emerges from the oven. Other versions include roasted corn and fresh basil in place of the sausage and pickled peppers; we've also been known to throw on some sautéed kale as well.

SERVES 2

1 (8-ounce / 230 g) ball (½ recipe) olive oil pizza dough (page 14) or store-bought dough

All-purpose flour, for the work surface

1 to 2 tablespoons extra-virgin olive oil

1 large garlic clove, thinly sliced

Kosher salt and freshly ground black pepper

3 ounces / 90 g fresh mozzarella, torn

⅓ cup / 70 g whole-milk ricotta, homemade (page 17) or store-bought

1 (6-ounce / 170 g) hot Italian sausage link, casings removed, browned, and crumbled

¼ cup / 40 g pickled sweet peppers, homemade (page 21) or store-bought

Position an oven rack on the very top rung of your oven. Place a pizza stone on the rack, if using. Preheat the oven to 450°F 45 to 60 minutes before you plan to bake the pizza. Move the rack to the top third of the oven when baking the pizza.

One hour before baking, remove the dough from the refrigerator and place on a well-floured countertop. After an hour, press out or roll out your dough to a 10-inch round. Place the dough on a flour-dusted pizza peel or the back of a baking sheet dusted with flour. Brush with olive oil, top with garlic, and sprinkle with salt and pepper. Add the mozzarella and ricotta and then the sausage and pickled sweet peppers.

Bake for 12 minutes, rotating halfway through. Turn the broiler to high and broil for 3 to 5 minutes, or until the cheese is bubbling and the crust is cooked through and deeply bronzed around the edges. Broiling at the end gives the crust a nice char that mimics the effect of a wood-fire oven.

Note: With this dough, the thinner you roll it, the crispier your pizza will be. It's a great dough for stretching and can be rolled or stretched to the point where you could read a book through it.

Using a pizza stone and preheating the oven for a long time also helps to get a good, crisp crust.

Salted Peanut Toffee Popcorn

There is no greater snack for snuggling up on the couch at the end of a hearty meal.

SERVES 4 TO 6

1 tablespoon canola oil

¼ cup / 65 g popcorn kernels (6 to 7 cups popped)

⅓ cup / 75 g unsalted butter

¾ cup / 150 g dark brown sugar

½ teaspoon kosher salt

2 tablespoons corn syrup

¼ cup / 65 g maple syrup

1 cup / 140 g roasted, salted peanuts

1 teaspoon flake salt or smoked flake salt, for finishing

Place the oil and popcorn in a large pot and cover with a lid. Place over medium-high heat. Shake the pot occasionally over the burner until the popping mostly subsides, about 2 seconds between pops. Pour the popcorn into a very large bowl.

Preheat the oven to 250°F. Line a baking sheet with parchment paper.

In a medium saucepan over medium-high heat, melt the butter with the brown sugar, salt, corn syrup, and maple syrup and bring to a boil. Gently boil for 5 minutes, stirring occasionally. Add the peanuts to the toffee and then drizzle over the popcorn. Stir carefully to evenly coat the popcorn. Spread onto the prepared baking sheet and bake for 1 hour, stirring and rotating the pan halfway through. Sprinkle with flake salt to finish and then let cool to room temperature.

The toffee popcorn can be made up to 3 days ahead. Store in an airtight container once thoroughly cooled.

A Flemish Feast

Bitter Greens with Mustard Vinaigrette
251

Belgian Frites
252

Flemish Beef Stew
254

Yeasted Belgian Waffles with
Ice Cream and Hot Fudge
257

I was on a mission. With less than twenty-four hours in Belgium and a long list of things that I needed to eat, there was little time to waste. While others may travel for monuments, architecture, or museums, I go for the food. Sure, I visit those sites too, but only between meals. I was determined, pushing through the bitter cold and an already full stomach in order to check off the items on my list: waffles, chocolate, beer, and fries, the necessities while in Belgium.

Belgium was a side trip taken while I spent a week in the Netherlands with my grandparents and a few other family members. I had come to visit the birthplace of my grandfather and to celebrate the marching band my great-grandfather had begun ninety years earlier. But I was there without my husband.

At Gabe's urging I had asked my grandparents if I could go with them on this trip, seizing the opportunity to go with my grandfather to his hometown for what was most likely his last trip home. I initially scoffed at Gabe's pleading, knowing full well that this would then leave him at home with three little kids for an entire week. I don't think I would have been as inclined as he was to push me out the door, but I knew he was doing it because he loved me, recognizing how important this trip was for me and sacrificing his desires for my joy.

So I went. The sacrifice Gabe made in order for me to be there made each moment of that trip more meaningful and gave me the desire not to waste a minute of it. When we arrived in Belgium late in the evening, I quickly dumped my bags on my bed in the hotel room, bundled in warm layers, and set out with my list in hand, determined to eat my way through the intoxicating country.

Following the curve of the iced-over canal, I traipsed along the cobbled streets in search of the five-century-old pub I had read about. When I finally found myself standing at its door, only to see the sign that read "closed," I placed my hand on the ancient, craggy stone that lined the door frame and continued to the next stop.

The painful chill in the air forced me into a nearby pub, which greeted me with a Belgian white beer that made all the others I had tried back home seem bland in comparison. Overwhelmed by the novel that was the menu, I asked the waiter for his advice on what to eat. The waiter offered his suggestion, and, only moments later, I met Flemish stew. I haven't been the same since.

The beef had stewed in a dark Belgian

ale along with onions and a few herbs; it was complex and hearty and chased away the bitter cold. And when I thought the meal couldn't get any better, I took a bite from my heaping bowl of fries with tangy mayonnaise for dipping.

I reveled at my classic Belgian dinner, but I longed more than anything to share it with my husband. In fact, there were countless times throughout the course of that week when I wanted so badly to experience this with him. The trip showed me my family's birthplace and answered many questions about my upbringing and who I am; it revealed new places and tastes that inspired and invigorated me. The trip changed me deeply, and not to have my husband, my best friend, there with me—well, I felt like I was missing something.

Gabe and I had tried being friends for quite a while before we jumped into dating. Everyone around us knew we were only kidding ourselves, but we insisted that we were "just good friends."

Starting our relationship as a friendship allowed us to be free of odd expectations that exist when dating. Our first date included a walk to the 7-Eleven for Slurpees in the middle of winter. Such an odd, simple activity, but somehow he made it fun. Now that I think about it, there may have been other people there, but for me it was only Gabe. That night I went to bed with a smile, and when I woke up it was still there.

When Ivy, our third and youngest, was one we somehow managed to steal away for an overnight trip. As usual the trip was based around a meal, and, although the food did not disappoint, what sticks out in my memory from that trip is the moment I looked into his eyes and remembered that nineteen-year-old with the aviators and pea coat.

In the midst of life, careers, having kids, and surviving, I had lost sight of him. I had forgotten that, before he was the father of my children and the guy I happen to live with, before he was my husband, he was my best friend. And he continues to be. In that moment, I looked at him and saw the man I fell in love with. It wasn't that I had fallen out of love with him—far from it. I just realized that, without even knowing it, I hadn't stopped to really see him and remember the basis of our marriage: our friendship.

As a young woman falling in love with a young man and imagining the possibility of spending forever with him, it was memories like that of our night at 7-Eleven that made my decision to say yes to his proposal so easy. If we could have the time of our lives on a freezing winter's walk to a convenience store, then surely forever with this man was an easy decision.

Gabe's ability to laugh at himself and pull me into it right along with him has proven vital in our marriage. Whereas I tend toward the serious, he remains even keeled and helps rein me in when necessary, which I'll admit, is quite often. I may roll my eyes at his antics, but they interrupt my frazzled state that so often accompanies daily life with three little ones and they remind me that sometimes all you can do is laugh.

Someday it will just be the two of us again. The kids will be grown and will eventually move out of the house. What will be left is us and our friendship. It's the constant in our marriage that takes time and energy to cultivate. It's not sustainable on its own and will not wait for us to find it. Without nourishing it, it deteriorates and leaves little behind.

A marriage with friendship at its core is what left me pining for my husband in a foreign country, wanting so badly to be sharing a bite of Flemish stew with him. To be lingering over conversation and Belgian beer.

I want my best friend alongside me no matter where I am. With him, I am a better person; without him, there's something missing.

TIMELINE

1 TO 3 DAYS IN ADVANCE

Make salad dressing

Make Flemish stew

Make waffle batter

Make hot fudge

DINNER TIME

Warm stew

Soak and fry frites

Dress salad

Make waffles

GROCERY

1 head frisée or other bitter green, such as kale, endive, or arugula

1 bunch fresh flat-leaf parsley

1 package or small bunch fresh thyme

1 large russet potato (about 1 pound)

½ pint / 225 g vanilla ice cream

1 pint / 470 ml heavy whipping cream

1½ pounds / 680 g beef chuck roast or well-marbled stew meat

Malt vinegar

Lyle's Golden Syrup or corn syrup

Cocoa powder

6 ounces / 170 g bittersweet chocolate

2 cups / 470 ml Belgian ale (such as Chimay)

PANTRY

1 large yellow onion

Garlic

Unsalted butter

Whole milk

Eggs

Kosher salt

Freshly ground black pepper

Dried bay leaves

Grainy mustard

Dijon mustard

Honey

Red wine vinegar

Extra-virgin olive oil

Vegetable oil

Mayonnaise

All-purpose flour

Dark brown sugar

Granulated sugar

Vanilla extract

Active dry yeast

Bitter Greens WITH Mustard Vinaigrette

Tangy vinaigrette cuts through the pleasant bitterness of the greens in this simple salad—a perfect way to start or end this hearty meal.

SERVES 2

1 tablespoon grainy mustard

1 teaspoon honey

2 tablespoons red wine vinegar

2 tablespoons extra-virgin olive oil

Kosher salt and freshly ground black pepper

2 cups / 60 g roughly chopped bitter greens, such as frisée, kale, endive, or arugula

Whisk together the mustard, honey, vinegar, and olive oil. Add salt and pepper to taste. The dressing can be made up to 3 days in advance and then refrigerated until ready to use. Toss the greens with enough dressing to coat. Taste and add more dressing, if desired. Serve immediately.

Belgian Frites

If the fuss of frying sounds too daunting, do not feel bad about serving the stew with simple roasted potatoes. It will be equally appreciated and delicious, I assure you. But if you do take the plunge, the secret to tender and crispy fries is to fry them twice: initially at a low temperature to cook them internally and then again at a higher temperature to give color and to crisp them. Serve these with malt vinegar–spiked mayonnaise as they do in Belgium.

SERVES 2

1 large russet potato, peeled

Vegetable oil, for frying

Kosher salt

Malt vinegar, for serving

Best-quality mayonnaise, for serving

Cut the potatoes into matchsticks about ¼ inch thick. Place in cold water for at least 20 minutes to remove some of the starch and to keep the fries from browning.

Fill a large heavy-bottomed pot at least 3 inches deep with oil, leaving 5 inches from the top of the pot, as the oil bubbles up rapidly while frying. Heat the oil to 325°F.

With a clean kitchen towel or paper towels, dry the potatoes thoroughly. Line a sheet tray with paper towels or a brown paper bag to absorb the extra oil after frying.

Working in small batches, fry until the potatoes are cooked through but not colored, about 5 minutes.

Remove to the prepared sheet tray.

When all the fries have been through the first fry, heat the oil up to 375°F and fry once more until they are deep golden all over, 3 to 5 minutes longer. Remove to the sheet tray and sprinkle liberally with salt.

The fries can sit after the first fry for an hour or two. Serve immediately after the second fry.

For vinegar mayo, I combine about 1 tablespoon malt vinegar or apple cider vinegar with ¼ cup / 60 g mayonnaise.

Flemish Beef Stew

This national dish of Belgium was one that was created to use cheap cuts of beef and flat beer. It is hearty, satisfying, and quick to throw together; the finished dish is very meaty, has very little liquid, and is intensely flavored. If you are out of the house all day, a crockpot works well for this.

This stew improves with a day in the fridge, so plan for some great leftovers or make the day before you eat.

SERVES 4 (OR IN OUR CASE, 2 WITH LEFTOVERS)

1½ pounds / 680 g beef chuck roast or well-marbled stew meat, cut into 1-inch cubes

1½ teaspoons kosher salt, divided

½ teaspoon freshly ground black pepper

2 tablespoons all-purpose flour

3 tablespoons unsalted butter

1 tablespoon olive oil

1 large yellow onion, thinly sliced

3 garlic cloves, chopped

2 cups / 470 ml Belgian ale (such as Chimay)

2 dried bay leaves

1 tablespoon chopped fresh parsley

1 teaspoon fresh thyme leaves

2 tablespoons red wine vinegar

2 tablespoons dark brown sugar

1 tablespoon Dijon mustard

In a large bowl, sprinkle the beef with 1 teaspoon salt, the pepper, and the flour. Toss to coat.

Add the butter and oil to a large pot or Dutch oven over high heat. When the butter has melted and bubbled and the pan is very hot, add the meat, cooking in two batches so as not to crowd the pan. Cook for 5 to 6 minutes per batch, turning over halfway through, until deeply browned on both sides. Remove the meat and set aside. Reduce the heat to medium low and add the onions and the remaining ½ teaspoon salt. Cook for 8 to 10 minutes, until golden and tender, stirring occasionally to scrape up the deeply flavored bits on the bottom of the pan while the onions sauté. Add the garlic and cook 2 minutes more.

Place the meat back in the pot and add the beer, herbs, vinegar, and brown sugar and bring the stew to a simmer over low heat. Place a wooden spoon in the pot and cover, with the spoon handle venting the lid a little. Simmer on the stove top for 3 hours, or until the meat is tender.

Alternatively, you may cook in the oven, venting the lid, at 325°F for 3 hours.

To finish, stir in the Dijon mustard and add salt and pepper to taste.

Stew can be made up to 2 days ahead and warmed over low heat on the stove top.

Yeasted Belgian Waffles WITH Ice Cream AND Hot Fudge

You can easily halve this batter, but I always make the full recipe and then plan to have waffles the next morning. They also freeze well and toast up nicely in the toaster or oven.

SERVES 4 TO 6

WAFFLES

½ cup / 115 g unsalted butter

1¾ cups / 410 ml whole milk

1 teaspoon vanilla extract

2 eggs

2 cups / 280 g all-purpose flour

⅓ cup / 60 g granulated sugar

1½ teaspoons kosher salt

1½ teaspoons active dry yeast

TO SERVE:

⅔ cup / Bittersweet Hot Fudge (recipe follows)

½ pint / 225 g vanilla ice cream (1 cup)

For the waffles:

In a small saucepan over medium heat, melt the butter and let cool for 10 minutes.

In a medium bowl, whisk together the milk, vanilla, and eggs and then slowly whisk in the melted butter.

In a large bowl, whisk together the flour, sugar, salt, and yeast. Pour in the wet ingredients. Mix until just combined.

Place in a container that leaves room for expansion and cover. Refrigerate overnight or for up to 4 days. If you are rushed, you can make this an hour in advance, but the flavor and texture is greatly improved after a good long rest in the fridge.

To serve:

Remove the batter from the fridge when you are ready to use and cook using your favorite waffle iron. Serve the waffles with the hot fudge and vanilla ice cream.

Note: Waffles can be frozen, well sealed, for up to 1 month. Pop them in the toaster for a quick weekday breakfast.

A FLEMISH FEAST

Bittersweet Hot Fudge

Hot fudge needs a bit of syrup to give it the classic soft, chewy texture. Most recipes call for corn syrup, and you can use that here if you'd like, but I prefer the taste of Lyle's Golden Syrup better. You can find it in many grocery stores or order it online. It's a syrup made from sugar, and it has a lovely amber color. The flavor is richer and more complex than corn syrup, while at the same time giving your hot fudge the perfect classic texture.

MAKES 2¼ CUPS

1½ cups / 360 ml heavy whipping cream

⅓ cup / 100 g Lyle's Golden Syrup or corn syrup

2 tablespoons dark brown sugar

¼ cup / 20 g cocoa powder

6 ounces / 170 g bittersweet chocolate, roughly chopped

2 tablespoons unsalted butter

¼ teaspoon kosher salt

1 teaspoon vanilla extract

In a saucepan, combine the cream, syrup, sugar, and cocoa powder. Bring to a boil, reduce the heat, and let simmer for 5 minutes, stirring occasionally.

Remove the pan from the heat and stir in the chocolate, butter, salt, and vanilla. Once the chocolate and the butter have melted, strain the entire mixture to ensure that no pesky cocoa powder clumps remain.

Let cool to room temperature. If you are making this in advance, refrigerate until ready to use and then gently reheat on the stove or in the microwave until the hot fudge is pourable. Store in the fridge for up to 2 weeks.

A Little French

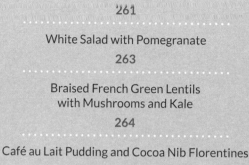

Grapefruit 75
261

White Salad with Pomegranate
263

Braised French Green Lentils
with Mushrooms and Kale
264

Café au Lait Pudding and Cocoa Nib Florentines
266

As I read over the ingredient list, I wonder if it's the same recipe I've made so many times before. It has been a while since I last made it, but I remember the flavor being so rich and full that I think there must be more to it than what I see in front of me. In spite of my skepticism, I slice the shallots and brush off the little clumps of dirt that cling to the mushrooms' tender flesh, and the familiarity of the recipe comes back as the butter melts and then browns in the pan. The ingredient list is simple, but the technique gives the dish its complexity.

The butter browns and the resulting flavor is nutty and more intense than that of melted butter. Shallots melt into a golden slump before I add the mushrooms and then cook until they match the nearly black earth they came from; the mushrooms almost look burnt, but their intensity gives a soft smokiness and dark sweetness born out of patience and a pan that's not too hot.

These meager lentils are comforting and nutritious without being obnoxiously so, simple and elegantly rustic: the best compliment when it comes to food, I think. It's simple food, my favorite, where a few seasonal ingredients come together in a way that highlights their unique flavor. They are all better for being together.

There are times, like with the lentils, when I forget just how effective simplicity can be. I mean, I've even complicated many of our date nights. There really doesn't have to be a cocktail, appetizer, side dish, main course, and dessert every week. Although most weeks I am eager for the presence of both a cocktail and dessert, the meal doesn't need to be one that starts days before the date day. In fact, the date doesn't even need to be a meal. We just really like to eat, so it works for us. But what if it was just a bit of time devoted to each other? What if it was as simple as turning off gadgets and TVs and tuning in to each other? What if it was simply two people looking into each other's eyes? Simple, and, yet after having been at this dating thing for a while, I would boldly proclaim that it's enough to solve a whole slew of complex issues.

Sometimes our dinners are multiple courses that require forethought in order for dinner to be on the table before midnight, and other times they are made up of a few simple ingredients put together in a way that creates a beautifully complex, yet comforting dish. Either way, it always ends up with us being together and connecting. Relationships can be complicated, but making a bit of time for each other is really quite simple.

TIMELINE

1 TO 3 DAYS IN ADVANCE

Make pudding

Make florentines

Cook lentils

DATE DAY

Make salad

DINNER TIME

Make cocktails

Cook lentil dish

GROCERY

1 grapefruit

2 ounces / 60 g celeriac

1 tart apple

1 small fennel bulb

1 small leek

1 shallot

8 ounces / 230 g assorted mushrooms
(such as cremini, porcini, and button)

½ bunch kale

2 ounces / 60 g aged white Cheddar (such
as Beecher's Flagship)

Parmesan (optional)

1 pint / 470 ml heavy whipping cream

¼ cup / 10 g pomegranate seeds

½ cup / 80 g dry French green lentils

¼ cup / 30 g cocoa nibs

Champagne

Bitters (optional)

Dry white wine

PANTRY

2 lemons

Garlic

Eggs

Unsalted butter

Extra-virgin olive oil

Kosher salt

Flake salt

Freshly ground black pepper

3 cups / 710 ml low-sodium chicken or
vegetable stock, homemade (page 18)
or store-bought

Coffee or espresso beans

Dark brown sugar

Granulated sugar

Cornstarch

All-purpose flour

Maple syrup

Vanilla extract

Gin

Grapefruit 75

The classic French 75, a bubbly gin drink with lemon juice and simple syrup, inspired this simple cocktail. It's best when everything is cold. I like to use a nice citrusy bitters here.

SERVES 2

3 ounces / 90 ml gin

1 ounce / 30 ml freshly squeezed grapefruit juice

8 ounces / 240 ml Champagne

Bitters (optional)

Grapefruit peel, for garnish

Divide the gin, grapefruit juice, and Champagne between two Champagne flutes or coupes. Finish with a couple drops of bitters and a twist of grapefruit.

White Salad with Pomegranate

Some of my favorite salad creations come out of the lack of seasonal produce available in the winter. I find the restriction forces me to be particularly creative. Every year, I settle on a version of this salad with stunning white produce cut very thinly and simply dressed. In this recipe, I add pomegranate seeds for a striking color contrast and sharp Cheddar for richness. In the past, I've left out the Cheddar and added crème fraîche to the dressing.

SERVES 2

1 tablespoon freshly squeezed lemon juice

½ teaspoon kosher salt

1½ tablespoons extra-virgin olive oil

2 ounces / 60 g celeriac, cut into matchsticks (about ¾ cup)

½ tart apple, cut into matchsticks (about ¾ cup)

¼ fennel bulb, thinly sliced (about ½ cup)

½ small leek, thinly sliced (white and light green parts) (about ¼ cup)

2 ounces / 60 g aged white Cheddar (such as Beecher's Flagship), cut into matchsticks (about ½ cup)

¼ cup / 10 g pomegranate seeds

Flake salt, for finishing

Freshly ground black pepper, for finishing

In a large bowl, whisk together the lemon juice, salt, and olive oil. Add the celeriac, apple, fennel, leek, and Cheddar. (I use a mandoline to make easy work of cutting the apple and celeriac into matchsticks.) Toss well to combine. Transfer to a serving dish and finish with pomegranate seeds, flake salt, and freshly ground black pepper.

The salad can be made 4 to 6 hours ahead and stored, covered, in the refrigerator.

Note: Leftover vegetables should be saved for making vegetable stock (page 18).

Braised French Green Lentils WITH Mushrooms AND Kale

This is one of my favorite winter meals. There's a good bit of nutrition in this bowl, as well as cream, to make it feel indulgent and comforting on a cold night. We top ours with a golden-yolked sunny-side-up egg because I think so much can be improved upon by the addition of an egg.

SERVES 2

½ cup / 80 g dry French green lentils

3 cups / 710 ml low-sodium chicken or vegetable stock (page 18)

3 tablespoons unsalted butter

1 small shallot, diced (¼ cup / 40 g)

8 ounces / 230 g assorted mushrooms (such as cremini, porcini, and button), cleaned and diced

1 teaspoon kosher salt, divided

3 garlic cloves, minced

¼ cup / 60 ml dry white wine

¾ cup / 180 ml heavy whipping cream

1 tablespoon extra-virgin olive oil

2 eggs

½ bunch kale, stems removed and chopped into quarter-size pieces

Parmesan, for finishing (optional)

Rinse lentils thoroughly. Place the chicken stock in a medium pot with the lentils and bring to a boil. Reduce to a simmer and cook, uncovered, for 25 to 30 minutes, until al dente. Drain, and if you're making the lentils ahead of time, pour them out onto a baking sheet to cool quickly. This step can be done 1 to 2 days ahead, and the lentils can be stored, covered, in the refrigerator.

In a large skillet over medium-high heat, add the butter and brown it (see page 11). Then add the shallot and cook for 1 minute.

Add the mushrooms and ½ teaspoon salt in an even layer to cover the bottom of the pan. Cook the mushrooms until deeply caramelized, about 7 to 9 minutes, stirring occasionally.

Add the garlic and cook for 1 minute. Deglaze the pan with white wine, scraping up all the flavorful brown bits from the bottom of the pan. Reduce the wine until no liquid remains.

Decrease the heat to medium-low and add the cream. Bring to a simmer and reduce for 2 minutes, then add the cooked lentils and remaining ½ teaspoon salt. Cover the pan with a lid and simmer for 5 minutes.

Meanwhile, prepare your eggs. I like mine sunny-side up so the yolk helps to sauce the lentils. In a nonstick skillet over medium heat, add 1 tablespoon oil. When the pan is nice and hot, crack in the eggs and sprinkle with salt. Turn down the heat and cook for 3 to 4 minutes, or until the whites are set. The eggs will do some carryover cooking, so turn off the heat before you think they are done. Remove the eggs to a clean plate to wait while you finish the lentils.

Add the chopped kale to the lentils. Cover and cook until tender but still bright green, about 3 to 5 minutes.

Taste and add more salt, if desired. Divide lentils into two bowls and top each with an egg. Finish with freshly grated Parmesan, if desired.

Café au Lait Pudding

This refreshingly rich dessert turns classic pudding into an adult favorite. Strong coffee mellowed with cool cream: a beautiful union.

SERVES 2

¾ cup / 180 ml heavy whipping cream

¼ cup / 60 ml espresso or strong-brewed coffee

2½ tablespoons / 30 g dark brown sugar

1 tablespoon cornstarch

Pinch of kosher salt

Whipped cream, for serving

Cocoa Nib Florentines (recipe follows), for serving

Place the cream and espresso in a small saucepan over medium heat.

In a small bowl, combine the brown sugar and cornstarch and stir until there are no lumps. Add the sugar mixture to the cream mixture and stir to combine. Bring to a boil and boil for 1 minute. Stir in the salt.

Divide the pudding between two bowls and cover the surface with plastic wrap to prevent a skin from forming.

Refrigerate until cold. Pudding can be made up to 2 days in advance.

Serve with whipped cream and florentines.

Cocoa Nib Florentines

A florentine is a lacy, sweet cookie with a crisp texture and almost caramel flavor. Classically they are made with almonds, but here I swap out the almonds and use cocoa nibs for a crunchy and bitter chocolate flavor.

MAKES 1 DOZEN

¼ cup / 30 g cocoa nibs

3 tablespoons all-purpose flour

¼ cup / 60 g unsalted butter, diced

6 tablespoons / 80 g granulated sugar

2 tablespoons heavy whipping cream

2 tablespoons maple syrup

½ teaspoon vanilla extract

¼ teaspoon kosher salt

Preheat the oven to 350°F.

Combine the cocoa nibs and flour in a medium bowl and set aside.

In a small saucepan, melt the butter, sugar, cream, and maple syrup together. Bring the ingredients to a full boil and boil for 1 minute. Remove the pan from the heat and carefully stir in the vanilla extract and salt.

Pour the butter mixture into the flour and cocoa nibs and whisk well to combine, making sure no lumps remain. It's a very wet batter that will thicken as it cools.

Line a baking sheet with parchment paper or a Silpat.

Scoop 1 teaspoon of batter per cookie (for 3-inch cookies) onto the prepared baking sheet, leaving about 3 to 4 inches between each cookie (they spread quite a bit). Bake for 8 to 10 minutes, or until the cookie is deeply golden.

Let cool on the tray for 5 minutes before transferring to a wire rack to cool completely. These cookies can be made up to 3 days in advance. Keep covered.

Note: Cocoa nibs are crushed roasted cocoa beans. They are nutty and crunchy while also buttery in texture. They aren't sweet, and yet they are reminiscent of bittersweet chocolate. I love them in salads, candied, and used as a dessert garnish or tossed into cookies for an unsweetened chocolate flavor. You can buy cocoa nibs in specialty grocery stores or online.

Renewal

Raclette with Butter and Shallot Poached
Potatoes, Charcuterie, Walnut Bread, and Apples
271

Salade Verte with Hazelnut Vinaigrette
274

Chocolat Chaud
274

Gabe, do you remember that night we ate melted cheese and drank Champagne at the bar? It was raining, I wore jeans and carried a few shopping bags from a little spree we had just had but probably shouldn't have had. We didn't plan to go out for a nice dinner, but the frigid wind and raindrops that felt like ice as they hit our faces forced us to tuck into the nearest restaurant. Opening the door to Le Pichet, we were welcomed by warmth and the scent of our future dinner.

As we nestled up to the bar, the older gentleman behind the counter greeted us and met our enthusiasm with recommendations that led us through glasses of Champagne, pâtés, warm Raclette pooling on our plate, piquant pickles, and chocolat chaud, the simple dessert that would continue to haunt me a decade later.

Just a few months before that dinner, we had made promises to each other and said "Yes!" to us on our wedding day. Now it's a decade later, and we're sitting around our dining room table while our three kids sleep upstairs, eating the same food we devoured on that cold, wet night; butter-coated potatoes, thin, fat-marbled pieces of ham, and little dimpled pickles to dip in a small copper pot filled with hot melted cheese. There's also the ruffly greens simply dressed and the tall glasses of Champagne with sparkling bubbles that tickle our noses as we drink, and soon there will be chocolat chaud with a generous dollop of cold cream, whipped just to the point where it holds its shape but melts into the chocolate as soon as they meet.

I don't remember exactly what I promised you in those vows, but I do remember that I made the biggest promise of all: that day after day, I would choose you. I would choose us. Barely old enough to drink and yet somehow I was smart enough to say yes to you. I'm so happy I did.

There are a few things that I'd like to add to what I said ten years ago because we've learned a lot, often as a result of our mistakes:

I will not keep a running list of things you've done wrong in order to prove myself right. Instead I will forgive freely.

I will ask for forgiveness too. Many, many times.

I will be vulnerable with you, let you in, and let you love me.

When you tell me I look beautiful, I will believe you. When you grab my butt in passing, I will try not to fret about how soft it is. Instead, I will be grateful that you still desire me and my butt.

I will finally recognize that you are not a mind reader; when you ask, "Is something wrong?" I will tell you the truth instead of hiding behind "I'm fine."

I will stop wishing you to be someone you're not. I will recognize that our differences make us pretty awesome, and, yes, sometimes they are maddening, but you're you and I'm me and we're we. And that's how it's supposed to be.

I promise to never stop learning about you and trying to know you better because you will change. When I said "I do," it meant that I will love you through the changes. I mean, when we were dating, you never watched football, and now our Sundays often involve the couch, the TV, and four quarters of a game I really don't understand and yet, I still love you.

I will lighten up and join you in your infectious laughter more often.

I will try to do a better job of putting aside my desires for yours. In the times I've done this, it has proven successful: it's how I learned to like sushi.

I will stop putting the pressure on you to make me happy. That's not your job (even though you do a pretty good job of it).

I will not judge you by the movies you watch nor by the food you eat, even when it's a bag of broken fortune cookies you got from the grocery store for $1.

I will notice you loving me in the small things.

I will stop taking it so personally when you put hot sauce all over the perfectly seasoned dinner I just made for you.

I will find your 30-minute coffee routine endearing rather than frustrating. Except when we are running late. Unlike my long-awaited coffee, I'm not strong enough to promise that. I also can't promise to stay away from bad puns, but seeing as you are the king of bad puns, I don't think this should be a problem.

I will look in your eyes more often. I don't remember exactly when it happened, but on a recent date night I stared into your eyes for a long time before I realized it had been a while since I'd done that. It's vulnerable and weird but important.

I will never stop dating you. There may not always be a fried chicken sandwich, beef tenderloin cooked to a pink perfection, creamy panna cotta topped with tangy roasted fruit, or even a homemade soda spiked with bourbon, but there will always be me, you, and time without distraction.

The main message remains the same: for as long as I'm alive, I will wake up every morning and say yes to you. Sometimes I will do it with a great joy pounding in my heart, and other times I will do it because of the promise we made so long ago. Regardless, I will continue to choose you over and over again.

TIMELINE

1 TO 3 DAYS IN ADVANCE
Make vinaigrette
Make chocolat chaud
Make walnut bread dough

DATE DAY
Bake walnut bread
Make butter-braised potatoes

DINNER TIME
Open Champagne
Toss salad
Assemble platter of Raclette
    accompaniments
Heat Raclette

PANTRY

Garlic
Unsalted butter
Whole milk
Kosher salt
Grainy mustard
Dijon mustard
Sherry vinegar
Honey
Extra-virgin olive oil
Unsweetened cocoa powder
All-purpose flour
Active dry yeast
Confectioners' sugar
Vanilla extract

GROCERY

1 apple
2 shallots
1 head butter lettuce
8 ounces / 230 g small new potatoes
4 ounces / 110 g Raclette (substitute
    Gruyère or fontina)
4 ounces / 110 g saucisson or other
    favorite sausage
1 small jar cornichons
5 ounces / 140 g bittersweet chocolate
    (60%)
1 cup / 85 g walnut halves
½ cup / 60 g hazelnuts
Champagne
Whipped cream

Raclette

There is no greater comfort than a meal of melted cheese and a platter of delicious things to dip into that cheese. I happen to find a meal eaten with your hands incredibly romantic, and this one speaks to me deeply. Traditionally, the Swiss melt Raclette over the fire. If you have a fireplace, I'd love it if you'd do it the traditional way. For us, we use a small pan and a hot oven; I still find it all romantic.

SERVES 2

1 recipe Butter and Shallot Poached Potatoes
   (recipe follows)

1 loaf Walnut Bread (recipe follows)

4 ounces / 110 g saucisson or other favorite
   sausages or meats

1 apple, sliced

½ cup / 60 g cornichons

Grainy mustard

4 ounces / 110 g Raclette (if you can't find
   Raclette, you can use Gruyère or fontina, or
   prepare a simple fondue)

Preheat the oven to 400°F.

Assemble a platter of your Raclette accompaniments: potatoes, chunks of walnut bread, sliced meats, apple, cornichons, and a dollop of grainy mustard.

Place the Raclette in a small skillet or baking dish and bake for 6 to 8 minutes, or until parts are melted and edges are starting to caramelize. Serve immediately. Return the pan to the oven to melt as it firms up.

Butter and Shallot Poached Potatoes

Of course, you could just boil or roast the potatoes and serve them alongside the cheese and be fine. Or you could poach them in butter and soft shallots so that a salty and rich glaze covers the exterior while leaving their insides fluffy and tender. I know what I'd choose to do.

SERVES 2

2 tablespoons unsalted butter

1 medium-size shallot, sliced

2 garlic cloves, roughly chopped

¼ teaspoon kosher salt

8 ounces / 230 g small new potatoes

½ cup / 120 ml water

Melt the butter in a small saucepan over medium heat. Add the shallot, garlic, and salt and sauté for 1 to 2 minutes, or until fragrant.

Add the potatoes and then stir to coat them in the butter. Add the water and bring to a boil. Reduce the heat to low and cover. Cook for 15 to 20 minutes, or until the potatoes are tender and cooked through.

Remove the lid, increase the heat to medium, and cook for 5 to 7 minutes, or until the liquid reduces and the potatoes are tender. Give the potatoes a couple gentle turns.

The potatoes can be made earlier in the day or the day before and refrigerated. Rewarm or bring to room temperature before serving.

Walnut Bread

I'm not one to jump on trends, but sometimes they stick around, long past the trendy season, to become so pivotal we wonder what we did before them. In this case I'm referring to, one: letting bread ferment slowly (of course, this isn't a new thing, but for most home bread bakers it is). And, two: baking a loaf of bread in a scorching hot pan. The idea for this, which was popularized by Jim Lahey, comes from mimicking the steam created in commercial bakery ovens. The lid traps the steam and helps to create a burnished, thick crust. The shape of the pot helps to control the shape of the loaf so you can use a very wet dough, which gives a wonderfully airy and soft texture to the finished bread. This is our standard loaf that I've made countless times. Sometimes there are toasted walnuts and other times not. Every time, the bread is gone by the end of the day.

MAKES 1 LOAF

3¼ cups / 460 g all-purpose flour, plus more for the work surface

1 teaspoon active dry yeast

2 teaspoons kosher salt

1½ cups / 360 ml lukewarm water

1 cup / 85 g walnut halves, toasted (see the technique on page 11)

In a large bowl, stir together the flour, yeast, salt, water, and walnuts. The dough will be slumped and very wet.

Cover the bowl with a clean kitchen towel or plastic wrap and let sit overnight. You can also refrigerate the dough for up to 3 days.

Grab a bowl a bit larger than the volume of the bread dough. Lay a clean towel in the bowl and cover the towel generously with flour.

Dump your dough onto a heavily floured surface and add more flour to the top of the dough so that your hands don't stick. The wetness of the dough creates a light and almost velvety texture to the final bread, but don't be afraid of using flour here so you aren't covered in wet dough.

Form the dough into a round by gently tucking the edges under while turning the dough.

Lay the round into the bowl with the floured cloth so the seam is exposed. Cover the dough and let rise for an hour or until it feels airy and light and slowly springs back when gently pressed.

While it rises, place a 4- or 5-quart oven-safe lidded pot in the oven and preheat to 450°F for 1 hour.

Carefully remove the hot pan from the oven. Place the round of bread into the pan seam-side down. There's no way to avoid this being a messy and awkward step. I assure you that even after dozens of homemade loaves, I still look a bit disheveled in this.

Give the pan a gentle tap on the counter to distribute the dough. Cover and return to the oven for 30 minutes. Remove the lid and continue to bake for 20 to 30 minutes, or until the crust is golden and the loaf sounds hollow when tapped.

Remove the loaf from the pan. If you want a deeper-set and more intensely caramelized crust, you can return the loaf to the oven outside the pan for another 5 to 10 minutes. Otherwise, let it cool completely on a rack before slicing and serving alongside the melted Raclette.

Salade Verte with Hazelnut Vinaigrette

This salad is just greens, dressed simply with a toasted hazelnut dressing.

SERVES 2

6 tablespoons / 60 g hazelnuts, toasted (see the technique on page 11), divided

1½ tablespoons chopped shallot

1½ teaspoons Dijon mustard

1½ tablespoons sherry vinegar

1 teaspoon honey

½ teaspoon kosher salt

3 tablespoons water

¼ cup / 60 ml extra-virgin olive oil

½ head butter lettuce, cleaned and well dried

In a food processor or blender, combine 3 tablespoons toasted hazelnuts, shallot, Dijon, sherry vinegar, honey, salt, and water until well puréed, about 1 minute. Add the oil and blend for another 15 seconds.

Place the butter lettuce leaves in a large bowl and add enough dressing to coat the leaves. Taste and add more dressing, if desired. Arrange the lettuce leaves on a platter and finish with the remaining 3 tablespoons hazelnuts, chopping them first.

The dressing can be made in advance and kept in the refrigerator for up to 1 week.

Chocolat Chaud

It's been ten years since I first enjoyed this dessert, and it continues to be my favorite.

SERVES 4

¼ cup / 20 g unsweetened cocoa powder

¼ cup / 25 g confectioners' sugar

2 cups / 470 ml whole milk

5 ounces / 140 g bittersweet chocolate (60%), roughly chopped

½ teaspoon vanilla extract

Pinch of kosher salt

Whipped cream, for serving

Combine the cocoa powder and confectioners' sugar in a small bowl and whisk to combine.

In a medium saucepan, bring the milk to a simmer over medium-low heat. Then whisk in the chocolate and the cocoa powder mixture. Whisk vigorously to combine. Bring to a boil and gently boil for 30 seconds while continuing to whisk. Remove from the heat and stir in the vanilla and salt. Pour this through a fine-mesh sieve to remove any small lumps.

Serve warm with a side of cold whipped cream, unsweetened or lightly sweetened.

This will keep, covered, in the fridge for up to 1 week. Reheat slowly on the stove top before serving.

Acknowledgments

They say it takes a village to raise a child, and now I realize the same goes for making a book. I set out on this process thinking it would mostly be a solitary experience. Luckily I was wrong, and now I know there is absolutely no way this book would be here without the help of a humbling number of people.

Stacey Glick, my agent, you pulled out of me words and confidence that I didn't know existed. You saw the story in this project and wouldn't settle until we had it right. I am so incredibly grateful that you did.

Kristen Green Wiewora, my editor at Running Press. Thank you for understanding my vision and saying yes to this book. You made me an author and that is a gift I will cherish forever.

To my ridiculously amazing team of recipe testers, you fine-tuned this book and asked the sort of questions that needed to be asked.

You have no idea how much you've taught me in the process. Your eagerness was always encouraging. Thank you to: Suzi Hubert, Daytona Strong, Cindy Rodriguez, Julie Hubert, Amy Vallejo, Kristal Wyman, Aimee Stark, Mary Brown, Andrew & Melissa Brown, Dana Wootton, Sara Newell, Brenna Mackenzie, Rachel Burke, Rachelle McGhee, Deborah Baron, Mindy Lee Irvine, Kay Baxter, Christine Goodrum, Megan Gordon, and Lindsay Attaway.

To my parents, Gerald and Lynne Baron. Mom, you taught me how to be fearless in the kitchen. Dad, you taught me how to be fearless in my career. I've needed both in order to create this book. Thank you for being my biggest cheerleaders. Also, thanks for letting me make a disaster in your kitchen for the photo shoots. At least you ate well, right?!

Sherry Yard, my mentor and friend. Thanks

for everything you taught me and continue to teach me.

To my dear friends: Julie & Zack Hubert, Sara & Hugh Forte, Amy Vallejo, Chris & Deborah Baron, Sara Newell, Mindy Lee Irvine, Lucy Shaw, Geoff & Amy Baron, Aimee & Jono Stark, Tara O'Brady, Shauna & Danny Ahern, Tara Austen Weaver, Stephanie Brubaker, Jenny Vorwaller, Aran Goyoaga, Lorraine Goldberg, Molly Wizenberg, Brandon Pettit, Brandi Henderson, Megan Gordan, Sam Schick, Niah Bystrom, Alicia Holsapple, Don and Kristy Riggs, Kirk and Faith Wimberley, and Steve & Jamie Moore. I've needed a lot of hand-holding, encouragement, and random favors in this process and you've all been there when I needed it most.

Jessie Blount, thanks for making my words more prettier.

Thanks for joining us on some of our dates to take beautiful images, Boone Rodriguez. I hope it wasn't too awkward.

To my readers, this book wouldn't be here if it wasn't for you. Your comments, emails, and encouragement made me see that it wasn't just Gabe and me who needed to continue to date, but that you all felt the same. Because of that this book exists. Thank you for reading the site, encouraging me daily, and walking with me in this. I'm honored to have you alongside me.

My children: Baron, Roman, and Ivy. You've been so incredibly patient with Mama through this; thank you for your grace. I hope that you've seen the benefit of working hard at a marriage and that you desire that for yourselves someday. Seeing your dad and I love each other selflessly and passionately is, I think, one of the best gifts we can give you.

Julie, oh Julie. Your talent and friendship is all over this book, and it is infinitely better because of that. You've carried me through the days when I wanted to start over and hooped and hollered with me when the recipes were flat-out amazing. Thank you for loving this project and loving me so well in the midst of it.

Finally, Gabe. Because of you I know love. Thank you for dating me.

But by the grace of God.

INDEX

A

Aioli

Tarragon Aioli, 32

Apple cider

Spiced Cider Toddy, 201

Apples

BBQ Pulled Pork Sandwiches with Apple and Radicchio Slaw, 220 (photo), 221–222, 223 (photo)

Grandma's Apple Cake with Maple Cream, 206

Kale with Apples, Currants, and Warm Pancetta Vinaigrette, 211

Roasted Apples, 184, 184 (photo)

Salad of Apples, Grapes, and Blue Cheese on Endive, 163

White Salad with Pomegranate, 262 (photo), 263

Apricots

Stewed Apricots with Cardamom Yogurt and Marcona Almonds, 229 (photo), 237

Artichoke hearts

Carciofi Fritti, 210

Arugula

Bitter Greens with Mustard Vinaigrette, 250 (photo), 251

Roast Beef Tenderloin Sandwiches with Caramelized Onions, Horseradish Mayonnaise, and Arugula, 81–83, 82 (photo)

Asparagus

Spring Vegetable Green Curry, 47 (photo), 51

Avocados

Avocado Salad with Fresh Herbs and Pepitas, 119 (photo), 122, 122 (photo)

Oranges with Avocado, Olives, and Mint, 225, 225 (photo)

B

Bacon and pancetta

Bacon and Leek Tart with Ricotta Custard, 164–165, 165 (photo)

Kale with Apples, Currants, and Warm Pancetta Vinaigrette, 211

Wedge Salad with Bacon Blue Cheese Dressing, 57, 57 (photo)

Beans

Baked Beans, 224

Lemony White Beans with Pecorino, 110, 111 (photo)

Pasta e Fagioli with Crispy Prosciutto, 70, 71 (photo)

White Bean and Pumpkin Gratin with Crispy Shallot Crumbs, 204, 205 (photo)

Beef

Flemish Beef Stew, 247 (photo), 254, 255 (photo)

Our Perfect Burger with Special Sauce, 150 (photo), 154–155, 155 (photo)

Roast Beef Tenderloin Sandwiches with Caramelized Onions, Horseradish Mayonnaise, and Arugula, 81–83, 82 (photo)

Beets

Fall Crudités with Creamy Olive Tapenade, 192 (photo), 193

Pickled Vegetable Salad, 169 (photo), 175

Bourbon

Basil Mint Jubilee, 171

Chocolate Pecan Ice Cream Pie with Bourbon Butterscotch and Pretzel Crust, 176–178, 177 (photo)

Kickin' Kentucky Mule, 76

Milk Punch, 226

Spiced Cider Toddy, 201

Breads, buns, and rolls

Black Pepper Biscuits, 172 (photo), 173

Burger Buns, 15

Pretzel Rolls, 100 (photo), 101

Walnut Bread, 272 (photo), 273

Brown sugar

Bourbon Butterscotch Sauce, 178

Brown Sugar Syrup, 143

Brussels sprouts

Brussels Sprouts Slaw with Grapes and Feta, 202, 203 (photo)

C

Cabbage

Mango Miso Slaw, 147, 147 (photo)

Candies

Ritz Cracker Mendiants, 218 (photo), 227, 227 (photo)

Carrots

Fresh Carrot Salad, 232 (photo), 233

Maple Coriander Roasted Carrots, 33, 33 (photo)

Pickled Vegetable Salad, 169 (photo), 175

Celeriac

White Salad with Pomegranate, 262 (photo), 263

Celery

Juniper-Pickled Celery, 60

Cheese

Baked Eggs with Spinach and Gruyère, 184 (photo), 185

Brussels Sprouts Slaw with Grapes and Feta, 202, 203 (photo)

Fire-Pit Fontina with Tomatoes, Rosemary, and Lemon, 99

Parmesan Frico, 212, 212 (photo)

Raclette, 271–273, 272 (photo)

Salad of Apples, Grapes, and Blue Cheese on Endive, 163

Cherries

Cherry Lime Soda, 90

Red Wine–Poached Cherries, 127 (photo), 128

Chicken

Caribbean-Style BBQ Chicken Legs, 145–146, 146 (photo)

Chicken Stock, 18

Fried Chicken Sandwiches on Black Pepper Biscuits, 172 (photo), 173–174

Herb-Butter Roasted Chicken, 30, 31 (photo)

Honey and Sriracha Chicken Wings, 58, 59 (photo)

Roasted Green Pozole with Chicken, 92 (photo), 93

Chocolate

Bittersweet Brownies with Salted Peanut Butter Frosting, 166 (photo), 166–167

Bittersweet Chocolate Malted Shakes, 156, 157 (photo)

Chocolate Chaud, 274, 275 (photo)

Chocolate Pecan Ice Cream Pie with Bourbon Butterscotch and Pretzel Crust, 176–178, 177 (photo)

Cocoa Nib Florentines, 267

Grapefruit and Olive Oil Cake with Bittersweet Chocolate, 65 (photo), 72

Mexican Chocolate Sorbet, 127, 127 (photo)

Ritz Cracker Mendiants, 218 (photo), 227, 227 (photo)

Salted Chocolate Chip Cookies, 84–85, 85 (photo)

S'mores Terrine with Smoked Salt, 104

Yeasted Belgian Waffles with Ice Cream and Hot Fudge, 256 (photo), 257–258

Coconut

Caramelized Pineapple Sundaes with Candied Coconut, 141 (photo), 148

Coconut milk

Thai Iced Coffee Affogato with Spiced Coconut Ice Cream, 52 (photo), 53

Coffee

Café au Lait Pudding, 266

Thai Iced Coffee Affogato with Spiced Coconut Ice Cream, 52 (photo), 53

Cookies

Cocoa Nib Florentines, 267

Salted Chocolate Chip Cookies, 84–85, 85 (photo)

Corn

Grilled Mexican Corn with Cotija and Lime, 90, 91 (photo)

Crab meat

Tomato and Fennel Gazpacho with Dungeness Crab, 131 (photo), 133

Cream cheese

Fresh Raspberry Tart with Lemon Cream Cheese Filling, 138

Crème Fraîche, 17

Crème Fraîche Panna Cotta with Ginger-Roasted Rhubarb, 44–45, 45 (photo)

Grandma's Apple Cake with Maple Cream, 206

Cucumbers

Fresh Spring Rolls with Ginger and Sesame, 49

Gordon's Cup with Caraway, 231

Mediterranean Lamb Tostadas, 234–236, 235 (photo)

Tzatziki Dressing, 236

Curry

Green Curry Paste, 50, 50 (photo)

Spring Vegetable Green Curry, 47 (photo), 51

D

Dates

Hot Dates with Olive Oil and Sea Salt, 39, 39 (photo)

Desserts

Bittersweet Brownies with Salted Peanut Butter Frosting, 166 (photo), 166–167

Café au Lait Pudding, 266

Chocolate Chaud, 274, 275 (photo)

Crème Fraîche Panna Cotta with Ginger-Roasted Rhubarb, 44–45, 45 (photo)

Fresh Raspberry Tart with Lemon Cream Cheese Filling, 138

Gingered Peaches and Cream with Browned-Butter Graham Crumbs, 116, 117 (photo)

Grandma's Apple Cake with Maple Cream, 206

Grapefruit and Olive Oil Cake with Bittersweet Chocolate, 65 (photo), 72

Rainbow Chip Cake, 61 (photo), 61–63, 63 (photo)

Red Wine–Poached Cherries, 127 (photo), 128

Salted Peanut Toffee Popcorn, 244, 245 (photo)

Shortcakes, 20

S'mores Terrine with Smoked Salt, 104

Stewed Apricots with Cardamom Yogurt and Marcona Almonds, 229 (photo), 237

Strawberry Shortcake Trifle, 34, 34 (photo)

See also Cookies; Ice cream and frozen desserts

Drinks

Aperol Spritz, 67, 67 (photo)

Apple Flip, 191, 191 (photo)

Basil Mint Jubilee, 171

Bittersweet Chocolate Malted Shakes, 156, 157 (photo)

Blood Orange Screwdrivers, 182, 182 (photo)

Cherry Lime Soda, 90

Gordon's Cup with Caraway, 231

Grapefruit 75, 261, 261 (photo)

Hemingway Punch, 140 (photo), 143

Homemade Cream Soda, 162, 162 (photo)

Kickin' Kentucky Mule, 76

Milk Punch, 226

Pineapple Rosarita, 121, 121 (photo)

Rhubarb Sour, 26 (photo), 27

Spiced Cider Toddy, 201

Sweet Plum Sangria, 130 (photo), 133

Thai Iced Coffee Affogato with Spiced Coconut Ice Cream, 52 (photo), 53

Thyme Lemonade, 108 (photo), 109

E

Eggs

Baked Eggs with Spinach and Gruyère, 184 (photo), 185

Braised French Green Lentils with Mushrooms and Kale, 264, 265 (photo)

Endive

Bitter Greens with Mustard Vinaigrette, 250 (photo), 251

Fall Crudités with Creamy Olive Tapenade, 192 (photo), 193

Salad of Apples, Grapes, and Blue Cheese on Endive, 163

F

Fennel bulb

Fall Crudités with Creamy Olive Tapenade, 192 (photo), 193

Tomato and Fennel Gazpacho with Dungeness Crab, 131 (photo), 133

White Salad with Pomegranate, 262 (photo), 263

Figs

Caramelized Figs Wrapped in Prosciutto, 111 (photo), 113

French toast

Croissant French Toast with Brown-Butter Maple Syrup, 186, 187 (photo)

G

Gin

Aperol Spritz, 67, 67 (photo)

Gordon's Cup with Caraway, 231

Grapefruit 75, 261, 261 (photo)

Rhubarb Sour, 26 (photo), 27

Grapefruit and grapefruit juice

Grapefruit 75, 261, 261 (photo)

Grapefruit and Olive Oil Cake with Bittersweet Chocolate, 65 (photo), 72

Hemingway Punch, 140 (photo), 143

Grapes

Brussels Sprouts Slaw with Grapes and Feta, 202, 203 (photo)

Salad of Apples, Grapes, and Blue Cheese on Endive, 163

Green beans

Braised Green Beans with Smashed Tomato Vinaigrette, 136, 137 (photo)

H

Hazelnuts

Nutella Semifreddo, 214 (photo), 215

Salade Verte with Hazelnut Vinaigrette, 274

Hominy

Roasted Green Pozole with Chicken, 92 (photo), 93

Horseradish

Roast Beef Tenderloin Sandwiches with Caramelized Onions, Horseradish Mayonnaise, and Arugula, 81–83, 82 (photo)

I

Ice cream and frozen desserts

Bittersweet Chocolate Malted Shakes, 156, 157 (photo)

Caramelized Pineapple Sundaes with Candied Coconut, 141 (photo), 148

Chocolate Pecan Ice Cream Pie with Bourbon Butterscotch and Pretzel Crust, 176–178, 177 (photo)

Dulce de Leche and Nectarine Creamsicles, 94, 94 (photo), 95 (photo)

Mexican Chocolate Sorbet, 127, 127 (photo)

Nutella Semifreddo, 214 (photo), 215

Thai Iced Coffee Affogato with Spiced Coconut Ice Cream, 52 (photo), 53

Yeasted Belgian Waffles with Ice Cream and Hot Fudge, 256 (photo), 257–258

J

Jams

Roasted Strawberry Jam, 16

K

Kale

Bitter Greens with Mustard Vinaigrette, 250 (photo), 251

Braised French Green Lentils with Mushrooms and Kale, 264, 265 (photo)

Kale with Apples, Currants, and Warm Pancetta Vinaigrette, 211

L

Lamb

Fennel-Crusted Lamb Chops, 42, 43 (photo)

Mediterranean Lamb Tostadas, 234–236, 235 (photo)

Leeks

Bacon and Leek Tart with Ricotta Custard, 164–165, 165 (photo)

White Salad with Pomegranate, 262 (photo), 263

Lemons and lemon juice

Lemony White Beans with Pecorino, 110, 111 (photo)

Thyme Lemonade, 108 (photo), 109

Lentils

Braised French Green Lentils with Mushrooms and Kale, 264, 265 (photo)

Limes and lime juice

Cherry Lime Soda, 90

Citrus Braised Pork, 126

Gordon's Cup with Caraway, 231

Hemingway Punch, 140 (photo), 143

M

Mangos

Mango Miso Slaw, 147, 147 (photo)

Maple syrup

Croissant French Toast with Brown-Butter Maple Syrup, 186, 187 (photo)

Grandma's Apple Cake with Maple Cream, 206

Maple Coriander Roasted Carrots, 33, 33 (photo)

Mayonnaise

Belgian Frites, 252

Horseradish Mayonnaise, 83

Special Sauce, 155

Milk

Chocolate Chaud, 274, 275 (photo)

Dulce de Leche and Nectarine Creamsicles, 94, 94 (photo), 95 (photo)

Milk Punch, 226

Mushrooms

Braised French Green Lentils with Mushrooms and Kale, 264, 265 (photo)

Chanterelle Pot Pie, 189 (photo), 196

N

Nectarines

Dulce de Leche and Nectarine Creamsicles, 94, 94 (photo), 95 (photo)

O

Olives

Fall Crudités with Creamy Olive Tapenade, 192 (photo), 193

Mediterranean Lamb Tostadas, 234–236, 235 (photo)

Orange and Red Chile–Marinated Olives, 112, 112 (photo)

Oranges with Avocado, Olives, and Mint, 225, 225 (photo)

Onions

Oven-Baked Onion Rings, 153

Pickled Red Onions, 125

Roast Beef Tenderloin Sandwiches with Caramelized Onions, Horseradish Mayonnaise, and Arugula, 81–83, 82 (photo)

Roasted Red Onions with Golden Raisin Gremolata, 194, 195 (photo)

Oranges and orange juice

Blood Orange Screwdrivers, 182, 182 (photo)

Citrus Braised Pork, 126

Oranges with Avocado, Olives, and Mint, 225, 225 (photo)

P

Pancetta

Kale with Apples, Currants, and Warm Pancetta Vinaigrette, 211

Pasta

Cacio e Pepe, 212, 213 (photo)

Pasta e Fagioli with Crispy Prosciutto, 70, 71 (photo)

Pastry

Quick Puff Pastry, 19

Peaches

Gingered Peaches and Cream with Browned-Butter Graham Crumbs, 116, 117 (photo)

Roasted Tomato and Peach Panzanella, 114, 115 (photo)

Peanut butter

Bittersweet Brownies with Salted Peanut Butter Frosting, 166 (photo), 166–167

Peanuts

Mango Miso Slaw, 147, 147 (photo)

Salted Peanut Toffee Popcorn, 244, 245 (photo)

Pears

Poached Pears in Muscat, 197, 197 (photo)

Peas

Crostini with Ricotta, Prosciutto, and Peas, 68 (photo), 69

Spring Vegetable Green Curry, 47 (photo), 51

Pecans

Chocolate Pecan Ice Cream Pie with Bourbon Butterscotch and Pretzel Crust, 176–178, 177 (photo)

Peppers

Pickled Sweet Peppers, 21

Roasted Red Peppers with Capers and Anchovy, 111 (photo), 113

Spring Vegetable Green Curry, 47 (photo), 51

White Pizza with Sausage and Pickled Peppers, 242 (photo), 243

Pickled dishes

Juniper-Pickled Celery, 60

Pickled Red Onions, 125

Pickled Sweet Peppers, 21

Pickled Vegetable Salad, 169 (photo), 175

Pineapple

Caramelized Pineapple Sundaes with Candied Coconut, 141 (photo), 148

Pineapple Rosarita, 121, 121 (photo)

Pizza

Olive Oil Pizza Dough, 14

White Pizza with Sausage and Pickled Peppers, 242 (photo), 243

Plums

Sweet Plum Sangria, 130 (photo), 133

Pomegranate seeds

White Salad with Pomegranate, 262 (photo), 263

Popcorn

Salted Peanut Toffee Popcorn, 244, 245 (photo)

Pork

BBQ Pulled Pork Sandwiches with Apple and Radicchio Slaw, 220 (photo), 221–222, 223 (photo)

Braised Pork Chilaquiles with Roasted Tomatilla Salsa and Pickled Red Onions, 119 (photo), 123 (photo), 123–126, 124 (photo)

Citrus Braised Pork, 126

Homemade Sausage Patties, 183, 183 (photo), 184 (photo)

Potatoes

Belgian Frites, 247 (photo), 252, 253 (photo)

Butter and Shallot Poached Potatoes, 271, 272 (photo)

Potato Chips with Fennel Coriander Salt, 78 (photo), 79

Raclette, 271–273, 272 (photo)

Smoky Potato Salad with Sour Cream and Dill, 102, 103 (photo)

Prosciutto

Caramelized Figs Wrapped in Prosciutto, 111 (photo), 113

Crostini with Ricotta, Prosciutto, and Peas, 68 (photo), 69

Pasta e Fagioli with Crispy Prosciutto, 70, 71 (photo)

Pumpkin

White Bean and Pumpkin Gratin with Crispy Shallot Crumbs, 204, 205 (photo)

R

Radicchio

BBQ Pulled Pork Sandwiches with Apple and Radicchio Slaw, 220 (photo), 221–222, 223 (photo)

Raspberries

Fresh Raspberry Tart with Lemon Cream Cheese Filling, 138

Rhubarb

Crème Fraîche Panna Cotta with Ginger-Roasted Rhubarb, 44–45, 45 (photo)

Ginger-Roasted Rhubarb, 45

Rhubarb Sour, 26 (photo), 27

Rhubarb Syrup, 27

Rice

Fresh Herb Risotto, 40 (photo), 41

Rice paper wrappers

Fresh Spring Rolls with Ginger and Sesame, 49

Ricotta, 17

Bacon and Leek Tart with Ricotta Custard, 164–165, 165 (photo)

Crostini with Ricotta, Prosciutto, and Peas, 68 (photo), 69

White Pizza with Sausage and Pickled Peppers, 242 (photo), 243

Rum

Hemingway Punch, 140 (photo), 143

S

Salad dressings and vinaigrettes

Bacon Blue Cheese Dressing, 57, 57 (photo)

Creamy Shallot Vinaigrette, 28

Hazelnut Vinaigrette, 274

Mustard Vinaigrette, 251

Salads

Apple and Radicchio Slaw, 222, 223 (photo)

Avocado Salad with Fresh Herbs and Pepitas, 119 (photo), 122, 122 (photo)

Bitter Greens with Mustard Vinaigrette, 250 (photo), 251

Brussels Sprouts Slaw with Grapes and Feta, 202, 203 (photo)

Fresh Carrot Salad, 232 (photo), 233

Kale with Apples, Currants, and Warm Pancetta Vinaigrette, 211

Mango Miso Slaw, 147, 147 (photo)

Salads (continued)

Oranges with Avocado, Olives, and Mint, 225, 225 (photo)

Pickled Vegetable Salad, 169 (photo), 175

Roasted Tomato and Peach Panzanella, 114, 115 (photo)

Salad of Apples, Grapes, and Blue Cheese on Endive, 163

Salade Verte with Hazelnut Vinaigrette, 274

Smoky Potato Salad with Sour Cream and Dill, 102, 103 (photo)

Spring Green Salad with Creamy Shallot Vinaigrette, 28, 29 (photo)

Sun-Dried Tomato Caesar with Parmesan Croutons, 239 (photo), 241

Wedge Salad with Bacon Blue Cheese Dressing, 57, 57 (photo)

White Salad with Pomegranate, 262 (photo), 263

Salmon

Salmon Cakes with Chile and Fresh Herbs, 134 (photo), 135

Sandwiches

BBQ Pulled Pork Sandwiches with Apple and Radicchio Slaw, 220 (photo), 221–222, 223 (photo)

Fried Chicken Sandwiches on Black Pepper Biscuits, 172 (photo), 173–174

German Pretzel Sandwiches, 100 (photo), 100–101

Our Perfect Burger with Special Sauce, 150 (photo), 154–155, 155 (photo)

Roast Beef Tenderloin Sandwiches with Caramelized Onions, Horseradish Mayonnaise, and Arugula, 81–83, 82 (photo)

Sausage

German Pretzel Sandwiches, 100 (photo), 100–101

Homemade Sausage Patties, 183, 183 (photo), 184 (photo)

White Pizza with Sausage and Pickled Peppers, 242 (photo), 243

Shakes

Bittersweet Chocolate Malted Shakes, 156, 157 (photo)

Shallots

Butter and Shallot Poached Potatoes, 271, 272 (photo)

Spring Green Salad with Creamy Shallot Vinaigrette, 28, 29 (photo)

White Bean and Pumpkin Gratin with Crispy Shallot Crumbs, 204, 205 (photo)

Soups

Pasta e Fagioli with Crispy Prosciutto, 70, 71 (photo)

Tomato and Fennel Gazpacho with Dungeness Crab, 131 (photo), 133

Spinach

Baked Eggs with Spinach and Gruyère, 184 (photo), 185

Starters and appetizers

Antipasto Salad, 110–113, 111 (photo), 112 (photo)

Carciofi Fritti, 210

Crostini with Ricotta, Prosciutto, and Peas, 68 (photo), 69

Fall Crudités with Creamy Olive Tapenade, 192 (photo), 193

Fire-Pit Fontina with Tomatoes, Rosemary, and Lemon, 99

Fresh Spring Rolls with Ginger and Sesame, 49

Hot Dates with Olive Oil and Sea Salt, 39, 39 (photo)

Stocks

Chicken Stock, 18

Vegetable Stock, 18

Strawberries

Roasted Strawberry Jam, 16

Strawberry Shortcake Trifle, 34, 34 (photo)

Sweet potatoes

Thyme and Parmesan Roasted Sweet Potatoes, 144, 144 (photo)

T

Tarts

Bacon and Leek Tart with Ricotta Custard, 164–165, 165 (photo)

Tomatillos

Roasted Green Pozole with Chicken, 92 (photo), 93

Roasted Tomatillo Salsa, 124 (photo), 125

Tomatoes

Braised Green Beans with Smashed Tomato Vinaigrette, 136, 137 (photo)

Fire-Pit Fontina with Tomatoes, Rosemary, and Lemon, 99

Roasted Tomato and Peach Panzanella, 114, 115 (photo)

Sun-Dried Tomato Caesar with Parmesan Croutons, 239 (photo), 241

Tomato and Fennel Gazpacho with Dungeness Crab, 131 (photo), 133

W

Waffles

Yeasted Belgian Waffles with Ice Cream and Hot Fudge, 256 (photo), 257–258

Y

Yogurt

Crème Fraîche, 17

Stewed Apricots with Cardamom Yogurt and Marcona Almonds, 229 (photo), 237

Tzatziki Dressing, 236

Z

Zucchini

Spring Vegetable Green Curry, 47 (photo), 51